Sun Tzu

AND THE

Art of

Modern

Warfare

For to win one hundred victories in one hundred battles
is not the acme of skill. To subdue the enemy without
fighting is the acme of skill.

—Sun Tzu

Also by Mark McNeilly
Sun Tzu and the Art of Business: Six Strategic Principles for Managers

SUN TZU

AND THE

ART OF

MODERN

WARFARE

Expanded Edition

NEW CHAPTER ON
USING SUN TZU'S
STRATEGIES TO FIGHT
THE WAR ON TERRORISM

MARK McNEILLY

OXFORD
UNIVERSITY PRESS

OXFORD
UNIVERSITY PRESS

Oxford   New York
Auckland   Bangkok   Buenos Aires   Cape Town
Chennai   Dar es Salaam   Delhi   Hong Kong   Istanbul   Karachi
Kolkata   Kuala Lumpur   Madrid   Melbourne   Mexico City   Mumbai   Nairobi
São Paulo   Shanghai   Taipei   Tokyo   Toronto

Copyright © 2001 by Oxford University Press, Inc.

First published by Oxford University Press, Inc., 2001
First issued as an Oxford University Press paperback, 2003
198 Madison Avenue, New York, New York 10016

www.oup.com

Library of Congress Cataloging-in-Publication Data
McNeilly, Mark.
Sun Tzu and the art of modern warfare / Mark McNeilly.
p. cm.
Includes a translation of the Art of war.
Includes bibliographical references and index.
ISBN 0-19-513340-4 (cloth) ISBN 0-19-516108-4 (pbk.)
1. Sunzi, 6th cent. B.C. Sunzi bing fa.
2. Military art and science.
I. Sunzi, 6th cent. B.C. Sunzi bing fa. English. 2001.
II. Title.

U102 .M54 2001
355.02—dc21   2001031410

1 3 5 7 9 8 6 4 2

Printed in the United States of America
on acid-free paper

PERSONAL DEDICATION

To my parents, James and Esperanza, for their love.
To my wife Sandy, for her help and support in all things.
To my children, Alex, Logan and Kenzie, for being themselves.
And to God, who makes all things possible.

DEDICATION TO POSTERITY

To the defenders of life, liberty and the pursuit of happiness throughout history.
To the defenders of the rule of law against the rule of man, past, present and future.
May your leaders always be worthy of you, May the people understand your sacrifice.
And may you use the ideas contained herein to protect freedom.

PREFACE TO THE EXPANDED PAPERBACK EDITION

Sun Tzu's *The Art of War* has proved to be a classic work on strategy, applicable to not only warfare but beyond that, statecraft. Its lessons have been applied in times both ancient and modern to win victory.

Given the terrorist attacks of September 11, 2001 it is clear that the need to study and understand warfare is as important now as ever. As the potential for terrorists and "rogue" nation states to acquire weapons of mass destruction increases, so does the imperative to learn essential principles of warfare.

The rise of China as a great power is almost assured over the next few decades. It has become increasingly important to understand her strategic and military heritage, as she, much more than other countries, relies on her ancient history to determine her future course.

While *The Art of War* contains much wisdom it is not a simple read. I have found that the people who have actually read *The Art of War* number far fewer than those who have purchased it. I believe this is due to the book's division into thirteen chapters consisting of a sequence of quotations and the use of ancient military examples. These factors can make the reading and comprehension of *The Art of War's* secrets a challenge.

The purpose of this book is therefore to make *The Art of War* more easily understood and applicable by soldiers, statesmen, historians, and those interested in strategy and warfare. This is accomplished by crystallizing the concepts and ideas put forth in *The Art of War* into six strategic principles, illustrating them with examples from history, and writing this book in a straightforward yet entertaining manner. Each of these six principles is captured in a separate chapter, with a seventh that discusses how to put the principles into practice. After the war on terrorism began in 2001, this edition has been expanded with a new eighth chapter dedicated to the application of Sun Tzu's ideas on fighting terror.

My interest in writing this book resulted from a deep interest in military history, my attraction to the ideas and concepts put forth by Sun Tzu, my experience as an infantry officer, and my time as a strategist for a major global corporation. These forces, plus the desire to ensure students of strategy have greater exposure to and understanding of Sun Tzu's holistic strategic philosophy, compelled me to pen this work.

I hope you find it useful and enjoyable.

M.R.M
Cary, North Carolina
August 2002

ACKNOWLEDGMENTS

I am very grateful to my editor Herb Addison for his excellent insights on improving this book. I would also like to thank the heirs of Samuel B. Griffith, who graciously allowed Griffith's translation to be a major part of this book. Lastly, I want to thank my wife, Sandy, and my children for their patience in dealing with my desire to complete this work.

If you browse the bibliography you will note I have referenced many excellent books. I have mined the richness of these histories to glean military examples that illustrate Sun Tzu's principles. I am grateful for the works of these authors, who have contributed not only to my learning but also the knowledge and history of the world. As I thank them for their scholarship I also must notify the reader that any and all comments, interpretations, and errors of fact contained within this book are entirely my own.

CONTENTS

CONTENTS

Sun Tzu

and the

Art of

Modern

Warfare

Introduction

The Relevance of Sun Tzu to Modern Warfare

As pilots from the Coalition Forces flew above, tanks, armored vehicles, and trucks below poured out flames and smoke. Known later to the world as the Highway of Death, the road out of Kuwait City was clogged with Iraqi forces trying to escape the Coalition Forces of Desert Storm. Instead, they had been turned into an inferno by the Coalition's air attacks. This dramatic scene symbolized the defeat that had overcome the formerly triumphant Iraqi Army. In less than one hundred hours the ground war phase of Desert Storm was over, with the Iraqi forces either destroyed, in retreat, or in shocked surrender. One of the keys to the amazing success of Desert Storm was the use by the Coalition strategists of a centuries-old text titled *The Art of War*, written by an ancient Chinese general, Sun Tzu.[1]

While some historians debate if and when a man named Sun Tzu actually existed, the great early Chinese historiographer Ssu-ma Ch'ien states that Sun Tzu was born in the state of Ch'i. Ssu-ma Ch'ien goes on to say that Sun Tzu became a general for the King of Wu during the Spring and Autumn period in China (722–481 B.C.) and won great victories for him. At this time he wrote *The Art of War*.

Other historians, based on the descriptions of warfare in his book, situate Sun Tzu's masterpiece in a period of China's history known as the Age of the Warring States (403–221 B.C.). This was a time of great

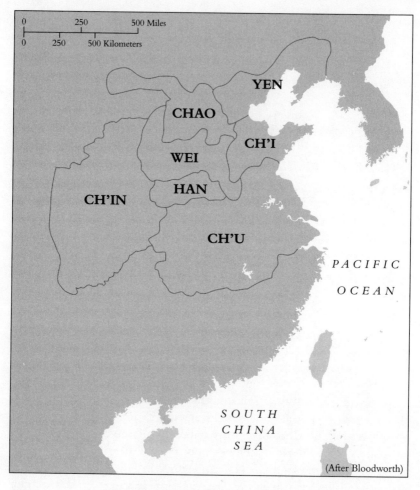

FIGURE I.1   Age of the Warring States

strife and conflict between seven states (Ch'in, Han, Chao, Wei, Ch'u, Yen and Ch'i), each trying to gain hegemony over all of China (see Figure I.1). Warfare and diplomacy, espionage and assassination . . . any and all means of winning were acceptable. It was an era of political and personal uncertainty in which only the wise and sagacious survived.

My view is that the discussion of if and when Sun Tzu lived is not a very interesting debate; what we can be sure of is that a book titled *The Art of War* most certainly exists and that the lessons it has to teach strategists are as deep and meaningful today as they were two thousand years ago. As proof of this, the thirteen chapters of this book are still in use by soldiers who fight not with chariots but with cruise missiles, and who communicate not by banners but by satellite.

The History of The Art of War

To hand down the wisdom he gained from his years in battle and his observation of state craft during the Age of the Warring States, Sun Tzu wrote *The Art of War*. His book, which details a complete philosophy of how to win decisive victories, became one of the classic works on strategy in China. Containing not only Sun Tzu's insights but also the elucidation by military commentators who came after him (such as Li Ch'uan, Tu Mu, and others), *The Art of War* has given guidance to military theorists and generals throughout time. In this classic treatise, military readers found an holistic approach to strategy that was at once powerful yet succinctly communicated—it is truly a masterpiece on strategy.

The Art of War became popular not only among military leaders but among leaders of the state. For contrary to its title, Sun Tzu's ideas cover not only warfare, but state craft; not only military strategy, but grand strategy. Whereas warfare deals only with the time during which the country is at war and is concerned essentially about the proper use of armed forces, state craft deals with successfully navigating relationships between nations to improve a nation's position. This broader scope encompasses warfare, peace, and diplomacy. Both state craft and *The Art of War* are concerned with the very survival, welfare, and prosperity of the state.

Thus it is of little surprise that the first Emperor of unified China, Qin Shihuang, studied *The Art of War* and used it to help him end the Age of the Warring States. Several centuries later, Mao Zedong used Sun Tzu's writings to defeat Chiang Kai-shek and the Nationalists in 1949, again reuniting China. Sun Tzu also influenced Mao's writings on guerrilla warfare, which in turn provided the strategy for communist insurgencies from Southeast Asia to the Americas.

Japan was introduced to Sun Tzu's writings around 760 A.D. and her generals quickly absorbed its lessons. The three most well-known samurai—Oda Nobunaga, Toyotomi Hideyoshi, and Tokugawa Ieyasu—all mastered *The Art of War*. This mastery enabled them to transform Japan from a collection of feudal states into a single nation.[2]

In the West, *The Art of War* first made its appearance in 1772 after being translated into French by a Jesuit missionary. B. H. Liddell Hart, the twentieth-century British military historian whose theories on armored warfare helped lead to the development of the Blitzkrieg concept, was amazed at the depth of Sun Tzu's military philosophy and instruction. Impressed by how closely Sun Tzu's ideas mirrored his own, he thought that had *The Art of War* been more widely read and accepted by World War I generals, much of the terrible slaughter of trench warfare could have been avoided. In fact, Germany's Kaiser Wilhelm is said to have stated, "I wish I had read *The Art of War* twenty years ago" before his defeat in the First World War.[3]

There is no exact equivalent to Sun Tzu's *The Art of War* in the West. In the scientific tradition of categorizing information, we separate politics and state craft from the military arts and warfare. Therefore, the West has two separate books dealing with each; the West's foremost military theorist, Carl von Clausewitz, discusses military theory in his book *On War*. Meanwhile, the West's most prominent political book, Niccolo Machiavelli's *The Prince*, deals with state craft (Machiavelli did discuss warfare in his book *The Art of War*, but it never enjoyed anywhere near the success of its sister book). Sun Tzu's *The Art of War* deals with both in an holistic fashion because state craft and warfare are intertwined. Like the Chinese yin-yang symbol, both make up half of the same whole and each contains part of the other.

The principles that lie buried in the text of *The Art of War* have been used successfully in countless battles throughout time. Speed was an essential facet in the victories of Genghis Khan and his Mongolian horde. Controlling their enemies by the skillful use of alliances allowed the Romans to expand and maintain their empire. Secrecy and deception were used in major World War II battles, both by the Japanese in their attack on Pearl Harbor and by the Allies to mislead the Germans about the exact location of their invasion of France. The use of intelligence was critical to American success in the Cuban missile crisis. The Viet Cong lived by the rule of avoiding strength and attacking weakness, while the Red Army used this principle to deal Germany's Sixth Army a devastating defeat at Stalingrad.

As mentioned above, Sun Tzu's principles were put to the test in Desert Storm. By controlling the air both to follow Iraqi movements and mask his own, General H. Norman Schwartzkopf fooled Saddam Hussein as to the location of his attack. Threatening an amphibious assault in the east, Schwartzkopf did an armored end-run on the Iraqi army in the west, thus winning a stunning victory with extremely low casualties. Deception, speed, and attacking the enemy's weakness—all part of Sun Tzu's philosophy—added up to amazing success. This was the reward for developing an awareness and understanding of Sun Tzu's concepts.

A modern understanding of *The Art of War* and its importance in Chinese history becomes more critical as China overcomes her troubles of the twentieth century and moves to attain potential superpower status as the new century dawns. The combination of China's huge population, increasing economic power, her move to modernize her military and sense of history and destiny as the leading power in Asia make it crucial that we learn as much as possible about her strategic philosophy. It is clear from the writings of hundreds of contemporary Chinese military experts that China's leaders will rely on strategic lessons from China's history to build their nation's strategy for the coming decades. These experts see a direct relationship between today's strategic environment and that of Sun Tzu's time. Furthermore, they see tremendous value in the teachings of Sun Tzu and China's other ancient strategists and will deploy them to guide the Chinese ship of state.[4]

Unfortunately, for many professional soldiers and others interested in military history and strategy, it is not easy to master *The Art of War* and apply it directly to battles past, present, and future. The original thirteen chapters consist of many quotations laced together; only ancient military examples are used, and no basic principles are elucidated. Therefore, I wrote this book with the goal of making Sun Tzu's ideas more widely available. The purpose of this book is to bring forth the basic concepts and underpinnings of Sun Tzu's masterpiece by setting down what I believe are the six principles of his holistic strategic philosophy. Each principle is then illuminated further with numerous examples from state craft and warfare throughout history. This use of historical examples follows the traditional Asian maxim, "use history as a mirror," meaning that ancient lessons can be applied to present and future challenges.[5]

The Six Principles and the Plan of This Book

To make *The Art of War* more understandable, applicable to modern warfare, and ultimately more useful to the reader of today and the future, I have extracted what I believe are the most important and pertinent strategic principles from Sun Tzu's work and devoted a chapter to each. These principles are:

I. Win All Without Fighting:
Achieving the Objective Without Destroying It

II. Avoid Strength, Attack Weakness:
Striking Where the Enemy Is Most Vulnerable

III. Deception and Foreknowledge:
Winning the Information War

IV. Speed and Preparation:
Moving Swiftly to Overcome Resistance

V. Shaping the Enemy:
Preparing the Battlefield

VI. Character-based Leadership:
Leading by Example

Each of the first six chapters discusses how these principles have been applied throughout history, using examples from ancient and modern battles, campaigns, and wars. These serve to illustrate how the understanding or ignorance of these principles has led to success or failure.

I developed these principles by combining careful reading and re-reading of *The Art of War* with a lifetime study of military history and strategy. With this background I was able to take key quotations from the book and group them, putting together those sections that shared a point-of-view on or clarified a major strategic concept or idea. Out of these groupings came the six principles. In this sense the principles formed themselves. The benefit of this approach is that it avoids the less useful and at times redundant (in my view) organization of the thirteen chapters, coalescing Sun Tzu's breakthrough ideas into six homogeneous areas of interest.

The final chapter culminates this comprehensive study of Sun Tzu's ideas by comparing the strategic philosophy of the East's most revered military theorist to that of West, namely, the Prussian Carl von Clause-witz. It also postulates how future changes in air power, sea power, weapons of mass destruction, missile technology, high-speed ubiquitous communications, space warfare, and international relations can be understood within the context of the six principles.

The Use of the Principles

As one reads the military examples I have used in the book, one will rightly ask, "Was the commander consciously using Sun Tzu's concepts? Was that commander even aware of *The Art of War*? If not, are the examples supportive of the principles or merely coincidental?" These are fair questions, but perhaps not the right ones.

The principles I have culled from *The Art of War* are much like the laws of physics; they exist whether we know of them or not. A scientist or engineer acting in accordance with the laws of physics, is successful. The same is true of a commander; using these principles of strategy, he too is successful. Conversely, if a commander is ignorant, does not understand or (worse) ignores these principles, he does so at his peril. The examples used to illustrate the principles throughout the book prove this point. As Sun Tzu said,

> ■ **If a general who heeds my strategy is employed he is certain to win. Retain him! When one who refuses to listen to my strategy is employed, he is certain to be defeated. Dismiss him!   (I.15)**

The principles and the strategic philosophy they represent have other benefits. The principles are practical and able to be readily put to use. They are holistic; one might think of them as cords in a rope. Individually each one is strong, but when interwoven and used together they become even more strong and useful. They are predictive in the sense that one can analyze a conflict and determine the future success or failure of a strategy based on its accordance with the principles. Finally, the principles are not a recipe for strategy and warfare—no fixed doctrine could ever be useful in the dynamic world of conflict between states. The successful use of the principles relies on strategic creativity and military genius.

It is for the above reasons that I chose to use the word "principle." The meaning of the word "principle" is "a basic law or truth" or "a rule about how things work." Also, "principle" comes from the Latin word "princeps," which means "first." Therefore, principle is the correct word to use, since these concepts are basic truths about how things work in strategy, and they are the first basis to which a leader should look for guidance when planning.

The Master Strategist

One final word before we begin. In Sun Tzu's time it was not unusual for leading thinkers to be employed as strategists by a sovereign, even if they came from a rival state. These men had a very specific and defined role, which was to provide creative ideas to the king on strategy. They even had a nickname, "Shi Ke," which means "Eating Guests." This name came from the fact that these strategists obtained position and sustenance from the king in exchange for their diplomatic, military, and political wisdom.[6]

In the West the position of strategist is not as well-defined and does not have an historical basis—nor is strategy itself held in much esteem. Instead, preference is given to action, preferably "bold" action. It is my view that we in the West would do well to cultivate understanding and respect for strategy, as well as for the position of strategist. To take a step in that direction, this book will provide examples of both excellent and poor strategists.

So, let us take the first step on the path to master strategist, beginning with the discussion of Sun Tzu's first principle.

1 ▪ Win All Without Fighting

Achieving the Objective Without Destroying It

At 2:45 in the morning of January 30, 1968, all hell broke loose at the United States embassy in Saigon, the capital city of what was then South Viet Nam. On Tet, the Vietnamese New Year, nineteen Viet Cong guerilla commandos shot their way into the embassy. Simultaneously, in the largest offensive of the war, eighty-four thousand Viet Cong and North Vietnamese troops threw themselves against the major towns and cities in South Viet Nam, using human wave tactics to overwhelm defenders and incite terror in the populace.

After overcoming their initial shock, the U.S. forces and the South Vietnamese troops recovered well, delivering major blows to the communists and retaking all captured cities and towns. The commando force that entered the embassy compound was wiped out. Overall, the communists suffered the loss of roughly forty thousand troops (almost half of the forces engaged) while the U.S. and ARVN (Army of the Republic of Viet Nam) forces losses amounted to only 3,400 men dead. If judged by a "body count" criteria, this was a major success for the U.S. and its ally. However, in warfare, body counts and casualty ratios do not determine success or failure. This war was not only being fought in the jungles and villages of Southeast Asia but also in the living rooms and student unions in the United States. More important than the reality on the Asian battlefields was the perception in American minds.

Promised that victory was within reach, many Americans, while un-happy about the war in Viet Nam, nevertheless supported it. As late as November 1967 the commander of the U.S. troops in Viet Nam, Gen-eral William Westmoreland, stated, "I have never been more encouraged in my four years in Viet Nam." He went on to tell Congress that the communists could not hold out much longer and that the U.S. forces could be brought home in two years. Therefore the Tet offensive, and especially the embassy raid, provided a rude shock, leading many to ques-tion if the government and the military were telling the truth.

While the United States was viewing the war as a problem to be solved by military means, the communists viewed the problem in its totality: militarily, politically, and psychologically. In preparation for Tet the communists reduced their attacks on U.S. and ARVN units. This was done to mislead the American and South Vietnamese leadership that they were indeed winning the war.

Thus when a ruined village in the central highlands was recaptured from the communists, comments from a U.S. Marine colonel to a news reporter that "we had to destroy the village to save it" convinced Americans that the war in Southeast Asia was not worth fighting. An editorial piece by Walter Cronkite immediately after Tet stated flatly to viewers that the only rational way out was negotiation. Scenes like this being beamed back to the States, combined with the psychological blow of the Tet offensive itself, turned opinion solidly against the war. This desire to totally withdraw from all involvement in Southeast Asia led not only to Nixon's "Vietnamization" policy (turning the war over to the ARVN to handle and reducing U.S. combat troops and air power significantly). It also led Congress in 1975 to renege on its prom-ise to South Viet Nam that the U.S. would come to its aid if the South were attacked conventionally by the North. This promise was part of the overall agreement that led the South to agree to peace. The com-munist strategy for Tet in 1968 set the stage for their eventual military victory seven years later. Meanwhile, America's failed strategy led to a turn inward, the willingness to achieve foreign policy goals through military means paralyzed until new leadership could revive it.[1]

■ **War is a matter of vital importance to the State; the province of life or death, the road to survival or ruin. It is mandatory that it be thoroughly studied. (I.1)**

The above statement was true in Sun Tzu's time, and in 1968—and remains true today. While many have prophesied that the end of the Cold War meant an end to future conflict between nation-states, those prophesies have proved hollow. Continued wars around the world (including Europe at the end of the twentieth century), the use of terrorism to achieve political, religious, or national aims, the rise to power of China, and the proliferation of nuclear weapons and other means of mass destruction have shown that war continues to be "a matter of vital importance to the State; the province of life or death, the road to survival or ruin." Therefore, it also follows that warfare must continue to be "thoroughly studied."

The Goal of Strategy: Take All-under-Heaven Intact

Many city-states, countries, and empires have been built by leaders who leveraged their nation's unique history, geography, and assets to control that state's environment and sphere of influence. These leaders were able to ensure their states' ability to survive, become stable, expand, dominate their neighbors, and ultimately prosper for hundreds of years.

The Roman Empire grew from a small area surrounding Rome, eventually extending from Britain to the Black Sea to Egypt to what would in the future be known as Gibraltar. It lasted over five hundred years. The Mongol Empire began with a single nomadic tribe in central Asia, but grew to rule lands from China to India to Europe. And, of course, the sun did not set on the British Empire for several centuries.

The goal of all these empires has been—like a living organism— to first survive, then to prosper. Today that goal remains for all countries.

If the goal of a country is to survive and prosper, then what is the goal of its strategy? Sun Tzu offers this advice:

- **Your aim must be to take All-under-Heaven intact. Thus your troops are not worn out and your gains will be complete. This is the art of offensive strategy.   (III.11)**

During the time of the Warring States, "All-under-Heaven" meant that one state would conquer the rest of civilized China (to them, the whole world) that is, the other six warring states. Thus, the goal of each state's strategy was to win control of China, thus bringing peace to the entire nation and putting order in place (of course, on the victor's terms). Capturing and consolidating All-under-Heaven was the key to ensuring both a single state's survival and prosperity as well as that of the "world" overall.

Today, in order to survive and prosper, the aim of a country's strategy must be the same. This means protecting the country's national interest while ensuring the nation's survival, and achieving the nation's policy goals to enhance prosperity. Another translation of the quotation "take All-under-Heaven intact" is "With his forces intact he disputes the mastery of the empire, and thus, without losing a man, his triumph is complete."[2] This is accomplished by being both powerful and wise enough to either control or strongly influence the nation's environment, "All-under-Heaven."

When speaking of this subject, Sun Tzu recognized that to take All-under-Heaven one needed to know more than just how to win wars. Thus his viewpoint of strategy went well beyond warfare and, despite its title, *The Art of War* reflects this. Sun Tzu's holistic view of strategy is characteristic of the East. In contrast, the West's two best classical theorists tend to divide this holistic view into two separate topics. The well-known Prussian theorist and author of *Vom Kriege* (*On War*), Carl von Clausewitz, only discusses military strategy, specifically the winning of wars through force. His famous quote "war is the continuation of politics by other means" leads only to a discussion of those other means. However, it does not say what a state should attempt to achieve by going to war in the first place or how to achieve the state's goals without war. Machiavelli, in *The Prince*, wrote primarily about directing domestic policy in order to remain in power, and managing relationships between states. He focused little on military strategy.

Sun Tzu takes a different approach, encompassing those areas and going beyond them to integrate his ideas. *The Art of War* not only speaks to all three, it also does so in an integrated fashion, showing how they are related and affect one another. Sun Tzu goes beyond domestic policy, military strategy, and foreign policy to advise us on "state craft." State craft entails achieving one's objectives in peace and in war—a country's objective in the relationship between states and the wise use of alliances. It includes the use of political, economic, psychological, moral, and military means to achieve goals. It encompasses the proper use and allocation of resources to accomplish aims. State craft includes looking beyond conflict to its resolution, ensuring a peace and system of interstate relationships more profitable to one's nation.

As such, Sun Tzu's insights are useful to both the general and the civilian leadership of the nation. Georges Clemenceau, the prime minister of France at the end of World War I, said that war was too serious a matter to leave to soldiers. The reverse is true as well; state craft and strategy is to important to be left only to politicians. They are deeply intertwined and one should not strive to understand one without understanding the other.

■ The Grand Duke said: "One who is confused in purpose cannot respond to his enemy." (III.23 Meng)

Implementing Strategy: Win All Without Fighting

Sun Tzu does not just say that one must capture All-under-Heaven, he states that one must "take All-under-Heaven *intact*" (my emphasis). This means that a nation's actions in diplomacy, warfare, and domestic policy should achieve its goals in a manner that improve the country's chances for future survival and prosperity; those actions must not lead to the destruction of the state through warfare or a peace that, through the loser's resentment, leads to a more vicious war later.

■ Generally in war the best policy is to take a state intact; to ruin it is inferior to this. To capture the enemy's army is better than to destroy it; to take intact a battalion, a company or a five-man squad is better than to destroy them. (III.1 and III.2)

So while the ability to control or significantly influence the nation's sphere of influence is critical, it should not be pursued blindly. It does no good to take All-under-Heaven if there is nothing left of it when one is done.

A seventeenth-century example of ignoring this concept was the Thirty Years War. This war had as its origins the desire of the Habsburgs to rebuild their authority in Germany by using their power bases in Spain and Austria. During this war all of Europe was subsumed and eighty battles or sieges were fought, creating losses in manpower totaling roughly twenty-five percent. Beyond the battle destruction were the other devastating effects of the prolonged war—disease, hunger, and inflation. This resulted in the loss of about a quarter of the civilian population in Germany, the elimination of much of the farmland, assets for production, housing, and food stores, and the loss of countless cultural treasures.

In the end, much of Germany was left a wasteland and subject to the power of France. Not until the end of the nineteenth century would Germany again have a major influence on Europe. The Habsburgs'— the originators of the war—were also greatly diminished in position. As a result of losses in the war Spanish power in Europe was broken;

that country was destined to never again be the leading power in Europe. The Dutch and the Swedes rose as trading and military rivals, respectively. A fitting epitaph to this war of devastation was penned by a young Silesian poet: "Hasten, use your common sense, before the whole of Europe goes up in smoke. Believe me, avoiding wars is more than a thousand victories."[3]

A more recent and familiar example of winning yet not keeping the end result intact is World War I. In 1914 Germany and Austria-Hungary went to war with Russia, France, and Great Britain over the assassination of Austria's Archduke Franz Ferdinand by a young Bosnian. A series of diplomatic blunders, mistakes, and misunderstandings lead quickly to war. The actual assassination of the Archduke was only possible due to his driver taking the wrong turn and stopping momentarily right in front of one of the plotters, who promptly took advantage of the situation to shoot the Archduke.

Four years later, over ten million men had died in combat, millions more were maimed, and much of Europe was starving. Furthermore, manufacturing output was a quarter lower than in 1914, the international monetary system was totally dislocated, and the souls of a generation were spent.

Germany's original aim in going to war was to achieve mastery in Central Europe and gain greater international respect. Austria-Hungary wished to expand its polyglot empire at its periphery. Russia and France strove to limit the power and expansion of the two German states. Great Britain desired to prevent any country from dominating Europe while her population (and that of the United States) hoped that by fighting the "Great War" they would end all wars. Those were the original objectives—but what was the situation at war's end? Germany lay devastated and dishonored. The Austro-Hungarian Empire was dismembered. Russia fell prey to revolution, internal fighting, and eventually suffered the bane of communism for seventy years. France lost an entire generation to the war and Great Britain lost over a million men. Both societies were so disillusioned with the experience of the Great War that they opted for an appeasement policy that allowed a resurgent Germany to rearm two decades later. A myriad of wars that followed in the twentieth century denied the world the dream that this war would end all wars.[4]

As *The Art of War* states:

- War is a grave matter; one is apprehensive lest men embark upon it without due reflection.   (I.1 Li Ch'üan)

Geoffrey Blainey's book *The Causes of War* illustrates that leaders of nations often have unrealistic expectations of their chances for success in war. A commonly held expectation by an aggressor nation is that the war will be won quickly. For example, Major John Pitcairn, a commander in the Royal Marines stationed in the American colonies in the late 1700s, expected that British troops would make short work of any rebellion by American patriots. He wrote, "I am satisfied that one active campaign, a smart action, and burning two or three of their towns, will set everything to rights." When shown his letter, British King George III agreed. However, by that time Major Pitcairn was dead, killed at the Battle of Bunker Hill. The war he and his King thought would be over quickly lasted seven years and cost many thousands of casualties.

Another common expectation leaders have is, of course, victory. One hundred years later, during the 1870 Franco-Prussian war, many French leaders counted on winning. As such, they issued to their officers no maps of France, only of Prussia. As is turned out, the smashing Prussian victory and entry into Paris made the French soldiers' Prussian maps an ironic joke.[5]

Think for a moment of the wagering that is done on sporting events. The rules of the game are set, all know which two teams are playing, and the individual strengths and weaknesses of each player have been tested in previous games. And yet millions of dollars are lost when the underdog upsets the favored team. Now compare this to war. The rules are never set; new weapons and technology come into play, the war expands to new theaters, and new tactics and strategies are deployed. The relative strengths of the contesting nations can turn out to be radically different than expected, since their armed forces may not have been tested in battle for years. Furthermore, the contestants can change significantly as well. New countries enter the fray while others leave or change sides. And unlike a game, the stakes in warfare are much higher; even the victor suffers casualties and destruction and expends national treasure.

Sun Tzu was cautiously respectful of war's awesome power and its ability to lead one to unforeseen circumstances. Thus one should not begin war lightly, without understanding how to achieve ones' goals "intact."

In contrast to the Thirty Years War and World War I there is the example of the peace following the end of the Napoleonic Wars. Napoleon's attempts to gain mastery of Europe embroiled the continent in warfare from 1803 to 1815. This eventually led to all the great powers of Europe combining against him. After finally joining forces to defeat Napoleon, the allies of the Sixth Coalition (Britain, Russia, Prussia, and Austria) met in Austria to create a system that would end the fighting and prevent future outbreaks of war.

At the Congress of Vienna the architecture of the future peace was designed. Two statesmen, Austrian Chancellor Prince Metternich and Viscount Castlereagh, the British foreign minister, combined intellects to construct this new international order. They devised a system built on great power conferences and a well-tuned balance of power that would prevent any one country from feeling strong enough to take on the rest. This concert of Europe would ensure harmony on the continent from 1815 to 1854, a major accomplishment.[6]

Similarly, even though World War II left the planet divided between democracy and communism, with each camp armed with nuclear weapons, the means of handling conflict were put in place. The United Nations and its Security Council provided an ongoing arena for dialogue and diplomacy. The "hotline" set up between the United States and the Soviet Union helped ensure that a future Armageddon would not happen through a miscommunication. Finally, in wars between allies the major powers worked hard to keep their own forces from fighting directly with one another. This system helped prevent nuclear war and eventually allowed the peaceful reintegration of Eastern Europe into the West.[7]

> ■ To triumph in battle and be universally acclaimed "Expert" is not the acme of skill, for to lift an autumn (rabbit's) down requires no strength, to distinguish between the sun and moon is no test of vision; to hear the thunderclap is no indication of acute hearing. . . . (IV.9)

> For to win one hundred victories in one hundred battles is not the acme of skill. To subdue the enemy without fighting is the acme of skill. (III.3)

To accomplish the nation's objectives while keeping one's victories intact, Sun Tzu advises us that battles are not necessarily the proper means. Instead, it is better to win "without fighting." One may think that this is a ridiculous proposition. With a book titled *The Art of War*, why would Sun Tzu say that the epitome of skill is to win without fighting? Similarly, isn't it the role of armies to fight in order to achieve the nation's goals? Sun Tzu provides additional insight:

■ Battles are dangerous affairs.   (III.6 Wang Hsi)

> Thus, those skilled in war subdue the enemy's army without battle. They capture his cities without assaulting them and overthrow his state without protracted operations. They conquer by strategy.   (III.10 Sun Tzu and Li Ch'uan)

This can be accomplished in two ways: through the use of political, economic, psychological, and moral means prior to resorting to military efforts, and then through the use of a wise war strategy when military means are called upon. The latter entails not just seeking to fight battles but utilizing intelligence, deception, surprise, speed, and other methods to either outmaneuver the enemy or to ensure that any battles will end in victory. Thus, the goal of strategy is not only to achieve the nation's aims through controlling or influencing its sphere of influence, but to do so without resorting to fighting.

Many have extolled the brilliant generalship and strategies of Napoleon, but few historians have viewed him as a statesman and evaluated the position of France after his reign. Fewer still have judged him according to Sun Tzu's view of strategy.

Despite Napoleon's outstanding generalship his penchant for continuous warfare ended in his personal humiliation and the humbling of France. It is indeed marvelous to stand beneath his Arc de Triomphe in Paris and get dizzy counting the numerous battles inscribed in the stone above, each one carrying the name of one of the Emperor's victories. However, those victories (and the defeats) led to almost one million dead in France, and a mortality rate of thirty-eight percent for the generation born between 1790 and 1795. That is fourteen percent higher than that inflicted on the generation that served in World War I. Europe's total dead during the Napoleonic Wars was five million.

The impact on the international stature of France was even greater. Although the Congress of Vienna eventually allowed her back into the fold of the big powers, territorially speaking she had nothing to show for the years of fighting and blood. One could even argue that after the Napoleonic wars France ceased to be the leading country in Europe. An increasingly powerful Prussia would defeat her in 1870, Britain captured the best overseas colonies to expand her empire, and it would take American help to save France in two world wars. Truly a high price to pay for glory.[8]

- Do not put a premium on killing. (III.1 Li Ch'uan)

  He who struggles for victory with naked blades is not a good general. (III.6 Chia Lin)

A sure way to violate the principle of winning without fighting is to follow a strategy of attrition, which by definition leads to protracted warfare.

- Victory is the main object in war. If this is long delayed, weapons are blunted and morale depressed. . . . (II.3)

  For there has never been a protracted war from which a country has benefited. (III.7)

While strategy in World War I exhibited failure from a state craft standpoint, it also highlights poor military strategy as well. After the initial maneuvering in World War I had stalemated into trench warfare, it was the strategy of the Western Allies to bleed the Germans into submission. This attrition strategy led to major attacks being launched each year, preceded by extensive artillery barrages. Through mine fields and barbed wire—no-man's land—and into the mouths of machine guns, the soldiers of France and Great Britain raced against Death. Hundreds of thousands lost the race, not even making it to the enemy trenches. Those that made it engaged in deadly hand-to-hand fighting, with trench knives, rifle butts, or entrenching tools. If they were lucky enough to take the trench, they regrouped for the inevitable German counterattack, preceded by artillery fire. Regardless of whether they held the trenches, until 1918 they could never quite break through those lines to win a major victory.

Germany also had an attrition strategy during one phase of the war. In 1916 the German Chief of General Staff, General Erich von Falkenhayn, believed that if he attacked the French fortress of Verdun, the French national character would demand strong resistance. He felt that an attack there would lead the French to feed troops into its defense, since Verdun symbolized France's pride, history, and independence. Falkenhayn could then pulverize those troops with massed artillery of 1,200 guns, bleeding France dry and breaking its spirit. He was correct on that point. However, Falkenhayn failed to realize he would also have to devote men and materiel to maintain the offensive pressure on Verdun. An initial nine hour artillery bombardment ripped open the ground and tore thousands of French troops, the *poilus*, asunder.

Then the German attack was pressed home. Initially good progress was made, but then resistance stiffened and the advance was halted. Three German army corps were added to the original three and another attack went in. The bloodshed continued from March through June, only to stop when the British opened their attack on the Somme (where the combatants would lose a total of one million men). In the end the French suffered 377,200 casualties defending the fort and their honor. However the German losses were 337,000—a price higher than she could afford, driven by a strategy of attrition that succeeded only in bleeding both sides white.[9]

American strategy in Viet Nam was also attrition-oriented, based on body counts. Pacification of the countryside was to be accomplished by bringing the Viet Cong guerillas and their North Vietnamese Army allies to battle and destroying them. Repeated bombing in North Viet Nam would reduce the North's capability to support the war in the South. However, even though the Tet offensive saw massive Viet Cong and NVA losses, in the end the grand strategy of the communists defeated the military attrition strategy of America. Sun Tzu proved correct again: victory was "long delayed" and "morale depressed." And truly the United States did not benefit from this protracted war.

Can attrition-based strategies win wars? Yes, in a sense. For example, eventually the Western Allies overcame the Central Powers in WWI, through blockades and four years of hard fighting in the trenches. However, looking at the final outcome and the cost, it is hard to say that even the victors truly won. Attrition-based strategies are extremely expensive for all participants, devouring resources measured in men, materiel, and morale. Since the goal of a country is to survive and prosper, an attrition-based strategy goes against this goal. In contrast Sun Tzu's philosophy, based on winning without fighting and avoiding attrition, uses resources wisely and economically to achieve objectives. This approach supports and reinforces the goal of survival and prosperity for a nation.

- **When the army engages in protracted campaigns the resources of the army will not suffice.   (II.4)**

  When your weapons are dulled and ardor damped, your strength exhausted and treasure spent, neighboring rulers will take advantage of your distress to act. And even though you have wise counsellors, none will be able to lay good plans for the future.   (II.5)

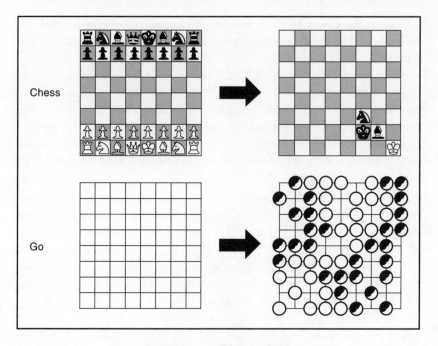

FIGURE 1.1   Chess and Go

This point can be illustrated by showing the difference between two popular games: Go, an Asian favorite, and chess, a Western one. In chess, the object is to destroy the opponent's pieces in an effort to "take" his King. In fact, the saying "checkmate" is derived from the original Persian "shah mat," meaning "the king is dead." In the beginning of the game, the board is full of pieces. However, by the end, chess resembles a medieval battlefield, with several dead pieces strewn about, one king taken, and the board empty except for the few men left standing (see Figure 1.1).

Contrast this to the ancient game of Go, which was invented in China over 4,000 years ago. One wins in Go by capturing and holding the greatest amount of territory with the smallest investment in pieces (either black or white stones). While each of the two players can surround an opponent's stones and capture them, in Go the destruction of an opponent's stones is secondary to the object of capturing territory. In games between masters, very few stones are taken.

Unlike chess, Go begins with the game board empty; the players then take turns placing their stones to control territory. Players can put their stones anywhere on the board, balancing the need to acquire territory against the possibility of overextension and capture. The best strategy is to claim the open areas of the board, then, as the board fills, to attack an opponent's unsupported pieces. One cannot win by being satisfied with merely defending a small piece of territory; one must defend by attacking, keeping one's opponent always on the defensive. Played by masters, the game will end with just enough pieces on the board to control the greatest amount of territory.

In strategy, one should follow the philosophy of Go rather than chess. One should seek to exert the most influence with the smallest investment, not to destroy one's opponent and one's own nation in endless fighting. It is best not to win by wiping out one's enemy but by avoiding fighting and moving strategically to achieve relative dominance, survival, and prosperity. This approach leaves the nation intact, allowing it to dominate a healthy peace rather than one which fosters resentment and poverty.

- Replace the enemy's flags and banners with your own, mix the captured chariots with yours, and mount them. Treat the captives well and care for them. This is called "winning a battle and becoming stronger." (II.18–20)

One can "win without fighting" in a number of ways, as the following examples illustrate. Subtle, indirect, and less directly threatening and visible attacks are much less likely to prompt a response. Obviously, any successful move that either delays or does not provoke a response will result in a gain by the attacker.

- Subtle and insubstantial, the expert leaves no trace; divinely mysterious, He is inaudible. Thus he is the master of the enemy's fate. (VI. 9)

Hitler used this method to rearm Germany, reoccupy the Rhineland, incorporate Austria into the Reich, and to partition and eventually occupy Czechoslovakia. These moves made Hitler and Germany stronger and improved her position militarily. However, Hitler was able to cloak these moves in diplomatic doublespeak while avoiding directly threatening France and the United Kingdom, thus achieving his objectives without fighting.[10]

- When he is united, divide him. Sometimes drive a wedge between a sovereign and his ministers; on other occasions separate his allies from him. Make them mutually suspicious so that they drift apart. Then you can plot against them. (I.25, I.25 Chang Yu)

Hitler's mistake was to continue to reach beyond what was possible and attack Poland. Bound by treaty to come to Poland's aid, Germany's overreaching finally drove Britain and France to war.

Another method of winning without fighting is to make strategic moves that are radically different from what a defender expects or are difficult for the defender to respond to. These will lead to a delay or even the absence of a response. During the Cuban Missile Crisis, for example, President Kennedy faced the installation of Soviet nuclear missiles in the Western Hemisphere. If launched from Cuba they were capable of hitting American cities in minutes. With a range of 2,200 miles, these missiles could even reach cities deep in the heartland.

Kennedy had a number of options. He could do nothing and potentially encourage further moves by the Soviets. He could react directly by invading Cuba, with the high probability of beginning a nuclear war. Instead he chose a more indirect path to which this opponent would have difficulty responding to. He implemented a blockade against any Soviet ships bringing offensive weapons into Cuba. Kennedy announced this to the American populace over television and ended his speech with an appeal to communist leader Kruschev to remove the weapons. Kennedy continued playing to international opinion and ratcheting down the rhetoric by describing the blockade (really an act of war) as a "quarantine," which has a less aggressive tone. Kruschev, lacking an oceangoing surface navy, had limited options; he was forced to choose between withdrawing the missiles or starting World War III. Due to this unexpected move by the United States, he withdrew the missiles.[11]

■ Attack where he is unprepared; sally out when he does not expect you. (I.26)

In contrast, high-profile attacks, direct attacks, attacks perceived as significant threats, and attacks that the defender believes can be responded to successfully are almost certain to elicit an aggressive response. For example, the Japanese attack on Pearl Harbor was a limited tactical success (limited by the fact that the American aircraft carriers were out to sea and therefore not damaged or sunk in the attack). However, it was a strategic failure since it forced the United States into the war and rallied the American people to fight with a vengeance. The war would terminate with Japan in ruins and two cities devastated by the atomic bomb.

- If not in the interests of the state, do not act. If you cannot succeed, do not use troops. If you are not in danger, do not fight.   (XII.17)

When one is weaker than the enemy, avoiding a decisive battle and going on the strategic defensive until the situation improves is another means of winning without fighting. Unfortunately, that strategy is not always followed.

It was a hot summer day in 216 B.C. as the Roman and Carthaginian armies faced one another at a place in called Cannae. The population of Rome had grown frustrated with the strategy of Fabius Verrucosus, whose policy of avoiding battles in order to weaken the Carthaginian general Hannibal had earned him the nickname of *Cunctator*, the Delayer. Fabius had lost popular support when Hannibal had wisely destroyed every estate in one area but his. Although the Fabian approach had kept Roman power intact and ensured her precious allies did not desert her, it proved unpopular with *Senatus Populusque Romanus*, the Senate and People of Rome. In place of Fabius the Roman people elected two consuls who promised that they would find Hannibal and attack him. The Roman Senate thus ordered that a decisive battle must take place to rid Rome of its scourge, Hannibal.

Although the Romans had recently lost over 30,000 men to Hannibal in an ambush at Lake Trasimene in central Italy, new legions were formed to replace them. Eight legions, the most Rome had ever put into the field, marched to attack the Carthaginian. The two armies met at a citadel and food source that Hannibal had taken: Cannae, near the east coast of Italy. The Romans and their allies, roughly 80,000 strong, lined up in characteristic Roman fashion, infantry in the center and cavalry on the sides to protect the flanks. Whereas in prior battles the Romans had either been ambushed or had fought on ground of Hannibal's choosing, this time neither factor was present. Furthermore, Hannibal only had 50,000 men. The omens looked propitious on this, the third day of August.

The Romans launched a direct attack into the center of Hannibal's line (see Figure 1.2). It was in the center that the Carthaginian general had put his Celtic and Spanish swordsmen, the weakest and most inexperienced troops. Their line was bowed out towards the Romans,

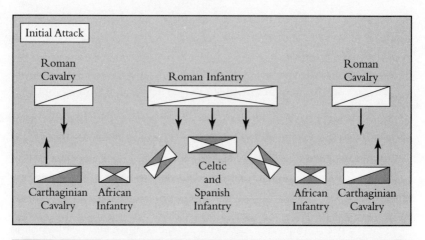

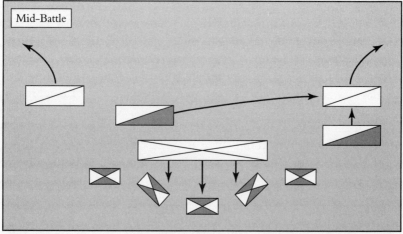

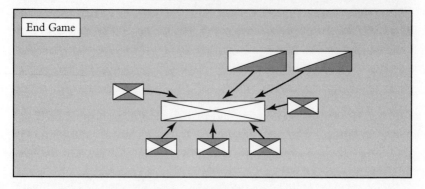

FIGURE 1.2   Battle of Cannae

anchored on both sides by phalanxes of African pikemen in column formation. On both flanks of the infantry line was cavalry, with that on the left being Hannibal's superb Numidian horsemen. As the Roman legions pressed forward, the Carthaginian line gave ground grudgingly. Meanwhile, the Numidian cavalry drove off that of the Romans and began to surround the legions. As the Romans moved further forward, they passed the African pikemen, whose phalanxes were now on the Roman flanks, completing the trap. As the legions turned to meet the threats from the new direction, the Celtic and Spanish infantry caught their breath and pushed forward. When the fighting was done it is estimated that up to 70,000 Romans met their death, the greatest defeat Rome would ever suffer. Rome would not win victory against Hannibal until several years later. In 206 B.C. the Roman general Scipio Africanus would avoid attacking Hannibal directly in Italy, instead capturing Hannibal's base in Spain. In 204 B.C. he sailed to attack Carthage itself. This indirect approach (which will be discussed in more detail later) forced Hannibal's recall from Italy to defend the homeland, where he would be defeated by Scipio on the plains of Zama.[12]

- ■ **Invincibility lies in the defense; the possibility of victory in the attack. (IV.5)**

This quote from Sun Tzu was true as well for General George Washington during the American Revolutionary War. After taking control of the Continental Army after the Battle of Bunker Hill in 1775, Washington was defeated many times by the British regulars and their American Tory allies. On a few occasions, such as Trenton, he was able to surprise and beat the British. However, his main achievement for six years was to keep his army intact. Thus he was able to keep the flame of Revolution alive and prevent King George's troops from extinguishing it. Ultimately, with crucial help from his country's ally France, he won the final victory at Yorktown in 1781. By keeping his army intact until the possibility of victory was within grasp, Washington helped create not just a new nation but *Novus Ordo Seclorum*, a New Order of the Ages. A picture with this motto would eventually be on one side of every U.S. dollar bill; on the other side would be Washington's.[13]

- ■ **Therefore, the enlightened ruler is prudent and the good general is warned against rash action. Thus the state is kept secure and the army is preserved. (XII.19)**

---

1. WIN ALL WITHOUT FIGHTING
Achieving the Objective Without Destroying It

---

2. AVOID STRENGTH/ATTACK WEAKNESS
Striking where the Enemy is Most Vulnerable

---

3. DECEPTION AND FOREKNOWLEDGE
Winning the Information War

---

4. SPEED AND PREPARATION
Moving Swiftly to Overcome Resistance

---

5. SHAPE YOUR OPPONENT
Preparing the Battlefield

---

6. CHARACTER-BASED LEADERSHIP
Leading by Example

FIGURE 1.3 Principles of *Sun Tzu and the Art of Modern Warfare*.

These quotations, illustrated with examples from history, make it clear that it is possible to win all without fighting. Thus one can win All-under-Heaven intact, achieve the nation's goals, and enable it to survive and prosper.

Sun Tzu's Remaining Principles

In this chapter we discussed the first principle, win all without fighting. This first principle is the overarching one; the other five principles provide the means of achieving it. (It is typical in Chinese philosophy to start first with the central idea and then expand from that point, laying out the viewpoint in an holistic manner.) The remainder of this book explains the other principles of *One Hundred Battles*, with a chapter devoted to each one. As you will see, each principle builds on and is supported by the others.

The second principle is an important tenet of this philosophy: avoid strength, attack weakness (see Figure 1.3).

- Now an army may be likened to water, for just as flowing water avoids the heights and hastens to the lowlands, so an army avoids strength and strikes weakness. (VI.27)

Although many generals prefer to attack each other head-on, this approach is very costly. As discussed earlier, wars of attrition can last for months and even years, leaving both sides in a weakened state. Instead, using the method of avoiding strength and attacking weakness maximizes gains while minimizing the use of the nation's resources. This, by definition, increases prosperity. This principle is discussed in detail in the next chapter.

To find and exploit an enemy's weakness requires a deep understanding of their leaders' strategy, capabilities, thoughts, and desires and a similar depth of knowledge of one's own strengths and weaknesses. It is critical to study the minds of the opposing generals and understand how they will react to one's moves. It is also important to understand the environment and terrain that will be contested.

- Therefore I say, "Know the enemy and know yourself; in a hundred battles you will never be in peril." (III.31)

It also demands a corresponding masking of one's plans.

- All warfare is based on deception. (I.17)

Chapter 3 sheds light on these topics. To fully utilize deception and foreknowledge effectively, it is critical to be able to act with blinding speed.

- Speed is the essence of war. Take advantage of the enemy's unpreparedness; travel by unexpected routes and strike him where has taken no precautions. (XI.29)

To move with such speed does not mean to do things hastily. In reality, speed requires much preparation. Reducing the time it takes to make decisions, develop new weapons, implement strategies, and respond to the enemy's moves is crucial. To think through and understand the opponent's reaction to one's possible moves also is essential.

■ To rely on rustics and not prepare is the greatest of crimes; to be prepared beforehand for any contingency is the greatest of Virtues.   (III.28 Ho Yen-hsi)

Chapter 4 expands on these topics. Putting all these factors into play successfully does not occur naturally. One must be able to "shape" the enemy.

■ And therefore those skilled in war bring the enemy to the field of battle and are not brought there by him.   (VI.2)

Shaping the enemy means changing the rules of the contest and making one's opponent conform to one's desires and actions. It means taking control of the situation away from the enemy. One way of shaping the enemy is by the skillful use of alliances. By building a strong web of alliances, the moves of the opponent can be limited. Also, by eliminating its alliances, one can weaken the enemy.

■ Look into the matter of his alliances and cause them to be severed and dissolved. If an enemy has alliances, the problem is grave and the enemy's position strong; if he has no alliances the problem is minor and the enemy's position weak.   (III.5 Wang Hsi)

By keeping plans and strategy closely held and using tactics to deceive the enemy about one's true intentions, one can continue to shape them by employing direct and indirect approaches.

■ He who knows the art of the direct (Cheng) and the indirect (Ch'i) approach will be victorious. Such is the art of maneuvering.   (VII.16)

A direct attack is one that occurs in an expected place at an expected time. An indirect assault is one that comes as a surprise, both in location and timing. By combining direct attacks on the enemy to fix their leaders' attention and deceive them, one can then use indirect attacks to win complete victory. By utilizing the indirect and direct approaches and skillfully crafting alliances the opponent can be put on the defensive and made more vulnerable to future attacks. Chapter 5 discusses this subject in more detail.

To achieve everything discussed so far takes a special kind of leader:

one who can see the correct course of action and take it immediately, who can relate to the military forces, other civilian leaders, and the population and gain commitment, who can empower subordinates to carry out the nation's strategy and who can use all personnel wisely. The attributes of this type of leader are discussed in detail in Chapter 6.

One more point must be made before continuing. Successful strategies are ones that are integrated and synergistic. Sun Tzu's strategic philosophy and approach is exactly that, with each principle interlocked with the others to form a sum greater than its parts.

Summary

Being able to dominate the environment to control or influence the nation's sphere of influence is the means, but survival and prosperity of the nation are the ends. This is done most economically by ensuring that the nation's goals are achieved in a way that leaves the environment intact (a peace in which the nation is in a better position than previously) and by winning without fighting, if possible. Fighting takes resources, which are limited and if used up, leave the nation defenseless. Continued fighting will destroy a country. To attack indirectly and win without fighting means the nation will use less resources and its goals will be achieved intact. It is then possible for the nation to dominate and prosper in a healthy environment instead of just surviving in a poor one.

- **Anciently, those called skilled in war conquered an enemy easily conquered.   (IV.10)**

  For he wins his victories without erring. "Without erring" means that whatever he does insures his victory; he conquers an enemy already defeated. Therefore the skillful commander takes up a position in which he cannot be defeated and misses no opportunity to master his enemy. Thus a victorious army wins its victories before seeking battle; an army destined to defeat fights in the hope of winning.   (IV. 12–14)

To do so requires a leader to seek and strike the enemy's weaknesses by shaping the mindsets of its leaders and making them conform to his wishes. To shape effectively, one must use knowledge of the enemy, the nation, and the world geopolitical and military situation. This allows one to launch direct attacks to fix the enemy's attention and then use deception and the indirect approach to close the battle. Speed and preparation, combined with excellent leadership, make this possible.

We have discussed the first principle of Sun Tzu's *Art of War*. With this foundation let us see how the Second Principle, Avoid Strength and Attack Weakness, helps us to win all without fighting and take all-under-Heaven intact.

2 ■ Avoid Strength, Attack Weakness
Striking Where the Enemy Is
Most Vulnerable

■ Now an army may be likened to water, for just as flowing water
avoids the heights and hastens to the lowlands, so an army avoids
strength and strikes weakness.   (VI.27)

Prior to the Persian Gulf War Saddam Hussein, leader of the nation of
Iraq, possessed the fourth largest army in the world. Its sixty-three divisions included eight elite Republican Guard units. Armed with the
latest Soviet tanks, South African artillery, Chinese and French anti-
ship missiles, Soviet and French fighter planes, SCUD regional missiles,
and chemical munitions capability, the Iraqi army had been tested in a
decade-long war with Iran. It was thus no surprise that it was able to
overrun its small neighbor Kuwait quite easily. This move in turn led
a coalition of nations, led by the United States, whose purpose was to
drive Iraq back and liberate Kuwait.

On February 24, 1991, the 1st and 2nd Divisions of the U.S. Marine
Corps launched their assault headlong into the Iraqi units blocking their
way to Kuwait City. The attack landed exactly where Saddam Hussein
expected it: along the most direct route the Americans could take to
liberate Kuwait. It was there that the Iraqi dictator had positioned the
majority of his million-man army. But it was two hundred miles to the
west that the real strike force of Desert Storm was located. One day

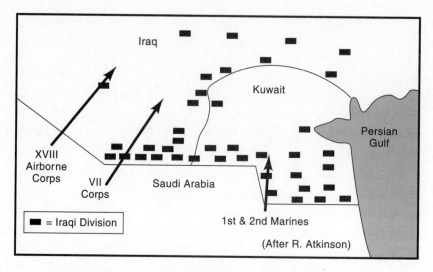

FIGURE 2.1   Operation Desert Storm: ground war attacks

after the Marines had fixed the attention of the Iraqis, a tempest of artillery fire announced the attack of the Coalition Army's Eighteenth Airborne Corps and Seventh Corps. Making easy work of the defenses in front of them, these two units performed an end run around the strongest part of Hussein's line (see Figure 2.1). Although outnumbered, by concentrating its strength against its opponent's weakness, the Coalition Army bagged thousands of prisoners, tons of military hardware, and brought Iraq to the peace table . . . all in one hundred hours.[1]

Avoid Strength

Avoid strength, strike weakness. This idea flows directly from the first principle of win all without fighting and the remaining principles flow from it. This principle enabled General Schwartzkopf's forces in the Persian Gulf War to defeat the Iraqis in four days while suffering almost no casualties.

If "win all without fighting" is the goal of the nation's strategy, then "avoid strength, attack weakness" is the key to achieving that goal. By focusing resources against the enemy's critical weak point, success is more easily achieved.

The reasoning behind this principle is simple: attacking the opponent's weak points is a much more effective and efficient use of the nation's resources than attacking its strength. Attacking weakness leverages the nation's limited resources; attacking strength wastes resources. Attacking weakness shortens the road to victory, while attacking strength makes it longer. Attacking weakness increases the value of the victory; attacking strength throws it away. Avoiding strength and attacking weakness achieves the maximum return for the least expenditure of resources in the shortest possible time.

Unfortunately, pitting strength against strength is often the preferred method of warfare among many Western countries. This is because the direct approach is strongly embedded in the Western mind. It makes its appearance in our legends, our sports, and, too often, our military adventures. It's the idea of two knights alone in armed combat, riding their chargers toward each other at high speed with the sole purpose of driving a lance through the opponent's heart. It's the shoot-out at OK Corral, the run-up-the-middle football mentality, the fight fire with fire approach. It's the frontal attack philosophy: impatient, unsubtle, and heads-down.

- **If the general is unable to control his impatience and orders his troops to swarm up the wall like ants, one-third of them will be killed without taking the city. Such is the calamity of these attacks. (III.9)**

So why then does the Western mind tend toward the direct attack approach? There are a number of reasons. One of the first is the heritage we have received from the Greeks. While the Greeks gave us many wonderful things, they also passed on to us their traditional means of warfare, which was the epitome of the direct approach. Herodotus, the early historian, quotes a contemporary of the early Greeks as saying this about the Greek philosophy of warfare: "And yet, I am told, these very Greeks are wont to wage war against one another in the most foolish way, through sheer perversity and doltishness. For no sooner is war proclaimed than they search out the smoothest and fairest plain that is to be found in all the land, and there they assemble and fight; whence it comes to pass that even the conquerors depart with great loss: I say nothing of the conquered, for they are destroyed altogether."[2]

Although perhaps somewhat exaggerated, this description of fifth-century B.C. Greek warfare is basically correct. Warfare only took place during the spring and summer. After a formal declaration of war, each city-state would send an army to meet on an open plain for the decisive battle. Ambushes, night attacks, and projectile weapons were looked upon as unfair and dishonorable means of fighting. Quick maneuvering to obtain an advantageous position was not attempted, as the goal was to meet at an agreed-to place. Instead, the warriors from each side—named hoplites after the round "hoplon" shield that they carried—would form up in phalanxes to do battle. The phalanx would be eight men deep, with each man's shield covering the next man's right arm, which held a spear for thrusting.[3] Although it came from an earlier time in Greek history, this description from Homer's *Iliad* most likely describes well what happened when the opposing armies met:

> That was how they closed with each other,
> And all their blind desire was to shred flesh
> With stropped bronze, eyes squinting against the glare
> Of helmets and corselets—just polished that morning—
> And the confusion of shields, like so many suns
> Shining through a bristling forest of spears.
> It was glorious to see—if your heart were iron,
> And you could keep from grieving at all the pain.

After the opposing formations collided, the *othismos* (the "push") would begin. The ranks of the two armies would dig in their feet and desperately try to force the other to back up and eventually break the enemy's formation. Again, Homer:

> When the two sides closed with each other
> They slammed together shields and spears,
> Rawhide ovals pressed close, bronze thoraxes
> Grinding against each other amid the groans
> And exultations of men being slain
> And of those slaying, as the earth ran with blood.[4]

The winner of the contest would be the army that stubbornly refused to break or give ground and eventually pushed hard enough to break the will and strength of the opponent. Once one formation broke there was little pursuit, due in part to lack of cavalry but also to the shared viewpoint that the defeated enemy would accept the result as final.

There were some very logical reasons for the Greeks to fight in this manner. For one thing, it limited the loss of civilian life and the destruction of property. More importantly, against non-Greeks the phalanx was undefeatable. From 650–350 B.C. no foreign army, no matter how strong, could stand up to a Grecian phalanx. From a less logical, more emotional standpoint, standing shoulder to shoulder to defend one's homeland served to uphold the Greek concept of honor and to bond citizens together. However, despite the passing of time and major changes in warfare, the Greek spirit of warfare lived on in the West. The desire for a decisive battle, the tendency to attack the enemy directly, and the view that the only honorable way of fighting was to push forward and not give up continued on through the Crusades and World War I up to the present day.[5]

Another source of the Western tendency of directly attacking strength is the popularity in military circles of Carl von Clausewitz's book *On War*. Clausewitz was a Prussian officer who fought against France during the Napoleonic wars. In those wars Clausewitz saw the new method of warfare introduced by France, which revolutionized the conduct of military operations. These cataclysmic changes had a huge impact on Clausewitz' theories.

Prior to the Napoleonic wars, armies were raised and supported by kings and princes. Composed of multiple nationalities and a mix of loyal men and mercenaries, their unwieldy organizational structures made them very inflexible. Tied by heavy logistical needs, they moved slowly and relied on stationary fortresses for supply. Once in battle they fought in parade-ground fashion and their tactics were time-consuming. Due to these limitations, and the assumption that warfare was used not to overthrow another sovereign but to merely to take land from him, warfare in pre–Revolutionary France had limited goals. These operational and objective limitations in turn called for limited resources.

The French Revolution changed all that. To defend against the counterrevolutionary forces of the European royalty, the entire nation was called to arms. The "levee en masse" drafted millions of citizen-soldiers to the French tricolor, creating the world's first instance of total warfare. Revolutionary fervor and the inspiration of nationalism provided the moral ingredient. The organization of the masses into more flexible division and corps formations and the ability to forage from the countryside dramatically increased the speed and mobility of the French army. The use of new tactics, such as the attack in column formation, massed artillery, and heavy cavalry attacks greatly increased shock and firepower. With this combination of moral and physical improvements the Napoleonic armies overcame the slower professional armies of ancient royal dynasties (such as Prussia's) like a tidal wave.

For Prussia to combat this new military model, Clausewitz and others recognized that the eighteenth-century methods of Frederick the Great were outmoded. Clausewitz became a leading reformer in the Prussian army, helping it to master the new tactics of nineteenth-century warfare. In 1807 he became secretary of the Prussian Reform Commission and lectured at the war college. These reforms enabled vanquished Prussia and her allies to turn the lessons of Napoleon against him and eventually defeat him. During that time Clausewitz rose to become a Prussian general, and fought against Napoleon's marshal Grouchy during the Waterloo campaign.

After the wars Clausewitz became the head of the Prussian War College, where he captured what he had learned and experienced during Napoleonic warfare in his book, *On War*. It has been said that *On War* is well-known but little read—probably because the book is a difficult read and was not completely finished. Furthermore, outside of Germany it was mostly read in translated form. However, this complex tome has significantly influenced western military thought for the last two centuries.

Clausewitz's viewpoint differs markedly from Sun Tzu's principles of win all without fighting and avoiding strength and attacking weakness. Because of his experience fighting against the French, Clausewitz strongly emphasized total mobilization of the country for warfare. He also believed in the need to seek a decisive battle (*Hauptschlacht*) in which one would annihilate the enemy:

1. Destruction of the enemy forces is the overriding principle of war, and so far as positive action is concerned, the principal way to achieve our object.

2. Such destruction of forces can *usually* be accomplished only by fighting.

3. Only major engagements involving all forces lead to major success.

4. The greatest successes are obtained where all engagements coalesce into one great battle.

5. Only in a great battle does the commander-in-chief control operations in person; it is only natural that he should prefer to entrust the direction of the battle to himself.[6]

This strategy of annihilation (*Vernichtungsstrategie*) dictated the need for extreme violence and destruction. Clausewitz has this to say when defining warfare: "Kindhearted people might think that there was some ingenious way to disarm or defeat an enemy without too much bloodshed and might imagine this is the true goal of the art of war. Pleasant as it sounds, this is a fallacy that must be exposed." He later states that "We are not interested in generals who win victories without bloodshed. The fact that slaughter is a horrifying spectacle must make us take war more seriously, but not provide an excuse for gradually blunting our swords in the name of humanity. Sooner or later someone will come along with a sharp sword and hack off our arms."

Finally, the Prussian military theorist did not believe in avoiding strength but in attacking it. "The scale of victory's sphere of influence depends, of course, on the scale of the victory, and that in turn depends on the size of the defeated force. For this reason, the blow from which the broadest and most favorable repercussions can be expected will be aimed against that area where the greatest concentration of enemy troops can be found; the larger the force with which the blow is struck, the surer its effect will be."

On War became extremely influential in Western military thought. The Chief of the Prussian General Staff, Helmuth von Moltke, ensured that the book permeated the thinking of the Prussian army. Moltke's success in the 1866 and 1870 German wars of unification made Clausewitz' ideas more popular in western military circles. Soldiers that they were, they missed the diplomatic moves made by Prussian Chancellor and statesman Otto von Bismarck that enabled those victories.

- For he wins his victories without erring. "Without erring" means that whatever he does ensures his victory; he conquers an enemy already defeated. (IV.12)

Lectures based on Clausewitz by Lucien Cardot at French École de Guerre made *On War* popular with Germany's ancient enemy, France. By the turn of the century the French military leadership was as enamored with the Prussian military theorist as that of his homeland.

Thus by the time of World War I, *On War* had become the Bible of the two main adversaries on what would soon become the Western Front. And like the Bible, few had read it while many extracted powerful passages out of context to support their positions. Focused on the precept of the total warfare, the goal of the decisive battle, the need for bloodshed, and the focus on attrition, Allied and German generals used Clausewitzian principles to build their plans. When those plans led to huge casualties, these same generals used Clausewitz again to justify the need to persevere and continue the bloody attacks. Merited or not, that was a major legacy of Clausewitz.

Another tendency toward direct, head-to-head combat comes not from Western history, but from our scientific approach. Answer this question: "What is the shortest distance between two points?" You will answer that it is a straight line. This line of reasoning has been so strongly indoctrinated into each Western child that our response to that question is immediate and unthinking. This is where we get into trouble, because while that answer is correct in a vacuum in space it is not necessarily true in the more complex real world.

Just because the shortest distance between two points is a straight line doesn't mean that following that line is the fastest, most profitable, and least resource-intensive means of achieving the objective. For example, let's assume that those two points are points on the earth; one in Beijing and one in Washington, D.C. To get from Washington to Beijing following a straight line would lead you to burrow directly through the center of the earth. However, as we all know, the fastest and least resource-intensive method is to go indirectly, flying over the curve of the earth.

In warfare too often it is assumed that the straight-line, direct attack is the fastest way to win victory. Marshaling greater numbers, the plan is to quickly overwhelm the enemy. However, the direct attack—the obvious attack—is what the enemy expects and is prepared for. Therefore, once the attack is launched it meets stiff resistance, which only increases over time. This leads to a war of attrition, not a war of maneuver, as there is no need to maneuver if one is going in a straight line. So you can see that the direct approach, while dangerously appealing, can be very misguided.

- In war, numbers alone confer no advantage. Do not advance relying on sheer military power. (IX.45)

    Although the troops of Yueh are many, of what benefit is this superiority in respect to the outcome? (VI.18)

The expectation on both sides at the beginning of the American Civil War was that it would be over quickly. The Southern view was that the Yankees did not have the stomach for war and could not stand up against soldiers molded in the military traditions of Dixie. Northerners believed that the South was either not serious about secession or that the rebellion would be quickly crushed. This belief was exemplified by the Federal government's initial action to call up as few as 75,000 troops to serve for a total of only ninety days. Before their three-month enlistments expired, these troops were expected to subdue an area the size of Western Europe containing 5.5 million people.

To achieve a quick victory the Union plan was to strike directly at the Confederate capital of Richmond. After all, it was only one hundred miles away from Washington, D.C., where the majority of Union troops were massing. It was believed by many that a major push south to capture Richmond would end the war in short order. The essence of this belief and strategy was summed up by famed newspaperman Horace Greeley's *New York Tribune* in the headline "On to Richmond!"

This simplistic approach backfired against the North, as the South was well-prepared for this strategy (after all, they just needed to read the newspaper to figure it out). First, the Confederates placed their strongest army, the Army of Northern Virginia, to defend the ground in front of Richmond. That army's left flank was protected by the Appalachian mountains, and it could use railroads to move troops quickly to defend against Union seaborne attempts to turn its right flank. The Army of Virginia could also use the Shenandoah Valley to threaten Washington, while Union troops defending this threat would be drawn away from Richmond. Finally, the ground to be defended was covered with natural obstacles such as rivers, hills, ridges, and woods, which the Southerners used to their advantage.

From 1861 to 1864 several battles were fought in this area between the Army of Northern Virginia and its opponent, the Union's Army of the Potomac. Their names ring throughout American history: Bull Run, the Seven Days, Fredericksburg, Chancellorsville, and other engagements. Despite great bravery, effort, and thousands of casualties, after three years of fighting Richmond still lay outside the Union Army's grasp. The direct approach proved not to be so quick after all. Only after General Grant was made commander of all Union forces and integrated the attacks in this theater with those of his other armies was the Confederacy broken. And even then Grant's aim in the East was not the city of Richmond itself, but the defeat and destruction of the Army of Northern Virginia. (Further proof that the fall of Richmond would not have caused the destruction of the rebellion was that in the summer of 1862, when the Army of the Potomac threatened to take Richmond, Confederate President Jeff Davis made plans to move the government. At no time was consideration given to the thought that abandoning the capital would lead to capitulation by the South.)

- A road, although it may be the shortest, is not to be followed if one knows it is dangerous and there is the contingency of ambush.

An army, although it may be attacked, is not to be attacked if it is in desperate circumstances and there is the possibility that the enemy will fight to the death.

A city, although isolated and susceptible to attack, is not to be attacked if there is the probability that it is well stocked with provisions, defended by crack troops under command of a wise general, that its ministers are loyal and their plans unfathomable.

Ground, although it may be contested, is not to be fought for if one knows that after getting it, it will be difficult to defend, or that he gains no advantage by obtaining it, but will probably be counterattacked and suffer casualties.   (VIII.11 Chia Lin)

This example illustrates the problem with the strength–against–strength approach: since it is not very creative nor based on attacking the enemy's weakness, it dooms a nation to a battle of attrition. The basic philosophy behind an attrition strategy is that the nation's resources will outlast those of the enemy. In practice, this means that one's country must not only have resources sufficient to overcome the opposing nation but also the will to expend them until its opponent capitulates.

■ Now when an army of one hundred thousand is raised and dispatched on a distant campaign the expenses borne by the people together with the disbursements of the treasury will amount to a thousand pieces of gold daily. There will be continuous commotion both at home and abroad, people will be exhausted by the requirements of transport, and the affairs of seven hundred thousand households will be disrupted.   (XIII.1)

Luckily the North had the resources to last through the first years of war and ultimately put together a more creative and successful strategy. But the price paid was high. Almost one million Americans ended up as casualties, the greatest number by far in any war fought by the U.S. The South was devastated and really only began to achieve its full potential one hundred years later, toward the end of the twentieth century. During the war there was civil unrest in the North, such as the draft riots in New York in 1863, that took 20,000 troops to quell. European powers took advantage of the war to meddle in affairs in the western hemisphere, with France setting up a puppet emperor in Mexico. Finally, the federal government took upon itself extraordinary powers outside the bounds of the Constitution, infringing on the rights of citizens and states, beginning a pattern of centralization of power.[7]

- Those adept in waging war do not require a second levy of conscripts nor more than one provisioning. (II.9)

Because strength-on-strength attacks are so direct, they can become imbued with meaning beyond that of a normal battle. This symbolic content can lead to decisions that make little strategic sense.

- The Emperor T'ai Wu led one hundred thousand troops to attack the Sung general Tsang Chih at Yu T'ai. The Emperor first asked Tsang Chih for some wine; as was customary before battle; Tsang Chih sealed up a pot full of urine and sent it to him. T'ai Wu was transported with rage and immediately attacked the city, ordering his troops to scale the walls and engage in close combat. Corpses piled up to the top of the walls and after thirty days of this the dead exceeded half his force. (III.9 Tu Mu)

Such was the case with the battle of Stalingrad in World War II. The defeat and destruction of the German Sixth Army at Stalingrad would prove to be a major blow to Hitler's plan to knock the Soviet Union out of the war. The loss of fifteen infantry divisions, three Panzer divisions, three motorized divisions, and one cavalry division through encirclement by the Red Army was the result of many mistakes. However, one crucial reason for the defeat was Hitler's personal insistence on taking the city.

As the fall of 1942 approached, German forces in southern Russia were stretched thin. On the right flank Army Group A was driving further south in an attempt to take the rich oil fields in the Caucasus. Simultaneously, Army Group B and the Sixth Army were pushing east with the aim of capturing Stalingrad. This would cut in half the Volga river, the Soviet Union's major water artery.

Initially, the push toward Stalingrad had been successful. However, as the Germans neared the city, the method of warfare turned from one of maneuver on the open Russian steppes to block-by-block fighting in the burnt and twisted rubble of demolished factories and houses. German Sixth Army commander Friedrich Paulus, whose objective was the capture of the city, launched a number of frontal assaults in the hope of taking Stalingrad quickly. However, Soviet resistance was fierce and the Red Army could not be dislodged. The Soviet Regional Party

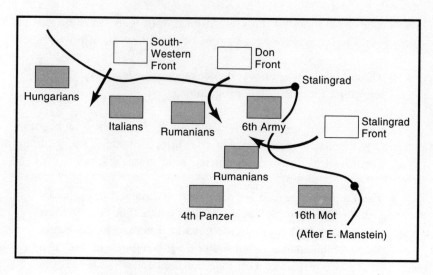

FIGURE 2.2   Soviet counterattack at Stalingrad

Committee issued a proclamation: "Comrades and citizens of Stalingrad! We shall never surrender the city of our birth to the depredations of the German invader. Each single one of us must apply himself to the task of defending our beloved town, our homes and our families. Let us barricade every street; transform every district, every block, every house, into an impregnable fortress."

In response, Hitler brought Paulus to his headquarters and directed that "the vital thing now was to concentrate every available man and capture as quickly as possible the whole of Stalingrad itself and the banks of the Volga." To rally the German people the Propaganda Ministry blared that the "greatest battle of attrition that the world has ever seen" was happening at Stalingrad and that the Russians were getting the worst of it. Just as Verdun in World War II had a magnetic effect on the French leadership, Stalingrad had a similar effect on Hitler. Part of his drive to take Stalingrad was strategic, but perhaps more important was its political symbolism. After all, the city was named after his nemesis, the Soviet dictator. Furthermore, Stalingrad had become the ultimate test of German arms. Failure here would destroy the aura of German invincibility. So in October, Paulus launched a frontal assault on the most heavily defended Soviet strong points in the northern part of Stalingrad. The bloody fighting went on for three weeks, gradually pushing the Red troops inch by inch back to the river.

However, the Russians were not losing the battle of attrition.

While feeding enough troops into Stalingrad to maintain a foothold in the city, they were building up huge reserves of fresh troops, tanks, and air forces. Composed of twenty-seven infantry divisions and nineteen armored brigades, these units were positioned on both flanks of the German thrust into Stalingrad. To lead them the top Soviet commanders from other fronts were brought in. In late November of 1942, the Soviets launched these units in two thrusts, one on either side of the Sixth Army (see Figure 2.2). Moving quickly they encircled the Sixth Army in a few short days, surrounding it in a ring of steel. To exacerbate the problem, Hitler refused to let the Sixth Army attempt to break out, believing that his strength of will would overcome the reality on the ground. And so despite attempts from German forces outside the ring to break in, the Sixth Army was lost. As a result a quarter of a million men perished, Germany lost all the ground captured in the summer campaign, and its army's aura of invincibility was broken.[8]

- Thus, those skilled in war subdue the enemy's army without battle. They capture his cities without assaulting them and overthrow his state without protracted operations. (III.10)

Attack Weakness

- The nature of water is that it avoids heights and hastens to the lowlands. When a dam is broken, the water cascades with irresistible force. Now the shape of an army resembles water. Take advantage of the enemy's unpreparedness; attack him when he does not expect it; avoid his strength and strike his emptiness, and like water, none can oppose you. (IV.20 Chang Yü)

Water takes the path of least resistance and flows with unstoppable force to reach its ultimate destination. The point made by the above quotation is that the same is true in the strategic realm; to achieve one's objective, take the path of least resistance. Then the mission will be accomplished and the nation will still have resources left for the next task.

The Western view might be that attacking weakness is somehow unfair or unsporting. However, the master strategist does not need to prove anything by taking the enemy head-on. Look at nature: even a lion doesn't go after the fastest antelope in the herd. Instead he runs down the slowest.

■ Create an invincible army and await the enemy's moment of vulnerability.   (III.28 Ch'ên Hao)

There are several ways a strategist can follow this principle and create a situation where a nation's strengths are applied against the enemy's weaknesses. One method is to attack the weakest part of the enemy's defenses. When the Red Army launched its encircling attacks on Stalingrad, the Soviets did not directly assault the battle-hardened German troops in Stalingrad. Instead the Red Army attacked the troops of Germany's allies, the poorly led and equipped Rumanian, Hungarian, and Italian troops on the flanks of the Sixth Army.

Still another method of attacking weakness is to select a key resource the enemy needs and deprive him of it. What is critical is to select the right resource and the proper means of denying it to the enemy. Ask yourself what country executed the most successful submarine campaign in World War II. What most likely comes to mind immediately is that of the German U-boats in the Atlantic. However, although coming close to cutting off supplies to Britain, in the end the U-boat campaign failed to achieve its objectives.

The most successful submarine campaign of World War II occurred in the Pacific theater, conducted by the United States against Japan. Despite a slow start due to a lack of submarines and malfunctioning torpedoes, the U.S. was eventually able to keep roughly seventy subs on patrol at war's end. With a range of 10,000 miles, these 1,500-ton fleet submarines were able to cut off the island of Japan from the resources of her newly captured possessions. While the subs were able to sink eight carriers and a battleship during the war, their primary contribution was to sink oil tankers and other merchant vessels. Operating in packs and armed with intelligence on the Japanese ships' positions, the U.S. subs were sinking ships faster than they could be replaced. Roughly a third of these were oil tankers. On more and more cruises, U.S. subs returned with a broom posted in their conning tower, signifying that the Japanese merchant fleet was being swept from the seas. This left Japan unable to acquire the resources to produce planes and ships necessary to continue war, or to power them if they were built. One Admiral stated that "the American submarine campaign against commerce was probably the most important single factor in the defeat of Japan."[9]

There are other ways to apply one's strengths against an enemy's weakness.

■ That you may march a thousand li [approximately one-third of
a mile] without wearying yourself is because you travel where
there is no enemy. Go into emptiness, strike voids, bypass what
he defends, hit him where he does not expect you. (VI.6 Sun
Tzu and Ts'ao Ts'ao)

One can "go into emptiness, strike voids, and bypass what he defends" by maneuvering around the enemy's strength. Warfare by maneuver is the antithesis of attrition warfare, as it substitutes swift
movement for overwhelming numbers.

In the First World War, the German army developed a new approach to break out of the trench warfare stalemate. It was called the
"stormtrooper" concept, and its basis was the *Sturmtruppen* unit. These
were small groups of highly trained, highly motivated soldiers who were
skilled in different weapons systems, such as machine guns, flame-
throwers, mortars, and mobile assault artillery. These specialists and their
weapons systems were integrated into assault teams that were trained
to work together and leverage one another's special capabilities.

Unlike Allied infantry, the stormtroopers did not advance in waves
of long lines, but crossed "no-man's-land" independently and in dispersed fashion. Preceded by a short but extremely intense artillery barrage, they moved by squads in short bounds. Their trademarks were
speed, surprise, and violence. Coordinating the use of their varied
weapons systems to support the advance, stormtroopers took the "combined arms" approach down to the smallest unit level possible.

The stormtroopers' mission was to first achieve a breakthrough in
the enemy's line of trenches. They sought not to attack Allied strong
points, but to instead maneuver around them and attack the rear areas.
Follow-on units of regular infantry would then mop up the remaining
isolated enemy strong points. Reinforcements would be fed not to
where enemy resistance was strongest and the attack had bogged down,
but instead to where success had been achieved. By these means the
momentum of the advance would be maintained and penetration of
the enemy's defenses would deepen.

■ To be certain to take what you attack is to attack a place the
enemy does not protect. To be certain to hold what you defend
is to defend a place the enemy does not attack. (VI.7)

While experimental attacks using the stormtrooper concept had
been launched as early as 1915, it was in 1918 that stormtroopers were

first used on a large scale on the Western Front. Early 1918 found Germany with one last opportunity to win the war. Numerous German divisions had been freed up from the Eastern front once Russia had been knocked out of the war, and 210 divisions were now assembled to strike in the West. However, it was critical that the attacks be launched before fresh units from the United States reach Europe in numbers large enough to tip the scales.

Germany's "Peace Offensives" comprised three separate assaults launched in the Spring of 1918. Using *Sturmtruppen* units as the spearheads of these attacks, the German Army captured ten times the amount of ground the Allies had in their 1917 offensives. The new tactics of the stormtroopers bewildered the Allied armies and sent them reeling. Germany came within a hairsbreadth of winning the war.

The new stormtroop tactics brought tactical mobility back to the battlefield and achieved success by using Sun Tzu's methods of going into emptiness, striking voids, and bypassing defenses. However, the German army lacked the tools to achieve strategic mobility. Once the breakthrough had been accomplished the infantry-based stormtroops were unable to exploit the opening and continue the pursuit. This lack of strategic mobility ultimately meant that the German peace offensives came up short.

The promise of the stormtroop concept would have to wait until World War II to be fulfilled. It would be done by the Germans, who would do so by adding to the concept the mobility of massed tanks, or Panzers. The Panzers, aided by the "flying artillery" of the Stuka divebomber, would evolve the stormtroop concept into that of the Blitzkrieg.

The Blitzkrieg ("Lightning War," a term coined most likely by American journalists) concept evolved during the interwar years through the ideas and experiments of German and British military theorists. British theorists J. F. C. Fuller and B. H. Liddell-Hart were the earliest proponents of mobile tank warfare, but the British army did not adopt their concepts. They and the French preferred to parcel out their tanks amongst their infantry. The result was that the tanks' power was diluted through dispersion and its mobility was limited to the speed of the foot soldier they accompanied.

The Germans, seeking a means to overcome the small professional army imposed on them by the Treaty of Versailles, eagerly accepted the new method of warfare. They understood that the new approach could combine the fluid tactics of the stormtroopers with the mobility and shock of armor and the devastating effects of air power.

The Blitzkrieg concept called for fast penetration of enemy lines followed by Panzer attacks against the "soft" targets in the rear areas. By using fast-moving, wide-ranging tank forces to destroy headquarters and supply units and encircle front-line units, the German army would overwhelm first the Poles in 1939, the French and British in 1940, and then the Russians in 1941. The idea was not to directly attack the enemy forces across a broad front, but instead attack through them at specific points to drive to the open spaces beyond. The goal was not the grinding physical destruction of the enemy but the disruption of their communications, the elimination of their ability to respond in coordinated fashion, and the collapse of their morale.[10]

- Troops thrown against the enemy as a grindstone against eggs is an example of a solid acting upon a void. Use the most solid to attack the most empty. (V.4 Sun Tzu and Ts'ao Ts'ao)

Using strength to attack weakness can also be used by a maritime power against a continental power. A maritime power is one whose military power is derived primarily from its naval forces, while a continental power is a country whose strength is based on its land forces. As one would expect, maritime powers have excellent access to the sea and are usually geographically isolated from land-based opponents. They tend to derive their wealth from commerce and their populaces are often freethinkers. Athens, Britain, and the United States are prototypical maritime powers. Continental powers typically share borders with one or more land-based powers that threaten them and historically have derived their wealth from agriculture. They are typically more hierarchically oriented and conformist. Sparta, Germany, and Russia are exemplars of continental powers.

Maritime powers, with seas to provide a defensive barrier from enemies and a navy to move troops about, can use their naval mobility to choose where they want to strike. To ensure greater chance of success in war, they often ally with a land-based power, many times providing funds to that ally to keep them engaged in the war. Britain has used this strategy several times throughout her history.

During the Napoleonic wars Britain used her navy to support her longtime trading partner and ally Portugal against France. Napoleon, trying to bolster his Continental System (which aimed at keeping European goods from reaching Britain and vice-versa), sent his troops through Spain to attack Portugal and staunch the flow of European products. While on their way they overthrew the Spanish government and installed Napoleon's brother Joseph.

Using naval capability, Britain sent General Arthur Wellesley (the future Duke of Wellington) to Portugal with 25,000 men to help protect it. While he and his Portuguese allies never numbered more than 60,000 men, they engaged twice their number of French troops. When the French besieged Wellesley's army, dug in at the Line of Torres Vedras, Wellesley was able to inflict 40,000 casualties at a cost of only 4,000 men.

As Henry IV of France was fond of saying, "Spain is a country where large armies starve and small armies get beaten." The French found this to be true as they tried to put down the Spanish guerillas while at the same time attempting to defeat the conventional army led by Wellesley. The ability of the British to sustain her forces via her navy in the Peninsular War was instrumental in Napoleon's defeat. While Britain could support her troops using open sea lanes from Britain to Portugal, France had to send her troops overland, fighting every inch of the way. The Peninsular War lasted six years, cost the French 400,000 casualties (as many as she lost in Russia in 1812), and destroyed Napoleon's aura of invincibility.[11]

> ■ And therefore those skilled in war avoid the enemy when his spirit is keen and attack him when it is sluggish and his soldiers homesick. This is control of the moral factor. In good order they await a disorderly enemy; in serenity, a clamorous one. This is control of the mental factor. Close to the field of battle, they await an enemy coming from afar; at rest, an exhausted enemy; with well-fed troops, hungry ones.   (VII.22–24)

Preemptive Strikes

Another method of utilizing this principle is to create a weakness through a preemptive strike. This is an especially useful tactic when one's enemy has greater material resources.

This was the strategy employed by the Israelis at the beginning of the Six Day War in 1967. After Egypt under Nassar requested the United Nations peacekeeping forces to leave the Sinai and he signed a joint defense pact with King Hussein of Jordan, Israel was in a perilous position. In addition to the 80,000 troops and 800 tanks on her southern flank in Egypt and the Jordanian forces to the east, Syria also threatened from the north. While the Arab regular forces could be kept in place for a sustained period, Israel could not afford to keep her reserves called up forever without destroying her economy. Furthermore, Israel had little territory and could not trade space for time. Finally, with a small population, heavy losses could not be sustained. With these considerations in mind, Israel's leaders opted for a preemptive air strike to create a weakness, which armored assaults and paratrooper landings could then exploit.

To mislead the Arabs as to their intentions, the Israelis put thousands of their soldiers on leave and made statements to the effect that the time for military action had passed. Then, at 7:45 A.M. on June 5, the Israeli airplanes hit Egypt's air fields. The time itself was selected to optimize surprise; 7:45 was three hours past dawn, dawn being the time the Egyptians expected that a surprise attack would come. It was also the time most of their officers were either at breakfast or driving to work. Finally, the early morning mist over the airfields had cleared and visibility was excellent, allowing targets to be seen and hit.

On the first day of the war the Israelis hit nineteen airfields and twenty-three radar sites. In the first three hours Israel's air force knocked out 300 of 340 Egyptian aircraft, leaving little more than ten percent of Egypt's air force left to fight. Few of the remaining planes were of modern vintage. Simultaneously with the air attack, Israel let loose her army.

By the end of day two the Arab forces had lost over 400 planes (the vast majority destroyed on the ground) and, lacking any air cover, her army lost the Sinai. By day three Israeli troops had captured Jerusalem. By the time the Arabs sued for peace on June 10, Israel had crippled the forces of Egypt, Syria, and Jordan, conquered territory that added greatly to military security, and humiliated the Arab forces and their Soviet allies. The tiny country had done so with fewer than 4,000 casualties.[12]

- Thus the potential of troops skillfully commanded in battle may be compared to that of round boulders which roll down from mountain heights. . . . Thus one need use but little strength to achieve much.   (V.25 Sun Tzu and Tu Mu)

As the example of the Six Day War shows, a properly executed preemptive strike can create a weakness (in this case, lack of air support) which can then be exploited. There is an advantage to being the one to strike first, to launch a preemptive attack to gain the advantage. (Interestingly, in the Asian game of Go, the advantage of first mover is acknowledged and accounted for. The game can be made even either by allowing the weaker player to move first or awarding the player who moves second additional points.) However, there are two caveats for a preemptive strike strategy.

First, it is imperative that the preemptive strike accomplish all its objectives. Japan's preemptive strike against Pearl Harbor succeeded in destroying the American Pacific Fleet's battleships. However, the U.S. aircraft carriers were at sea and left untouched. As a result, the Japanese admiral Nagumo had to flee the scene to avoid allowing his force to be attacked by planes from the U.S. carriers. This in turn meant that the oil and dock facilities at Pearl Harbor were not hit as planned. Japan could have totally wiped out the entire Pacific Fleet and forced the U.S. to begin the war with the West Coast as her starting point. Instead, Japan succeeded only in arousing the fighting spirit of America while leaving the U.S. carrier forces intact and an American operational base far out in the Pacific to support them. The objectives of the planned preemptive strike were not totally achieved.[13]

The second caveat is that if the preemptive attack is successful, it may make sense to use the temporary advantage to offer magnanimous terms and build a lasting peace. This is where Israel may have made a mistake. Rather than use her newly won position to come to terms with her Arab enemies, she made no serious effort to do so. So the Six Day War, while it enabled Israel to continue to survive, did not allow a lasting peace. Fewer than six years would pass before the country would again be at war with its neighbors.[14]

Attacking Weaknesses at Boundary Points

Another place weaknesses occur is at the boundaries points. In war, these boundaries occur where two unit's areas of responsibility meet. In these boundary areas, responsibility for coverage may be unclear, coordination is difficult, gaps between units may appear, and weaknesses develop. Strategically it is wise to seek out these boundary points and attack them as there is a higher probability of achieving a breakthrough. Furthermore, once a breakthrough is achieved, there is a strong urge for each unit being attacked to retreat away from one another to protect their rear areas. This results in opening the gap further and creates the possibility of defeating each unit separately. Finally, because the attack is occurring between two areas of responsibility, it is more difficult for the two units to coordinate a joint defense or mount a combined coun-terattack.

On the eve of May 10, 1940, Germany was fresh from victory in Poland. Now her army faced that of the Western allies, and was outnumbered. Roughly 2.8 million Germans with 2,600 tanks and 7,700 artillery pieces were opposed by 3.7 million men backed by 3,600 tanks and 11,500 artillery pieces. Aircraft was the only area in which Germany had numerical superiority (3,700 to 1,800)—yet to be successful, it had to take the offensive.

In a few short weeks Germany had achieved that success against the odds, and had done so in devastating fashion. The German armed forces had knocked France, Holland, and Belgium out of the war and pushed Britain off the continent. They did so by utilizing the principle of attacking weakness and striking at key boundary points.

The German attack was focused at a point where the right flank of the French Ninth Army touched the left flank of the French Second Army. This point was not only a boundary where two armies met. It was also the point where the static Maginot line fortifications to the south ended and the mobile forces of the north began. This area was also a place through which the Western Allies never expected an attack; thus they left it defended by a few weak units.

The area was the Ardennes, a heavily wooded and hilly area that was thought to be too difficult for mobile offensive operations. In the Ardennes were packed the bulk of Germany's new armored force. Composed of seven Panzer and three motorized divisions, the formation was named Panzer Group Kleist, after its commander. Supporting these elite units were another thirty-five regular infantry divisions, while opposing this massive armored fist were French troops of poor quality with limited mobility and firepower.

And so on May 10 the German offensive began. By feinting with a strong attack in Belgium to the north, the Germans led French and British forces to move in that direction. Meanwhile, in the south, Panzer Group Kleist drove through the weak French defenses defending the route from the Ardennes. Although Kleist's Panzers were constantly being reined in by a nervous Hitler, they nevertheless continued their relentless drive to the Channel coast. By pushing toward that objective they forced the British and other units in the north to retreat to the coast. Meanwhile, the French forces in the south had to move in the opposite direction to protect Paris and the part of France that remained free. This opened the gap even further, allowing Panzer Group Kleist to reach the Channel by May 20.

After eliminating over a million Allied troops from the equation and forcing the remaining troops in the north to evacuate to Britain minus their heavy equipment, the Germans reorganized and faced south. On June 5 they attacked the remaining French forces, who were without air cover and now outnumbered two to one. In short order it was over; Paris fell on June 14 and was granted an armistice on June 22. German losses for the lightning forty-six-day campaign were less than 160,000 men.[15]

While the Germans successfully utilized strength against weakness and attacked the enemy at a crucial boundary point, there are other types of boundary points a strategist can take advantage of. These can take several forms. One might be enemy combined arms actions, such as an infantry unit using close-air support. Or it might be a joint effort between branches of service, such as a navy–army operation. Wherever two or more units (especially units of different types or nationalities) have to coordinate, the probability of a weakness occurring is high; the strategist need only look for them and think how best to take advantage of them.

Attacking Nonmaterial Weaknesses

For attacks to be successful, they do not necessarily have to attack a physical weakness. They can be psychologically based, directed at the mind and morale of the enemy.

- ■ **Anger his general and confuse him. Pretend inferiority and encourage his arrogance. Keep him under strain and wear him down. (I.22–24)**

In early 1942 the fortunes of war were not smiling on the U.S. armed forces. Pearl Harbor contained the hulks of many of America's battleships, several island possessions had been captured, and Japan now ruled from Hong Kong and Malaysia to Wake Island and the Philippines. But America was about to strike back with a bold air attack on Japan itself.

On April Fool's Day, sixteen B-25 bombers were put aboard the aircraft carrier *Hornet*. Commanding the B-25s was Lieutenant Colonel James H. Doolittle, a former world speed record holder. The task force, composed of the *Hornet* and the *Enterprise*, planned to close within three hundred miles before launching the bombers. However, the American naval forces were seen by a Japanese ship seven hundred miles out and to protect the vital carriers it was necessary to launch the planes immediately.

Thirteen of the bombers hit Tokyo and the rest hit other cities. While the physical damage inflicted was minimal, the psychological impact was huge. The populace was shocked and the leaders were extremely upset. As a result the leadership overreacted, with Admiral Yamamoto changing Japan's strategy of invading Hawaii and Australia. Instead, he planned to destroy American naval power in a decisive battle near Midway Island. This would end the naval threat to the home islands of Japan.

This change in strategy to a quest for the decisive battle at Midway proved disastrous for Japan. The Battle of Midway resulted in a huge defeat for Japan and proved to be the major turning point of the war in the Pacific. Japan lost four carriers and numerous air crews and her aura of invincibility was shattered. The materiel advantage now went the United States. The lesson to learn is that even though an attack may not inflict major physical damage, it can be used to manipulate the enemy's emotions. If aroused enough, these emotions will overcome logic and negatively affect strategy.[16]

Selecting and Concentrating the Attack: The Schwerpunkt

One of the intrinsic values of "avoid strength, attack weakness" is that it does not take great resources to apply it. In fact, having substantially greater resources than the enemy may even be a hindrance to creative strategy, since the temptation is to rely on overwhelming force instead of cleverness. What is critical, especially if one has limited resources, is that one apply the right amount of resources at exactly the right spot. Then, with a little push, an avalanche is released.

- Therefore when using troops, one must take advantage of the situation exactly as if he were setting a ball in motion on a steep slope. The force applied is minute, but the results are enormous. (V.25 Chang Yu)

During World War II, German forces called this point of attack the *schwerpunkt*. It means "the center of gravity" and is the place where one concentrates the most resources to achieve the greatest impact. Through intelligence one must determine this point of weakness in the enemy and amass power accordingly. For example, in the Gulf War the F-117A "Stealth" bomber constituted less than three percent of U.S. air power. However, the United States leveraged this secret weapon's tremendous strength of radar invisibility to carry out thirty-one percent of all air attacks on the first day of the air campaign.[17]

As discussed earlier in the chapter, there are many potential places where weaknesses reside; one must decide which weakness would be the most effective to attack. This is done by balancing the vulnerability of a weakness against the potential damage to the enemy. Obviously, the best weakness to attack would be one that not only is extremely vulnerable but, if attacked successfully, would be especially damaging to the enemy.

- **Thus a victorious army is as a hundredweight balanced against a grain; a defeated army as a grain balanced against a hundredweight.   (IV.19)**

This weak point is precisely where the *schwerpunkt* must be. It is essential to concentrate the physical resources and efforts in time and space here; all other efforts must be secondary. Again, the Gulf War provides an excellent example. The main strike force of Desert Storm was the Seventh Corps, which had the mission of sweeping around the Iraqi right flank and destroying the Republican Guard divisions. This Corps contained 1,300 high-tech Abrams and Challenger tanks, the largest amount of armor ever assembled in a corps in the history of warfare. This powerful force was concentrated at the most vulnerable point of the Iraqi line, and it proved also to be the point where the Coalition Army could inflict the most damage.

At this point, one may be thinking that Sun Tzu's philosophy means that one should not make the effort to improve those parts of the nation's military that are weak or failing. This is not the case. Strength and weaknesses are relative. Therefore, if critical areas of the nation's defenses are obsolete, they should be upgraded. Resources should be expended to bring them up to par. However, the majority of the nation's resources must be concentrated to build a strength that can be used against the enemy's weak point. Only in that fashion can they be used most effectively. To parcel out resources in an attempt to make every service "world class" is wasteful. No nation in the world has the resources to do that. The drive to be strong in all areas was a mistake Germany made prior to the First World War. This mistake led both to the creation of alliances against her and the dispersion of crucial resources.

One of the causes of World War I was Germany's naval buildup. The new Kaiser, after reading Captain Alfred Mahan's book *The Influ-*

ence of Sea Power Upon History, 1660–1783, was enamored with creating a strong German navy. He was encouraged in this by his chief naval officer, Admiral Alfred von Tirpitz. Although Germany was primarily a continental power whose strength lay in her army, Kaiser Wilhelm II believed that a strong navy would enable Germany to obtain colonies like those of Britain and France. These colonies would validate Germany as both a true empire and a world power.

However, Germany's drive to build a navy that could rival Great Britain's ultimately led to negative consequences. Britain could not afford to allow Germany to overtake her in naval strength, so the navy was upgraded. Also, Britain made agreements with the United States and Japan to minimize the naval threat from those two countries. That enabled Britain to concentrate power in the North Atlantic against Germany. Furthermore, Germany's aggressive move to create a high seas fleet drove Britain to make an alliance with France and Russia. Finally, diverting resources away from the army to the navy seriously limited Germany's ability to successfully carry out a two-front war. Here the Kaiser ignored the country's traditional reliance on its land forces and Bismarck's strategy for balancing rival powers to achieve leadership on the continent. Bismarck was dismissed by the Kaiser in 1890. Bismarck knew that Germany's strength depended on having a strong army and invested resources to ensure that this would always be the case. Bismarck's confidence in Germany's land-based superiority was such that, when it was thought that Britain might land troops on the German coast, Bismarck reportedly said that he would send a policeman to arrest it.

In the end, Germany's High Seas Fleet only went to sea for one major battle, the Battle of Jutland in 1916. The battle was unsuccessful in breaking the Allied blockade, which continued to create critical shortages both at the front and at home. Meanwhile, the German Army failed in its attempt to end the war quickly and ultimately surrendered in November 1918.[18]

The Attack/Defend/Attack Cycle

In battle there will be times one may not have the strength to attack. The enemy may have the advantage and one may need to gain time to secure allies or build reserves. In these times it will be necessary to go on the defensive and hold on for survival, wearing down the enemy and husbanding resources in preparation for attacks that will eventually enable victory. This is especially true when forces are rebelling against

the government or fighting a much stronger foreign power using guerilla tactics.

- **One defends when his strength is inadequate; he attacks when
  it is abundant.   (IV.6)**

In late 1780 the war was not going well for the American rebels
against the British. The main British effort had moved to the southern
colonies, where Lord Charles Cornwallis used his army to capture
Charleston, South Carolina. The British objective in moving in this
direction was to subjugate the south while at the same time getting
thousands of loyalist Tories to rally to the Crown's cause.

In the process of taking Charleston, Cornwallis captured 5,500 regular American troops, almost 400 guns, and tons of other weapons and
supplies. These were resources the rebel forces could ill afford to lose.
Cornwallis then moved north and defeated another rebel army under
Horatio Gates at Camden, South Carolina. As British successes continued more Tories rallied to the British flag. One of the most notorious
flags to which they flocked belonged to Colonel Benastre Tarleton.

Tarleton was a man with a reputation for ruthlessness. "Tarleton's
Quarter" was a term that came into use after Tarleton's Legion slaughtered defenseless rebels who were trying to surrender at the Battle of
the Waxhaws. However, Tarleton was also an excellent tactician and
became a leader Cornwallis depended on to help subjugate the Carolinas.

To stop Cornwallis, George Washington sent a trusted lieutenant
and his best commander, Nathanael Greene. In addition to this former
Quaker the American commander-in-chief also sent another general by
the name of Daniel Morgan. Together they assembled the remnants of
the rebel army and allowed it to rest for a few weeks before joining
battle with the British.

Nathanael Greene's strategy was to split his forces in two in order
to enable them to more easily supply themselves and to better respond
to any of Cornwallis' potential moves. Greene took the easternmost
force, while the one in the west was commanded by Morgan. Cornwallis' response was to split his forces into three. He detached one force
to take up a blocking position to protect Camden and then took the
major part of his army north to conquer North Carolina. Finally, he
split off Tarleton to eliminate the threat from Morgan. These two subordinates and their relatively small units, whom Cornwallis and Greene

had set in motion, were fated to have a major impact on the outcome of the war.

After trailing Morgan for a number of days, on January 17, 1781, Tarleton's small army caught up with Morgan's at a place called Cowpens. Although any retreat by Morgan was made impossible by the Broad River, it was a place of Morgan's own choosing. As his force was composed to a large extent of less-trained militia, Morgan wanted to ensure they were incapable of running away.

- Throw the troops into a position from which there is no escape and even when faced with death they will not flee. For if prepared to die what can they not achieve? Then officers and men together put forth their utmost efforts. In a desperate situation they fear nothing; when there is no way out they stand firm. (XI.33)

Morgan was a plainspoken man who wore a rifleman's frock just like his men. He was a big man who always sought out the most dangerous part of the battlefield. Morgan led by example, yet was also an extremely capable strategist.

He had thought through how Tarleton would fight the battle. Morgan knew that Tarleton would strike with his cavalry on the flanks and infantry in the middle, supported by artillery. Using the shock effect of his horsemen and the power of British regulars, Tarleton expected to quickly scatter the rebels and then run them to ground as they attempted to get away. To take advantage of this knowledge of his enemy, Morgan put his militia in the front ranks, with his Continental regulars behind them. Finally, he kept his cavalry in reserve (see Figure 2.3).

Morgan knew that the militia could not stand up against Tarleton's cavalry, so he told them to fire two volleys and then retire behind the regulars as another reserve. They were also told to aim first at the British officers. Morgan informed his regulars to expect the retreat of the militia, so they would not think the militia was breaking and running away.

Expecting an easy victory, Tarleton launched his attack. As the British approached the militia fired their two volleys. These volleys were effective in eliminating Tarleton's cavalry from the equation. Although some of the cavalry broke through and hit the militia as it was reforming, Morgan's cavalry reserve drove them off. As the British in-

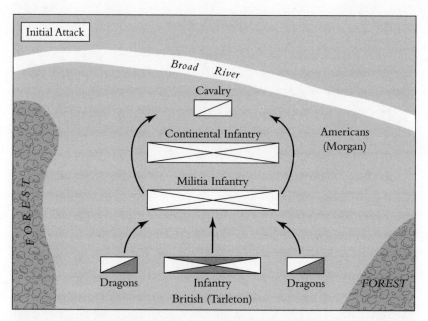

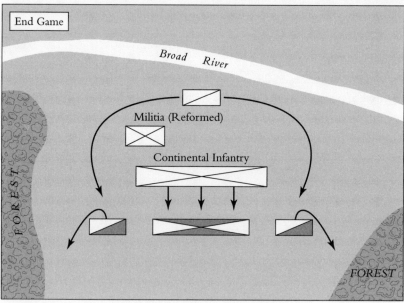

FIGURE 2.3   Battle of Cowpens

fantry lunged forward to take advantage of the militia's supposed retreat, they were shocked to see the line of Continental regulars behind them. For a moment they paused and were further disconcerted when the militia regrouped off to their flank. Nevertheless, the British line re-formed and moved forward again.

At this point the Continentals, composed of companies from Delaware, Virginia, and Maryland, let loose their volley. One militiaman reported that "when the regulars fired, it seemed like one sheet of flame from right to left." As the British closed with them, the Continentals continued to pour fire into them, and the slaughter on both sides was great.

At this point a misunderstood order almost led to disaster for the Americans. The result of the misunderstanding was that the right flank of the Continentals turned around and began retreating. The British sensed victory and pressed forward, hoping to overrun the Americans. However, the American officers regained control and ordered an about-face, the Continental troops having reloaded as they retired. The Continentals turned and released a volley right into the faces of the surging British, then lowered their bayonets and charged. Simultaneously, Morgan's cavalry reserve hit the British left flank and the militia rejoined the fray.

The result was a British collapse and victory for the Americans. Roughly ninety percent of the British force was killed or captured while the Americans suffered twelve killed and sixty wounded. More importantly, the Battle of Cowpens deprived Cornwallis of his light troops, which meant that he no longer had the resources to pursue Greene's army. After some inconclusive battles Cornwallis moved to Virginia to resupply, fortifying his position at a place called Yorktown.

Greene's army was then joined by Washington's northern army, reinforced by French troops. This army, working together with the French fleet, besieged Cornwallis at Yorktown, forcing his surrender on October 19, 1781. This major defeat essentially ended British hopes of winning back the colonies, and the Revolutionary War formally ended in 1783. As the British marched out to surrender their arms to the Americans their band played a popular tune called "The World Turned Upside Down." Its lyrics captured the moment:

> If ponies rode men and grass ate cows
> And cats should be chased into holes by the mouse
> If summer were spring and the other way round
> Then all the world would be upside down.

The battle of Cowpens was instrumental in enabling the ultimate victory of the Americans at Yorktown. Is also supports Sun Tzu's point that one may need to go on the defensive when "strength is inadequate" but then go over to the attack "when it is abundant."[19]

■ **Invincibility lies in the defense; the possibility of victory in the attack. (IV.5)**

The other situation that calls for defense is immediately following a successful assault. Executing fast-paced, high-tempo operations to throw the enemy off balance cannot be maintained indefinitely. Troops wear down, equipment wears out, and enemy lines of supply shorten while the victor's get longer. At this point one must go on the defensive, fortifying the new gains, resting one's personnel, and preparing for counterattacks. In this way it is possible to retain the ground captured.

Germany was taught this lesson by the Soviets in World War II when the Wehrmacht became overextended in the vast expanse of the Russian steppes. There, after major early successes in its summer campaign, the Wehrmacht was caught by a vicious Soviet winter counterattack at Moscow in 1941. After Operation Typhoon, the final German push to capture Moscow, petered out due to extremely tough weather conditions and lack of supply, the Russians counterattacked. Realizing the Germans were at the end of their rope and close to breaking, the Soviets used newly arrived Mongolian reinforcements to launch a pincer movement composed of a half a million men against the Germans on a 600-mile front. Barely able to survive, much less fight, and under threat of being cut off, the German army was forced to retreat up to 200 miles.

This lesson was repeated by the Soviets at Stalingrad in 1942. Later in the war the Germans hit the Soviets hard when they overextended themselves after their successes. In 1944 the Germans taught the Western Allies the same lesson. The Western Allies had outrun their supply lines in France. Simultaneously, the Germans had shortened their lines of supply as both their western and eastern fronts were pushed back toward Germany. This enabled Hitler to amass large enough reserves to launch another attack through the Ardennes against the Western Allies. During the Battle of the Bulge once again the Allies were surprised and thrown on the defensive, at least until they could halt the German attack and launch a counterattack of their own.[20]

Therefore the strategist must be prepared for the ebb and flow between offensive and defensive operations. The question is not which is the strongest, offense or defense, but which will enable the achievement of objectives. By being able to move quickly from one to the other, the shrewd strategist can take advantage of each inherent strength to achieve victory.

■ **Anciently the skillful warriors first made themselves invincible and awaited the enemy's moment of vulnerability. (IV.1)**

Final Considerations

As a strategist, it is critical not only to determine where weakness exists and attack there, but also that one have the personal fortitude to avoid attacking when the situation has changed. Often the government or the populace is clamoring for action. They demand a victory. The pressure to attack can be immense.

That was the situation that faced General Ambrose Burnside in November 1862. The previous commander of the Army of the Potomac, McClellan, had just been dismissed by President Lincoln for not being aggressive enough in bringing the Confederates to battle. Meanwhile, Union newspapers and citizens were demanding a major victory. Lincoln wanted Burnside because he had a reputation as an aggressive fighter. That reputation may not have been well-earned, as at the Battle of Antietam two months earlier Burnside's performance had been lackluster. He had shown no initiative or creativity, following orders to the letter and doing nothing more.

Burnside had been offered command of the army by Lincoln three times and had turned it down each time. Although Burnside considered the job too big for him (the thought of it made him physically sick) he finally reconsidered and accepted it to prevent rival Major General Joseph Hooker from getting it.

In response to the pressure for a victory Burnside developed an aggressive plan to take Richmond. Although by this time Lincoln understood that General Robert E. Lee's Army of Northern Virginia was the proper target, he agreed to the plan so as not to demoralize his already self-doubting general. Lincoln's only stipulation was that Burnside move quickly, stating that he thought the plan "will succeed, if you move rapidly; otherwise not."

Burnside's plan was to feint to the southwest, hoping to convince Lee that the Union forces would continue the line of attack that McClellan had taken previously. Burnside would then move quickly to the southeast, crossing the Rappahannock River before the Confederates could contest his crossing. The campaign would end with a speedy march south to capture Richmond.

Initially the plan went well and the Army of Northern Virginia was misled. As the first major Union forces neared Fredericksburg on November 17, only a few Confederate units held the heights beyond it. The closest major rebel forces, a corps under James Longstreet, were thirty miles away. Burnsides' subordinates pressed him to move quickly to cross the Rappahannock.

Instead Burnside held back, waiting for the river to get lower and pontoon bridges to arrive. As he waited Longstreet's corps arrived, followed by "Stonewall" Thomas J. Jackson's troops on November 29. After attempting to cross downstream, Burnside decided to send troops across on December 11. Realizing that his plan to move quickly had been thwarted, Burnside faced two choices. He could either retreat to face the wrath of Lincoln, the government, and the people or attack. He chose the latter.

After a one-hundred gun bombardment of the town, heavy fighting, and heroic efforts by Union engineers to build the pontoon bridges, Union troops flowed across the river in the late afternoon. The next day Burnside had difficulty determining what to do. Meanwhile, Lee was busy fortifying the ridge behind Fredericksburg called Marye's Heights and bringing up more troops to defend it and the ground to the south.

Finally, on December 13, Burnside made his attack. In Fredericksburg he had 57,000 men facing Longstreet's 41,000, and further south were 51,000 Union troops arrayed against Jackson's 39,000. The Union attack in the south was implemented in piecemeal and uncoordinated fashion. After a series of attacks and counterattacks, the combatants ended up in their starting positions with a few thousand casualties each. However, the situation in the northern part of the battlefield by Fredericksburg was very different.

Near Fredericksburg, Burnside threw his soldiers into a frontal assault on Marye's Heights. To reach the heights where the enemy infantry and artillery was entrenched the Union troops had to cross 200 yards of open plain. Then they had to file across three bridges to get over a water-filled ditch. Once on the other side, they would then have to cover another 350 yards of open ground before they could come to grips with the enemy. All this time the enemy would be firing upon them. As the Confederate artillery chief Colonel E. Porter Alexander said, ". . . we cover that ground now so well that we will comb it as with a fine-tooth comb. A chicken could not live on that field when we open on it."

The artillery chief's words proved prophetic. Seven divisions were sent in fourteen separate waves against the Rebel position, but none ever reached it. The closest one Federal soldier got was thirty yards, but most got no closer than one hundred yards. Another Union soldier had this observation of the assault: "At noon the slaughter began, and we witnessed the sacrifice of French's and Hancock's divisions of our corps, as one, following the other, was led across the canal, swept by hundreds of cannon, and gallantly rushed against the stone wall at the foot of Marye's Heights, which sheltered as heavy a force of Confederate infantry as could operate behind it, while the face of the hill in the rear was terraced with lines of breastworks, manned by Longstreet's Veteran Corps, being able to fire from each line of works over the heads of the lines in front. It was murder to attempt such an assault. . . . But the orders were imperative, and were obeyed."

Seven thousand Union soldiers ended up as casualties as a result of the attack on Marye's Heights and the morale of the Army of the Potomac was broken. Burnsides' subordinates refused his entreaties to renew the attack the next day, despite an offer by Burnside that he himself would lead it. Shortly thereafter, Lincoln relieved Burnside of command of the Army of the Potomac, describing Burnside's failed efforts in the Fredericksburg campaign as "snatching defeat from the jaws of victory."[21]

> ■ A general who is stupid and courageous is a calamity. Wu Ch'i said: When people discuss a general they always pay attention to his courage. As far as a general is concerned, courage is but one quality. Now a valiant general will be certain to enter an engagement recklessly and if he does so he will not appreciate what is advantageous.   (VIII.18 Tu Mu)

The lesson from this example is clear: if the enemy is too strong to attack at the moment, stand firm and refrain from ordering an immediate assault that is destined to fail.

> ■ They do not engage an enemy advancing with well-ordered banners nor one whose formations are in impressive array. Therefore, the art of employing troops is that when the enemy

occupies high ground, do not confront him; with his back resting on hills, do not oppose him.   (VII.25–26)

One must be able to recognize a situation where it is not the appropriate time to attack, nor the appropriate place. Instead, it is better to wait until a weakness can be found and then attack.

- If your troops do not equal his, temporarily avoid his initial onrush. Probably later you can take advantage of a soft spot. Then rouse yourself and seek victory with determined spirit.   (III.16 Tu Mu)

Given the great risks of entering battle, one must carefully weigh the potential gains against the chance of loss. Do so without emotion but with deep thought. Remember, the wise strategist will not attack unless victory is ensured.

Summary

A crucial tenet of Sun Tzu's philosophy that will enable a leader to win "All-under-Heaven" is to avoid strength and strike weakness. Unfortunately, too often Western culture shows a preference for the opposite, a direct attack upon the enemy's strength.

The situation the strategist must create is the application of the nation's strength against the enemy's weak point. This principle maximizes the use of resources and avoids long and costly wars of attrition. It forces one to constantly look for new openings to exploit and demands creativity. It is perhaps a more Eastern—and certainly more subtle—approach than the frontal attack, but it is both more efficient and effective.

- Thus, those skilled in war subdue the enemy's army without battle. They capture his cities without assaulting them and overthrow his state without protracted operations.   (III.10)

Success can be accomplished in several ways. One can attack the weakest enemy troops, destroy critical war-making resources, utilize land or sea-based mobility, launch a preemptive strike, attack boundary points, or deliver a psychological attack. The key is knowing where the weaknesses are and when to release the attack. Attacking only when one has found the right weakness will dramatically improve the chances for victory.

- **When he concentrates, prepare against him: where he is strong, avoid him.** (I.21)

To find those weaknesses and keep the enemy from discovering one's own is the subject of the next chapter, which discusses deception and foreknowledge. Let us now explore this principle.

3 ▪ Deception and Foreknowledge
Winning the Information War

- ▪ Now the reason the enlightened prince and the wise general
  conquer the enemy whenever they move and their achievements
  surpass those of ordinary men is foreknowledge.   (XIII.3)

As Sun Tzu states, to defeat the enemy and achieve the nation's goals, one must have "foreknowledge." Sun Tzu then explains exactly what foreknowledge is:

- ▪ What is called "foreknowledge" cannot be elicited from spirits,
  nor from gods, nor by analogy with past events, nor from calculations. It must be obtained from men who know the enemy
  situation.   (XIII.4)

What Sun Tzu is saying is that foreknowledge is not simply projecting the future based on the past, nor is it simple analysis of the enemy's order of battle. Foreknowledge is firsthand insight and a deep understanding of three things—the enemy, one's own strengths and weaknesses, and the environment. The first of these is the enemy.

Know the Enemy

Rome faced a major challenge in defeating Carthage, its new rival in the First Punic War. While Rome was all-powerful on land, Carthage ruled the seas. Thus, to win Rome had to cease being solely a continental power and become a sea power as well. To effectively do so Rome had to learn from its enemy.

At the beginning of the war Roman forces had found a Carthaginian *quinquereme* (a warship with five rows of oars) that had grounded during a storm. Using it as a model to build her ships and train her crews, Rome was able to launch a fleet within two months. However, Roman builders did more than just copy the warship. To take advantage of their army's superiority the Romans added a hook to the bow of their ships. Called a "corvus," or beak, it would be dropped onto the enemy warship to prevent its escape. Next, Roman soldiers would cross a drawbridge to the enemy ship and eliminate the crew. Although Rome would lose many ships to the learning process and the Carthaginian navy, eventually she would win a decisive victory over her enemy at the sea battle of Aegusa.[1]

- It is a doctrine of war not to assume the enemy will not come, but rather to rely on one's readiness to meet him; not to presume that he will not attack, but rather to make one's self invincible. (VIII.16)

As this example illustrates, to defeat the enemy one must first understand him. To win the overall war one must first win the "intelligence war." This entails research and analysis. It must be completely and thoroughly done and must not lack for detail. Unfortunately, even today much of what passes for military and diplomatic intelligence can be very shallow.

On May 7, 1999, a U.S. B-2 Stealth bomber laid its deadly payload on a building in Belgrade. The mission targeted the Yugoslav Federal Directorate of Supply and Procurement headquarters. It was authorized as part of the NATO effort to keep the peace by forcing Yugoslavian forces out of Serbia. However, the supposed Yugoslavian government building turned out to be the embassy of China. After the smoke cleared, three Chinese were killed and twenty were injured. Also damaged were U.S. and Chinese relations, as well as the standing of the United States in the eyes of the world.

- One ignorant of the plans of neighboring states cannot prepare alliances in good time; if ignorant of the conditions of mountains, forests, dangerous defiles, swamps and marshes he cannot conduct the march of an army; if he fails to make use of native guides he cannot gain the advantages of the ground. A general ignorant of even one of these three matters is unfit to command the armies of a Hegemonic King.   (XI.51)

How, in the era of GPS locators, satellite photos, and phone books with addresses could a mistake like this be made? It was the result of bad intelligence. The country with the most sophisticated intelligence agencies and systems had its major intelligence agency, the CIA, using outdated maps.

Intelligence can be defined as "processed, accurate information, presented in sufficient time to enable a decision-maker to take whatever action is required."[2] Poor intelligence is the result of several factors: the lack of intelligence funding or skills; limited methods for gathering, analyzing, or disseminating intelligence; the lack of understanding by the leadership of the importance of intelligence; or the political leaderships' belief that intelligence gathering is unfair or unethical. In the latter case, there is the example of Henry L. Stimson, the U.S. Secretary of State who closed down his code-breaking department, stating that "gentlemen do not read other gentlemen's mail." These factors and others can lead to a skin-deep analysis of the enemy and the situation. Whatever the reason, the lack of good intelligence is a betrayal to the nation and its armed services, placing the population and the military in grave danger. It is not enough for an intelligence officer to satisfy the leadership by providing shallow facts and analysis of the potential threats, thus allowing them to pretend to fashion effective strategies and predict the responses of the opponent. To be satisfied with such a simplistic level of analysis is to invite disaster.

On November 21, 1970, American special forces troops attacked a prisoner of war camp in North Viet Nam with the mission of freeing U.S. prisoners. After weeks of preparation, the raid on Sontay went like clockwork; total time on the ground was only twenty-six minutes. The guards were quickly dispatched and the only casualty in the strike force was a badly sprained ankle. However, there was just one problem: the prisoners had been moved out of the camp weeks before, so no POWs were rescued. A lack of intelligence preempted what could have been a major coup for the American forces in Viet Nam and instead led to failure.[3]

■ Generally in the case of armies you wish to strike, cities you wish to attack, and people you wish to assassinate, you must know the names of the garrison commander, the staff officers, the ushers, the gatekeepers, and the bodyguards. You must instruct your agents to inquire into these matters in minute detail.   (XIII.16)

To be successful, to find weaknesses, a leader must do as Sun Tzu states: one must elicit knowledge "from men who know the enemy situation." One must "inquire into these matters in the most minute detail." As a starting point, one must begin with the enemy's *capabilities*. Analysis of the enemy's capabilities provides insight into the enemy's *potential* for action—its ability to attack other nations and/or defend itself. One looks at such things as the size of the enemy's military forces, their level of modernization, their training, and troop movements.

However, analysis of enemy capabilities is the easy part. More importantly, one must assess the enemy's *intentions*. This provides insight beyond what the enemy *can* do to provide understanding of what the enemy *will* do. Intentions analysis reviews the opponent's objectives and plans to achieve them; in other words, the enemy's strategy.

In November of 1950 American, South Korean, and other United Nations forces were approaching the Yalu River in North Korea, the latter's border with its communist cousin, China. Only a few months before the Allied troops had their backs to the wall, fighting for their last toehold in South Korea in the Pusan Perimeter. General Douglas MacArthur, Supreme Commander of the Allied Armies, had gotten around the rear of the attacking North Korean People's Army via an amphibious landing north at Inchon. This assault, combined with attacks out of Pusan, pushed the North Korean invaders back. First to fall was Seoul, the capitol of South Korea. It was quickly followed by Pyongyang, the North Korean capitol. As they rolled through the rest of North Korea and approached the Yalu, many American GIs thought the war might be done by Christmas.

This euphoria was shared at headquarters in Tokyo. Therefore, when General MacArthur began receiving reports about the appearance of Chinese communist troops from his front lines, he knew they must be false. While MacArthur believed that Chinese forces were massing across the Yalu in China's province of Manchuria, he felt that China's chance to affect the war had long passed. Furthermore, MacArthur felt that his air reconnaissance flights would quickly pick up any sign of Chinese troops in North Korea and so far those scouting efforts had shown no sign of the "Chicoms."

However, danger signs had begun to appear. Chinese soldiers had been captured in October and interrogation of these prisoners revealed the potential presence of six Chinese field armies on the Korean side of the Yalu. This was a total of 180,000 men, as yet undetected or ignored by UN Intelligence. On November 6, attacks against the Australians north of the Chungchon River by Chinese forces caused concern at MacArthur's headquarters. But over the next few days the attacks ceased and the attackers disappeared into the hills. MacArthur assumed it to be a bluff and called for the resumed march to the Yalu.

If the high command was not worried, the troops on the ground were. Although their fast advance had scattered many of its units, the U.S. Marines ensured that they controlled an open lane to the sea should a retreat be necessary. On the opposite side of North Korea in the west the Eighth Army slowed, then stopped, its advance. Events would prove that these were indeed wise precautions.

Right after Thanksgiving Day, 1950, the Chinese communists launched their attack. With tens of thousands of troops they hit both the Marines in the east and the Eighth Army in the west. Allied units that had reached as close as seventy-five yards from the Yalu were sent reeling back. The Marines fought their way to the sea and safety, suffering 5,500 casualties but inflicting severe losses on the enemy and maintaining their élan and honor. The Eighth Army had to evacuate X Corps by sea, while the rest of the army fell back on land. A further Chinese offensive on New Year's Eve pushed the Allies back farther, forcing them to evacuate hard-won Seoul to the communists.

In the final analysis, the lack of understanding the Chinese enemy and misreading his intentions cost the Allies thousands of casualties. It also led to the loss of Korean territory and caused a huge drop in military and civilian morale. Finally, these crucial mistakes were a key factor in General MacArthur being relieved of his command, the last he would hold in his career.[4]

■ When the trees are seen to move the enemy is advancing. When many obstacles have been placed in the undergrowth, it is for the purpose of deception. Birds rising in flight is a sign that the enemy is lying in ambush; when wild animals are startled and flee he is trying to take you unaware. Dust spurting upward in high, straight columns indicates the approach of chariots. When it hangs low and is widespread infantry is approaching.   (IX.20–23)

"Knowing the enemy" played a crucial role in the diplomatic intrigues of the First World War. As the war progressed it was clear to the German leaders that unrestricted submarine warfare against Britain could severely cripple or even force Britain out of the war. Yet at the same time, allowing German subs to attack neutral ships could bring the United States into the war on the side of the Allies. Germany's new Foreign Minister, Arthur Zimmerman, believed he had a plan that would both implement unrestricted submarine warfare while keeping the U.S. out of the war.

Zimmerman's plan was to entice Mexico to attack the United States by promising her aid and, should Mexico be successful, reclaim the territories she had lost in the Mexican–American War. In addition, Zimmerman wanted Mexico to join Germany in persuading Japan to attack the U.S. as well. These attacks would keep the U.S. occupied and unable to enter the war against Germany, even in the face of submarine attacks against her shipping.

Zimmerman made his intentions clear in a telegram to his ambassador in Mexico:

> We intend to begin unrestricted submarine warfare on the first of February. We shall endeavour in spite of this to keep the United States neutral. In the event of this not succeeding, we make Mexico a proposal of alliance on the following basis: make war together, make peace together, generous financial support, and an understanding on our part that Mexico is to reconquer the lost territory in Texas, New Mexico and Arizona. The settlement in detail is left to you.
>
> You will inform the President (of Mexico) of the above most secretly, as soon as the outbreak of war with the United States is certain, and add the suggestion that he should, on his own initiative, invite Japan to immediate adherence and at the same time mediate between Japan and ourselves.
>
> Please call the President's attention to the fact that the unrestricted employment of our submarines now offers the prospect of compelling England to make peace within a few months. Acknowledge receipt.
>
> Zimmerman

Unfortunately for Germany, Britain had the capability to intercept her enemy's communications. As the war began the British ship *Telconia* cut Germany's transatlantic cables, forcing Germany to route her communications through other more insecure means, lines which went through Britain. As a result, the Zimmerman telegram ended up in "Room 40," the British Admiralty's code-breaking center, where the main contents were known within hours.

At this point Britain faced a dilemma: if the Americans were told of the contents of the telegram, then Germany would know its code was broken. This would lead Germany to begin using more secure codes and potentially end Britain's ability to read intercepted messages. On the other hand, if the information wasn't shared with the United States, the latter might still not enter the war as an ally.

In the end Britain was forced to use the secret contained in the telegram. After the United States decided to remain neutral in the face of Germany's declaration of unrestricted submarine warfare on February 1, 1917, Britain played her card. The British ambassador handed the Zimmerman telegram over to his American counterpart, who in turn showed it to U.S. President Wilson. The telegram was also released to the press, who trumpeted it to the American people. And when Zimmerman admitted to the world that the telegram was authentic the die was cast. On April 2, 1917, Wilson asked Congress for a declaration of war against Germany. In this case, intelligence and knowing the enemy was crucial to Britain's success.[5]

> ■ When the enemy's envoys speak in humble terms but he continues his preparations, he will advance. When their language is deceptive but the enemy pretentiously advances, he will retreat. When the envoys speak in apologetic terms, he wishes a respite. When without a previous understanding the enemy asks for a a truce, he is plotting. (IX.25–28)

As the above examples illustrate, it is essential to look beneath the facts and surface information and carefully consider the minds of the enemy's leaders. One must learn as much as possible about the culture of the enemy nation and the mindset and assumptions of those who run it if one is to be prepared for conflict.

> ■ If you wish to conduct offensive war you must know the men employed by the enemy. Are they wise or stupid, clever or clumsy? Having assessed their qualities, you prepare appropriate measures. (XIII.16 Tu Mu)

An excellent example of this comes from ancient Chinese history, that of Sun Pin and P'ang Chuan. Sun Pin was reputed to be a direct descendant of Sun Tzu and would eventually write his own book on strategy, *Military Methods*.

Sun Pin and P'ang Chuan studied military strategy together and P'ang Chuan grew to envy Sun Pin's expertise. While serving the King of Wei, P'ang Chuan intrigued against Sun Pin and had him convicted: in punishment, Sun Pin's feet were cut off and his face branded. With this punishment Sun Pin was forbidden to serve the King of Wei.

However, the state of Ch'i learned of Sun Pin and engaged his services, bringing him secretly back to their capitol. There he served the King of Ch'i for many years as the army's strategist. Many years later the kingdom of Wei went to war with the state of Ch'i. Leading Wei's army was none other than P'ang Chuan, while that of Ch'i was lead by Sun Pin. Knowing P'ang Chuan's traits and also the fact that he considered the soldiers of Ch'i cowardly, Sun Pin laid his trap.

Leading an army into Wei, Sun Pin encamped, giving direction that one hundred thousand cooking fires be lit that evening. The next evening Sun Pin ordered that only fifty thousand fires be lit, and the next evening only thirty thousand. Hearing the news P'ang Chuan was ecstatic, believing that the army of Ch'i was melting away through desertion. Therefore he took only his fastest troops and pursued the army of Ch'i.

Sun Pin, knowing the ground, estimated the time that P'ang Chuan's army would arrive at the highly constricted Ma-ling Pass. There he deployed ten thousand crossbowmen to wait in ambush, to wait for the army of Wei. Next, Sun Pin scraped onto a large tree the words "P'ang Chuan will die beneath this tree." Sun Pin's final preparation was to order his men not to fire until dusk, aiming all their arrows at the place where they would see a fire being lit.

As night fell P'ang Chuan's army reached the pass. Seeing some sort of writing on a tree, P'ang Chuan lit a torch. At that moment ten thousand arrows flew and Wei's army was trapped. As his men died around him, P'ang Chuan lamented, "I have established this clod's fame," then cut his own throat.[6]

By knowing his enemy well Sun Pin was able to defeat him, save his adopted country, and extract revenge. That is why one must find out not only the names of the enemy leaders but what experiences have molded them, where they get their information, how they view the current situation, the degree of risk they are willing to take, how important different goals are to them, and what their ambitions are. This will enable the projection of how one's enemy will react in various situations and the probability of success.

■ When the King of Han sent Han Hsin, Ts'ao Ts'an, and Kuan
Ying to attack Wei Pao he asked: "Who is the commander-in-
chief of Wei?" The reply was: "Po Chih." The King said: "His
mouth still smells of his mother's milk. He cannot equal Han
Hsin. Who is their cavalry commander?" The reply was: "Feng
Ching." The King said: "He is the son of General Feng Wu-che
of Ch'in. Although worthy, he is not the equal of Kuan Ying.
And who is the infantry commander?" The reply was: "Hsiang
T'o." The King said: "He is no match for Ts'ao Ts'an. I have
nothing to worry about."   (XIII.16 Tu Mu)

By the end of 1776, the American revolutionary cause was at a low
ebb. On Friday, December 13, the British had just captured the American general that many thought should replace Washington, General
Charles Lee. Compounding that setback was the fact that January 1,
1777, would find many rebel soldiers' enlistments expiring. Essentially,
by the first of the new year the American army would most likely cease
to exist, and the revolution would evaporate with it. A morale-boosting
victory was needed to turn the situation around, and fast.

Washington decided to strike one of the isolated British outposts
that his adversary, General William Howe, had posted in winter quarters. He chose the Hessian garrison at Trenton, New Jersey, led by
Colonel Johann Rall. This leader of the German mercenaries was
known by Washington to have a very low regard for the fighting capabilities of the Americans. In fact, he held them in such contempt that
he refused subordinates' requests to fortify the Trenton ferry or the
town itself.

To learn more about the Hessian defenses Washington recruited a
supposed Loyalist who was also thought to be a British spy. Washington
told this double agent, John Honeyman, to go to Rall and ask him if
wanted to buy Honeyman's cattle to feed Rall's soldiers. Honeyman
used this guise to collect intelligence on Hessian routines and defenses.
After doing so, Honeyman arranged to be "captured" by American
troops and was taken to Washington. To maintain Honeyman's cover,
Washington pretended to be incensed with the supposed British spy
and interrogated him personally. He then had Honeyman taken to the
guardhouse, but slipped him a key. The key enabled Honeyman to
"escape" and go back to Rall with tales of how weak and dispirited
the American forces were. This made Rall even more overconfident
and relaxed.

■ Therefore, when capable, feign incapacity: when active, inactivity. When near, make it appear that you are far away; when far away, that you are near. Offer the enemy a bait to lure him; feign disorder and strike him.   (I.18–20)

On Christmas Day, 1776, Rall was expecting an enjoyable celebration, instead of a rebel attack. Especially not in the snowstorm that was blowing. When a messenger came with a note stating that the American army was moving toward him, Rall stuck it in his pocket without looking at the contents.

Out of the blinding snow, the Americans attacked the Trenton garrison. As the Hessian troops ran out of their barracks, the Americans fired two cannon that they had placed at the end of the street. This was quickly followed by a bayonet charge. When it was all over the Americans had captured over 900 Hessians and inflicted over 100 casualties. Among them was Colonel Rall, dead—with the unread note still in his pocket.

Washington's use of spies such as Honeyman was crucial to his success at Trenton and maintaining the momentum of the American Revolution.

■ We select men who are clever, talented, wise, and able to gain access to those of the enemy who are intimate with the sovereign and members of the nobility. Thus they are able to observe the enemy's movements and to learn of his doings and his plans. Having learned the true state of affairs they return and tell us.   (XIII.11 Tu Yu)

The use of Honeyman to gather intelligence for the Trenton raid was representative of Washington's use of spies and agents. He preferred written over verbal reports, was adamant that intelligence be expedited, and used special funds (including gold) to pay for secrets. He also jealously guarded his list of intelligence assets, to the point of not committing their names to paper.[7]

■ Of all those in the army close to the commander none is more intimate than the secret agent; of all rewards none more liberal than those given to secret agents; of all matters none is more confidential than those relating to secret operations.   (XIII.12)

In Sun Tzu's day the means of gathering intelligence was primarily through human observation of enemy activities or obtaining information through others. As the example above shows, this method (human intelligence, or "humint") is an excellent means of gathering information about enemy intentions.

> ■ Among the official class there are worthy men who have been deprived of office; others who have committed errors and have been punished. There are sycophants and minions who are covetous of wealth. There are those who wrongly remain long in lowly office . . . As far as all such are concerned you can secretly inquire after their welfare, reward them liberally with gold and silk, and so tie them to you. Then you may rely on them to seek out the real facts of the situation in their country and to ascertain the plans directed against you.   (XIII.8 Tu Mu)

As Sun Tzu states, there are several reasons a military or government official could be recruited to provide secrets to another nation. Modern spymasters have coined the acronym MICE (Money, Ideology, Conscience, and Ego) as major reasons for doing so. Whatever the cause, this type of intelligence can be invaluable in providing insight into the opponent's intentions.

Shortly after the United States won its independence from England, it began to look westward to expand. The most promising area for expansion was the Northwest Territory (composed of the present-day states of Ohio, Indiana, Illinois, Michigan, and Wisconsin), awarded to the U.S. as a result of the Treaty of Paris, which ended the Revolutionary War. However, standing in the way of settling that territory were the Indian tribes of the Ohio valley, led by the Miamis but also including their Shawnee, Delaware, and Wyandot allies. Behind the Indians stood the British, who were interested in maintaining the fur trading posts and using the Indians to limit the expansion of the fledgling American nation.

In 1790 conflicts between settlers and the Indians increased. To defend the settlers President Washington sent a small army under General Josiah Harmar into the Ohio country. Defending their lands, the Miamis and their allies were led by Chief Little Turtle, who defeated Harmar's small army easily.

Washington saw the need for a stronger effort and authorized the governor of the territory, Arthur St. Clair, to build a 3,000-man army to push the Indians back. Naming him the commander of the new force, Washington's last words of advice to St. Clair were "beware of surprise!"

St. Clair took little time to train his troops, instead pushing them into a campaign before many had mastered the basics of soldiering. As he began his march into the Northwest Territory St. Clair's army was tracked every step of the way by Indian scouts. As the army progressed, the lack of training and discipline began to show. Officers bickered, food was short, and many troops became ill. Desertions grew.

On the other side, Little Turtle knew St. Clair's every move and the condition of his troops. On November 3, 1791, St. Clair's army was encamped near the modern-day Ohio–Indiana border. Down to 1,400 soldiers, St. Clair posted sentries, but they spent most of their time trying to keep warm. Early the next morning Little Turtle's 1,200 warriors attacked the camp. Caught by surprise, St. Clair's inexperienced army disintegrated. Before noon half of the American army was dead on the field and the rest had fled, leaving their wounded behind. St. Clair's troops abandoned eight cannon, 1,200 muskets,, and assorted other equipment. Little Turtle suffered only about sixty casualties. St. Clair's lack of preparedness, combined with Little Turtle's knowledge of his enemy, led to the single greatest defeat of an American army by Indians.

Washington, furious with St. Clair's bungling and refusal to heed the President's advice to avoid a surprise attack, named General "Mad" Anthony Wayne to take command. Wayne got his nickname from a night bayonet attack he led against the British during the Revolutionary War. Contrary to his nickname, Wayne was keenly intelligent.

Unlike St. Clair, Wayne spent several months training his new force, the core of which were regular troops he named the Legion of the United States. With tough discipline he taught his troops to stand firm, maneuver as a unit, and deliver well-placed volleys of fire against the enemy. Rather than marching pell-mell into Indian territory without a good source of supply, Wayne built a series of three forts to support his drive deep into the Ohio country. Finally, Wayne had a special source of information on his Indian enemy, William Wells.

Wells was a settler's son who was captured by Miami Indians at age twelve. Adopted by Chief Little Turtle, Wells became a Miami warrior and fought against St. Clair's forces in 1791. However, Wells had a change of heart following the battle and after talking with Little Turtle, went over to the American side. Wells provided a wealth of knowledge about the Indian style of warfare and tactics. He also served as a scout ahead of Wayne's forces as they entered Indian country.

Intelligence and preparation were key to Wayne's success at the
Battle of Fallen Timbers. Hoping to repeat his ambush of St. Clair with
Wayne, Little Turtle set a trap at an opening in the woods where a
tornado had knocked down hundreds of trees. The initial volley by the
Indians forced the scouts and vanguard of Kentucky militia back, but
the rest of Wayne's force moved forward. Wayne sent the regulars of
the Legion forward in two lines with bayonets fixed while sending his
dragoons around the Indian's flank. This combination of the Legion's
bayonets and the dragoons' sabers caught the Indians in a vise, and the
Indian force broke and ran. The victory at the Battle of Fallen Timbers
opened the Northwest Territory to settlement and enabled the United
States to expand and grow stronger.[8]

Beyond *humint*, modern technologies have added new methods of
gathering intelligence. One can learn enemy capabilities and intentions
by monitoring their level of communications activity (signals intelligence, or *sigint*). Observation by agents is also augmented through airplane and satellite observation, or imagery.

> ■ Therefore in the enemy's country, the mountains, rivers, high-
> lands, lowlands, and hills which he can defend as strategic points;
> the forests, reeds, rushes and luxuriant grasses in which he can
> conceal himself; the distances over the roads and paths, the size
> of cities and towns, the extent of the villages, the fertility or
> barrenness of the fields, the depth of irrigation works, the
> amounts of stores, the size of the opposing army, the keenness
> of weapons; all must be fully known. Then we have the enemy
> in our sights and he can be easily taken.   (VII.11 Ho Yen-hsi)

Additional sources of intelligence can be gained through diplomatic
contacts, military sources, and allies, and there are "open" sources such
as the news media or, most recently, the Internet. All of these have
increased the amount of information available to the strategist many
times over, and make the collation and interpretation of the data increasingly important.

Analyzing several modern surprise attacks such as Barbarossa (the
German attack on the USSR), Pearl Harbor, and the Yom Kippur War
proves that having more data and information may not necessarily lead
to better strategic analysis and decisions. Despite receiving a copy of
the German battle plans from both their attaché in Berlin and from the
American ambassador and a direct letter from Winston Churchill about
German intentions, Stalin refused to believe that Hitler would attack.

Stalin's refusal to listen to the warnings led to the loss of millions of troops and critical materiel in the first year of the war. In spite of Japanese signals that lack of progress in talks with the U.S. would lead directly to war, the lack of a national intelligence infrastructure meant that the United States was surprised by Pearl Harbor, leading to the loss of eighteen major ships, 188 aircraft and 2,403 men. Because Israeli and American planners were able to convince themselves that Arab moves were defensive in nature, they were unable to predict the surprise Arab attack on Yom Kippur, the Jewish Day of Atonement. The increased amount of data and information that new sources provide make it more important than ever to avoid preconceptions of the enemy's plans.[9]

To determine the enemy's plans one may need to probe the enemy or find a means of eliciting a response. Forcing action can provide insight into what the enemy's plans are or how they might respond to one's moves. Also, it is important to look closely at the enemy's past behavior: how has the enemy responded to attacks? How have they launched and executed attacks? What signs have its leaders given before taking an action? Did they provide warnings and make deployments ahead of time? Or is there a pattern of surprise? When one finds a pattern, it can be used to predict how the enemy will react at a later time. It is then possible to take advantage of this new knowledge.

- Agitate him and ascertain the pattern of his movement. Determine his dispositions and so ascertain the field of battle. Probe him and learn where his strength is abundant and where deficient. (VI.21–23)

Mid-1942 found the Americans and their allies still on the defensive in the Pacific. Although the Doolittle raid had buoyed Americans' spirits, almost no material damage had actually been done to Japan or her armed forces. Rather, Japan was now planning to strike hard at the American fleet, hoping for a decisive battle that would weaken the U.S. significantly and perhaps even drive it out of the war. Admiral Isoroku Yamamotos's plan to do so centered on drawing the U.S. Pacific Fleet out to do battle over the island of Midway.

His U.S. adversary, Admiral Chester W. Nimitz, knew an attack was coming but did not know where. This is where intelligence became critical. Luckily for Nimitz, U.S. Naval Intelligence had broken the Japanese codes and knew the attack was planned on a place the Japanese termed "AF." The analysts thought that AF might mean Midway Island, but were not sure. So they had the garrison at Midway send a message in the clear that their water-distilling machinery was out of order. Sure enough, this message was soon followed by a Japanese coded message stating that "AF was short on water." The scene of the battle was set and an American force sent to take on the Japanese. The battle was indeed decisive, with U.S. intelligence enabling a major American victory.[10]

- Therefore, determine the enemy's plans and you will know which strategy will be successful and which will not. (VI.20)

Knowing the Environment

In addition to knowing the strengths and weaknesses of one's own forces and the enemy's, it is also essential to know the terrain on which the battle will occur, the environment in which one will operate.

- When employing troops it is essential to know beforehand the conditions of the terrain. Knowing the distances, one can make use of an indirect or a direct plan. If he knows the degree of ease or difficulty of traversing the ground he can estimate the advantages of using infantry or cavalry. If one knows where the ground is constricted and where open he can calculate the size of force appropriate. If he knows where he will give battle he knows when to concentrate or divide his forces. (I.6 Mei Yao-ch'en)

Knowing the terrain is crucial to knowing where to deploy one's forces for maximum effect. Terrain will determine if an area is defensible or not, whether one can move rapidly to surprise the enemy, the logistical requirements, and likely enemy avenues of approach.

- Conformation of the ground is of the greatest assistance in battle. Therefore, to estimate the enemy situation and to calculate distances and the degree of difficulty of the terrain so as to control victory are virtues of the superior general. He who fights with a full knowledge of these factors is certain to win; he who does not will surely be defeated. (X.17)

During Desert Storm, General Fred Franks ensured he knew the ground he would fight on. As commander of the VII Corps, the main punch of Desert Storm, Franks led the massive armored fist that would swing around the right flank of the Iraqi Army. To prepare for the battle he would "meditate" on the terrain. He would sit down in front of maps of the battleground and study them intently, look away for a moment, then study the maps again. Knowing the terrain and his deployments in such detail allowed General Franks to notice that he could rehearse his upcoming attack as his troops moved to their jump-off line. This rehearsal served to better prepare his troops and to react quickly to changes in situation as the battle progressed.[11]

- Generally, the commander must thoroughly acquaint himself beforehand with the maps so that he knows dangerous places for chariots and carts, where the water is too deep for wagons; passes in famous mountains, the principal rivers, the locations of highlands and hills; where rushes, forests, and reeds are luxuriant; the road distances; the size of cities and towns; well-known cities and abandoned ones, and where there are flourishing orchards. All this must be known, as well as the way boundaries run in and out. All these facts the general must store in his mind; only then will he not lose the advantage of the ground. (VII.11 Tu Mu)

The "environment" includes not only the terrain but, by extension, the effects of weather as well. The two are tightly related. Combined with knowledge of the enemy, understanding of the terrain and the weather will provide insight into the proper strategy.

- By weather I mean the interaction of natural forces; the effects of winter's cold and summer's heat and the conduct of military operations in accordance with the seasons. (I.5)

Although their attacks were separated by more than a century, both Napoleon and Hitler underestimated the impact of Russia's winter on their chances for success. Weather played a major role in both campaigns, reducing mobility, creating logistical problems, and causing huge losses in men and materiel. Both Napoleon and Hitler launched their invasions of Russia on June 22, the former in 1812 and the latter in 1941. The French Army left middle Europe with 400,000 men and returned after winter with less than a tenth of that. The losses Napoleon suffered, both materially and to his reputation, eventually led to the loss of his empire.

By the end of 1941 the German Army had killed four million Red Army soldiers and captured another 3.5 million. However, it still had not achieved its key objectives; the Red Army was still fighting and Moscow, Leningrad, and Stalingrad were still in Soviet hands. Winter 1941 came and, stuck in the snows of the Eastern front, the German Army still wore its summer clothing. Its soldiers were freezing, its weapons didn't work, and the tanks would not start. As a result of the winter of 1941 the German Army lost a quarter of a million men, 35,000 motor vehicles, and 1,800 tanks. In the end it would be Berlin and not Moscow that would feel the tread of the enemy's boots.[12]

It is not only major seasonal patterns that need to be considered; even daily weather conditions can have an impact on operations. On the morning of June 5, 1944, General Eisenhower had to make an excruciatingly difficult decision. As Supreme Commander of the military forces preparing to invade Europe, Eisenhower had decided the previous day to postpone the "Overlord" operation due to bad weather. Overlord depended on a passable English Channel in order to get the invasion force from England to Normandy, in France. A major storm had made it impossible for the landing craft to put to sea. The same storm also grounded aircraft, negating a major allied advantage, one that would be crucial in isolating the invasion spot and stopping the Germans from reinforcing it quickly. The dilemma Eisenhower faced was that if he delayed Overlord much longer, the secrecy of Overlord's timing and point of attack would be gone. It would prove impossible for a movement of that size to remain concealed. However, if he gave the order to proceed, he risked the chance that the invasion force would be severely damaged in the crossing and be unable to gain a foothold on the continent.

To help him make his decision, Eisenhower had an ace in his hand. He had access to weather intelligence that forecast a break in the storm for the following day, the sixth. Relying on this crucial piece of intelligence, Eisenhower ordered the commencement of Operation Overlord. Lacking Eisenhower's weather forecast, the Germans were taken completely by surprise. Because of the storm they had determined that no attack could possibly come on June 6, and stood down. According to the account of a German private in Normandy, "On that night of 6 June none of us expected an invasion any more. There was a strong wind, thick cloud cover, and the enemy aircraft had not bothered us more that day than usual. But then—in the night—the air was full of innumerable planes. We thought, 'What are they demolishing tonight?' But then it started. I was at the wireless set myself. One message followed another. Parachutists landed here—gliders reported there,' and finally 'Landing craft approaching.' Some of our guns fired as best they could. In the morning a huge naval force was sighted—that would be the last report our advanced observation posts could send us, before they were overwhelmed."

And so, as a result of this crucial piece of weather intelligence the Western Allies were able to gain precious time to establish a beachhead in Europe. It was one that they would never relinquish.[13]

Know Yourself

Despite the shock of the Japanese surprise attack in Asia and the fact that the resources of the Empire were strained by the requirements of the war's expansion into another hemisphere, the British were heartened by the entry of the Americans into World War II. Furthermore, the British had the utmost confidence that their "impregnable fortress" of Singapore would not only hold out against the Japanese onslaught, but serve as a base to strike back at them. In British minds Singapore was a bastion, with huge guns and a new naval base to defend it; it was considered the "Gibraltar of the East."

It therefore came as a huge surprise to Winston Churchill, the British government, the people, and the Empire when Singapore fell after only a little more than a month after it came under attack. Even more surprising was the fact that Singapore fell with 130,000 well-supplied troops to 35,000 Japanese troops at the end of a 500 mile-long supply line. How could this happen?

The reality was that Singapore was not a Gibraltar; in fact its defenses were either inadequate or built on false assumptions. Because the British expected any assault to come from the sea, no defenses were prepared against an attack from the land side across the strait. As a cable from General Sir Archibald Wavell to Churchill stated:

> Until quite recently all plans were based on repulsing sea borne attacks on the Island and holding land attack in Johore or farther North, and little or nothing was done to construct defences on the North side of Island to prevent crossing Johore Straits . . .

Furthermore, the naval base and the island defenses had totally inadequate air protection. British eyes were opened to this when, after a morale-building visit to Singapore, the battleship *Prince of Wales* and her escort *Repulse* were sunk by Japanese air attacks. Lacking adequate air cover meant that the destruction of the naval facilities, city infrastructure, and whatever land defenses there were was only a matter of time.

The loss of Singapore was a disaster from both a morale and a strategic standpoint. The shock dealt a huge blow to British morale when their morale was already extremely low. The loss of a military base and Malaysia as a source of rubber and other materials was a major one from a strategic standpoint. This was directly due to the British military's lack of knowledge about its own defenses—a major mistake.[14]

- Therefore I say, "Know the enemy and know yourself; in a hundred battles you will never be in peril. When you are ignorant of the enemy but know yourself, your chances of winning or losing are equal. If ignorant both of your enemy and yourself, you are certain in every battle to be in peril." (III.31–33)

Foreknowledge does not stop at knowing the enemy. One must also know the strengths and weaknesses of one's nation. To pit one's strengths against the enemy's weakness and avoid getting surprised by their attacks, it is critical to realize both where one is strong and where one is weak. The leader must understand a broad array of items, such as the capabilities of his forces, the ability of the economy to sustain a war, and the commitment of allies. It is crucial to know this information in detail and have access to it on a real-time basis.

- If I know that the enemy is vulnerable to attack, but do not know that my troops are incapable of striking him, my chance of victory is but half. (X.23)

Modern communist China's security analysts take extreme steps to calculate the balance of power between itself and different nations. To measure what it calls "Comprehensive National Power," Chinese analysts calculate the leading countries' levels of natural resources, economic capability, scientific and technological capability, social development, governmental power, foreign affairs capacity, and military strength. With this information, looking both at current positions and trends in these areas, the Chinese analyze the hierarchy of nations and the power of potential allies and rivals, and predict who will win future wars. This enables the Chinese government to conduct its foreign policy and make plans for future investments. In fact, this methodology results from the Chinese government's reliance on its heritage of ancient strategic thought, including Sun Tzu's *Art of War*.

■ Now if the estimates made in the temple before hostilities indicate victory it is because calculations show one's strength to be superior to that of his enemy; if they indicate defeat, it is because calculations show that one is inferior. With many calculations, one can win; with few calculations, one cannot. How much less chance of victory has one who makes none at all! By this means I examine the situation and the outcome will be clearly apparent.   (I.28)

Faced with a United States that exhibited the power of technology and weaponry over Iraq during the Persian Gulf War, modern China has focused on identifying U.S. weaknesses. The Chinese believe that their only means of successfully winning a war with the United States is by taking advantage of those weaknesses. Specifically, Chinese analysts have determined that the American military suffers from interservice rivalry, insufficient funding, overly complex technology, military arrogance, logistical weaknesses, and vulnerable communications networks. To exploit these weaknesses China is evolving strategies to take advantage of them.[15]

To calculate opposing strengths and weaknesses it is important to have a process for integrating and analyzing the correlation of opposing forces, and an intelligence infrastructure to support that process. The intelligence process can be thought of in five steps: command direction, information collection, information collation, data interpretation, and dissemination of intelligence. The first action a commander must take is to provide guidance to the intelligence community on what he needs to know. This guidance determines what information needs to be collected. Once the information is collected, it must be categorized and provided to the analysts. The analysts interpret all the information and turn it into "intelligence." Finally, the intelligence is then disseminated to the commanders who need it.[16]

To support this process it is critical to have an intelligence infrastructure. It is amazing how many times throughout history key information was available but did not get to the decision-makers. By infrastructure, I mean formal processes that exist to link up the sources of information and intelligence with the analysts who can interpret the data, and who then bring that information to leaders for action on a timely basis.

In well-run military organizations, data-gathering infrastructures include processes that train individual soldiers to look for key enemy information and bring it back to teams of intelligence analysts, who visit the front-line units on a regular basis. The infrastructure also provides for the collection of data from satellites and listening posts that pick up signs and signals of larger enemy movements. These two types of data are then pieced together to form a complete, holistic picture of the situation.

For example, during Desert Storm, the American intelligence team in Riyadh, Saudi Arabia, developed a unique approach for assessing the damage Allied aircraft were inflicting on the Iraqi army. Combining interviews with pilots and gun-camera footage with satellite and aerial photos, they were able to fashion a sophisticated and accurate method of understanding the fast-moving battlefield dynamics. To communicate this intelligence to General Schwartzkopf, they created a simple color-coded scheme that could tell him at a glance the state of the forces that opposed him. The ground-attack portion of Desert Storm proved that this information system provided excellent and accurate data, while that compiled by the CIA solely by satellite back in Washington, D.C., was off by a factor of two to three times.[17]

Deception

It is not enough to know one's strengths and weaknesses, the environment, and the enemy. The other side of the equation is ensuring that the opponent is denied access to that same information. This is where deception comes in.

The history of deception goes back far into China's history. One of the legends is that of Chuko Liang and the Empty Fortress, from the time of the battles between the Three Kingdoms. Charged with holding a key city against overwhelming enemy forces, Chuko Liang needed to resort to stratagems and deception to save it. The city was protected by strong walls, but Chuko Liang did not have enough troops to man them. Therefore he lowered his army's banners, put his troops in hiding, opens the city gates and waited outside the walls by himself for the enemy. The enemy, seeing Chuko Liang basking in the sun and the city seemingly defenseless, assumed Liang had laid a trap and left. The city was saved through deception.[18]

■ **All warfare is based on deception.** (I.17)

By leaving the Trojan horse "abandoned" outside the walls of Troy and supposedly sailing away, the Greeks deceived the Trojans into bringing the horse within their city. After night fell, the Greeks emerged from the horse and sacked Troy. By using his cavalry to screen his quick movements and deny his enemy knowledge of his intentions, Robert E. Lee kept the Union's numerically stronger Army of the Potomac on the defensive for most of the Civil War.

- The ultimate in disposing one's troops is to be without ascertainable shape. Then the most penetrating spies cannot pry in nor can the wise lay plans against you.   (VI.24)

The logic is straightforward. To defeat the enemy one must first deceive its leaders about the true nature of one's plans. If they do not know where the next attack will land, they will be confused and unable to respond effectively.

- The enemy must not know where I intend to give battle. For if he does not know where I intend to give battle he must prepare in a great many places. And when he prepares in a great many places, those I have to fight in any one place will be few.   (VI.14)

Before Eisenhower launched the invasion of France, the Allies prepared a massive deception plan. As it was clear to the Axis powers that the Western Allies would invade in the summer of 1944, the objective of the "Bodyguard" deception plan was to keep the German leadership in the dark as to the exact location of the invasion. By doing so the Allies would force the Germans to disperse their forces prior to invasion, protecting and defending places the Allies would not attack. After the invasion the Allies would continue the deception to gain valuable time for the Allies to solidify their beachhead.

- For if he prepares to the front his rear will be weak, and if to the rear, his front will be fragile. If he prepares to the left, his right will be vulnerable and if to the right, there will be few on his left. And when he prepares everywhere he will be weak everywhere.   (VI.15)

To create Bodyguard the Allies used Ultra, their system for breaking the German Enigma coding system. By knowing what intelligence the Germans sought the Allies were able to craft a series of signals to lead the Nazis to think the attack would land in Pas de Calais area, not the actual invasion site of Normandy. These signals would be delivered by various means and "confirmed" by a number of German spies the British had captured and turned into double agents. The level of Bodyguard's sophistication is borne out by the fact that it was composed of sixteen major stratagems. Each of these stratagems reinforced the others and fed German preconceptions as to where and when the attack would come.

> ■ Lay on many deceptive operations. Be seen in the west and march out of the east; lure him in the north and strike in the south. Drive him crazy and bewilder him so that he disperses his forces in confusion.   (XI.26 Meng)

The Germans were predisposed to believe that the invasion would be at Pas de Calais. This area was the most direct route to Berlin, its port of Antwerp would provide the finest harbor in Europe, the English Channel was at its narrowest, and the flat terrain was excellent for tanks. Bodyguard's objective was to reinforce the German's assumption that Pas de Calais would be the landing area (see Figure 3.1).

Bodyguard's deceptions included the creation of a fake invasion force, First U.S. Army Group, or FUSAG. It was made known to the Germans that the commander of FUSAG would be General George Patton, the man the German high command considered the best Allied commander. FUSAG contained a mix of real and fictional units and was positioned across the Channel from Calais. Its presence was communicated to the Germans by heavy radio traffic, which the German Army picked up through signals intelligence. Believing in the existence of FUSAG, German intelligence "identified" twice as many divisions as the Allies really had and therefore were sure that their target was Calais.

> ■ He changes his methods and alters his plans so that people have no knowledge of what he is doing. He alters his camp-sites and marches by devious routes, and thus makes it impossible for others to anticipate his purpose.   (XI.45–46)

The final pre-invasion deception was the use of Garbo, a double agent highly trusted by the Germans. As the invasion fleet sailed, Garbo sent a message to the German high command announcing its imminent arrival in Normandy. However, Garbo's message made it clear that the

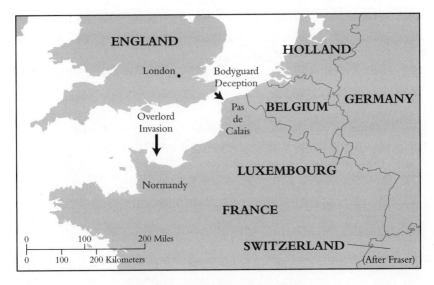

FIGURE 3.1 Bodyguard Deception

Normandy invasion was a diversion, whose objective was to lead the Germans to move troops from Calais. As a result of Garbo's message, Hitler stopped the movement of Panzer divisions to Normandy, over-ruling his commander, Field Marshal Erwin Rommel.

> ■ I make the enemy see my strengths as weaknesses and my weak-nesses as strengths while I cause his strengths to become weak-nesses and discover where he is not strong. I conceal my tracks so that none can discern them; I keep silence so that none can hear me.   (VI.9 Ho Yen-hsi)

After the invasion the deception continued. Double-cross agents continued to warn the Germans of potential amphibious or paratroop landings. Given that German intelligence overestimated the number of Allied divisions, these warnings made sense. Ultra confirmed that these warnings kept strong German forces in the Calais region as late as the end of July.

The result of Bodyguard's stratagems was the success of the Nor-mandy invasion and the eventual defeat of Germany. Through deception Bodyguard enabled a highly vulnerable force to establish itself in force on a beachhead against a numerically superior enemy. Without these deceptions, the invasion of France may have resulted in defeat for the Allies; certainly it saved countless lives of American, British, Canadian, and Polish soldiers.[19]

- Therefore, against those skilled in attack, an enemy does not know where to defend; against the experts in defence, the enemy does not know where to attack.   (VI.8)

  They make it impossible for an enemy to know where to prepare. They release the attack like a lightning bolt from above the nine-layered ground.   (IV.7 Tu Yu)

To pull off a deception as sophisticated as Bodyguard takes great skill and discipline. In fact, any deception plan requires a deep understanding of the enemy's state of mind, use of reinforcing strategies, and heavy security to guard the deception. Without these, the deception plan will fail.

- Apparent confusion is a product of good order: apparent cowardice, of courage, apparent weakness, of strength.   (V.18)

An additional means of enabling deception is to not release the orders for an attack until immediately before it begins. When Germany unleashed its Blitzkrieg invasion of France on May 10, 1940, the majority of its officers did not receive their orders until at or after midday on May 9. Although well-prepared by wargames and exercises, keeping the actual day and hour of the advance secret maintained the element of surprise.[20]

- He should be capable of keeping his officers and men in ignorance of his plans. . . . His troops may join him in rejoicing at the accomplishment, but they cannot join him in laying the plans.   (XI.43 Sun Tzu and Ts'ao Ts'ao)

Constraints on Deception

The form of government a nation has (democracy, dictatorship) will determine to an extent its ability to practice deception. Unless its very existence is threatened, in most instances the need for openness in a democracy will limit its ability to keep secrets. Conversely, totalitarian regimes by their very nature may be more effective at maintaining secrecy.

Furthermore, as media coverage of events becomes increasingly real-time, practicing deception is even more difficult. For example, during the Persian Gulf War in the early 1990s the "CNN effect" meant that continuous newscasts about the war provided both sides with real-time intelligence. To help maintain better control over what information reached both the home front and the enemy, the U.S. military rotated reporters in pools which controlled their access yet provided great pictures for propaganda value. This method contrasted sharply to the practice in Viet Nam, in which reporters were given fairly free rein.[21]

With methods such as these, plus the practice of solid security discipline and a sophisticated deception program, even a republic can effectively practice deception.

Information Warfare

Learning the enemy's intentions in Sun Tzu's day was accomplished using one's eyes and ears. Keeping the nation's secrets secret was enabled through the use of relatively simple codes and severe punishment for those who betrayed them. To signal orders and commands to subordinates units, soldiers would beat drums and wave flags.

> ■ Now when masses of troops are employed, certainly they are widely separated, and ears are not able to hear acutely nor eyes to see clearly. Therefore officers and men are ordered to advance or retreat by observing the flags and banners and to move or stop by signals of bells and drums . . . (V.2 Chang Yü)

Today—and even more so in the future—the tasks of eliciting intelligence, monitoring the situation, commanding subordinate units securely, and denying the enemy those same capabilities will be done electronically. Multitudes of sensing and input devices will feed data into both highly mobile and stationary computers via high-speed communications networks, updating access devices that graphically depict the battle environment. "Stealth" submarines, planes, tanks, and other units, using radar/sonar-absorbing materials and super-quiet engines, will seek to avoid detection. Simultaneously, the opposing forces will be launching attacks on their enemy's information infrastructure, either by eliminating nodes, jamming communications or (more insidiously) providing false data to the enemy's access devices to mislead their opponent. This struggle between opposing forces to understand their enemy's plans and the evolving situation while at the same time keeping their opponent in the dark is the essence of information warfare.

Clarifying the concept of information warfare are these excerpts from a working definition of it, as recognized by the School of Information Warfare of the National Defense University as of November 16, 1996. The definition begins with "Information-based warfare is an approach to armed conflict focusing on the management and use of information in all its forms and at all levels to achieve a decisive military advantage. . . ." This sentence makes clear that winning the battle and the war will be possible only if one is better than the enemy at gathering, analyzing, and acting on information, both tactically and strategically.

Achieving information superiority means that one understands the changes in the situation and responds more effectively to those changes than the enemy. Furthermore, attaining information dominance means that one prevents the enemy from achieving a similar understanding, thus making him incapable of responding appropriately to one's moves.

> ■ When you are ignorant of the enemy but know yourself, your chances of winning or losing are equal. If ignorant of both your enemy and yourself, you are certain in every battle to be in peril.   (III.32–33)

A later excerpt from the definition states, "While ultimately military in nature, information based-warfare is also waged in political, economic and social arenas and is applicable over the entire national security continuum from peace to war and from 'tooth to tail.' "[22]

The above passage points out that information warfare is not limited to occurring during a military conflict. With the advent of the Internet and the increasing reliance by modern countries on their information infrastructure to function, information warfare becomes an alternative to direct military confrontation. By launching information war attacks against another country, it is possible for the "aggressor" nation to inflict severe damage without being found out—or, if found out, attack will likely be considered below the threshold of a military response.

Economic institutions and major businesses can have their information technology assets attacked, brought down, or fed false information. Think for a moment what the impact could be on financial markets if false information is spread throughout the network over a long enough time period. A nation can also use the Internet to foster worldwide sympathy for its objectives or to hack into its opponent's web sites to deface them or destroy them. For example, during tensions between Taiwan and China in 1999, both sides fought a cyberwar, posting propaganda on one another's web sites. Also in 1999, Serbian hackers attacked a NATO web site, knocking it out of service. These simple and relatively harmless attacks are minor precursors to the damage a full-scale information war could bring about.

Since Sun Tzu's time, winning the information war has been critical to winning the overall war. The increasing speed with which new technology is emerging, the sensitivity of that technology to disruption and subversion, and the power of that technology when employed as an interconnected system has made winning the information war that much more important and that much more difficult.

- **He who knows when he can fight and when he cannot will be victorious.   (III.25)**

Summary

To conquer, one must combine foreknowledge and deception. Learn everything possible about the enemy: troop levels, technological advancements, economic strengths, their leadership. This intelligence gives insight into not just the enemy's capabilities, but its intentions as well.

Foreknowledge also means knowing one's own capabilities as well as the enemy's. Comparison of strengths and weaknesses will provide an understanding of the correlation of forces.

Know the impact of terrain and weather on one's strategy and plans. Understand how they may affect the outcome of the battle. Build an intelligence infrastructure to provide this knowledge.

Lastly, practice deception where prudent to mask one's intentions from your enemy. Keep their leadership in the dark and ignorant about one's movements. Do not let them know the time and the place of the attack.

Foreknowledge and deception provide the advantage. As the next chapter illustrates, speed and preparation allow one to capitalize on it.

4 ■ Speed and Preparation

Moving Swiftly to Overcome Resistance

■ Speed is the essence of war. Take advantage of the enemy's unpreparedness; travel by unexpected routes and strike him where he has taken no precautions.   (XI.29)

In war, speed is essential. Armies must move rapidly to secure ground that favors them in battle, maneuver quickly around the enemy to hit his flanks, exploit breakthroughs, and pursue enemies in retreat. Furthermore, the very nature of warfare is constant change, which tests a leader's and an army's ability to quickly respond, adjust, and take advantage of it.

Speed in warfare provides four advantages: it is a substitute for resources, it shocks and surprises the enemy, it is critical to exploiting weaknesses and opportunities, and it builds momentum (see Figure 4.1). Let us examine each aspect of speed in detail.

Speed Is a Substitute for Resources

Speed is a substitute for resources. In warfare a smaller, more mobile army can defeat a much larger one by rapid movement. Moving quickly to attack parts of the larger one before it can react and coordinate its forces, the smaller army defeats the enemy "in detail," essentially

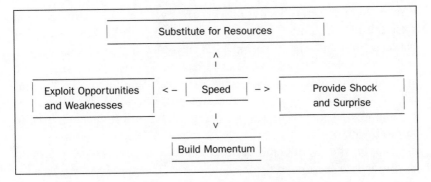

FIGURE 4.1   The Importance of Speed

destroying each piece of the opposing army before others can come to its aid.

- If I am able to determine the enemy's dispositions while at the same time I conceal my own then I can concentrate and he must divide. And if I concentrate while he divides, I can use my entire strength to attack a fraction of his. There, I will be numerically superior. Then, if I am able to use many to strike few at the selected point, those I deal with will be in dire straits. (VI.13)

Although General Stonewall Jackson earned his name by having his troops stand "like a stone wall" at the first battle of Bull Run, his true genius was his ability to plan and execute quick-hitting, highly mobile operations. Those campaigns exemplify the substitution of speed for resources.

One of those operations was Jackson's seven-week campaign in the Shenandoah Valley in 1862. The situation facing the South that April was grim. The Union's new "Napoleon," General George B. Mc-Clellan, had concentrated 65,000 men around the Confederate capitol of Richmond, far outnumbering the Rebels 24,000. Something needed to be done to relieve the pressure on Richmond.

The Confederate commander on the spot, General Joe Johnston, wanted to recall as many troops to defend the capitol. However, General Robert E. Lee, at the time the military advisor to President Jeff Davis, had another idea. Lee wanted to combine a defensive posture around Richmond while unleashing a diversionary attack in the North. The man he chose to lead the attack was General Stonewall Jackson.

Jackson had trained his infantry to march quickly and they had earned the nickname "Jackson's foot cavalry." First he marched them west and hit the Union troops under General John C. Fremont. After handing Fremont a nasty defeat, Jackson turned his army against General Nathaniel P. Banks and dealt him several blows. With these two armies reeling, the Union leadership feared that Washington itself might fall. As a result Lincoln refused to send General Irvin McDowell's corps to reinforce McClellan, instead sending McDowell in a futile attempt to catch Jackson.

Jackson then scampered back to join forces with the army around Richmond to help defend the capital city. The speed with which he carried out his mission was instrumental in ultimately convincing McClellan that he was heavily outnumbered and could not take Richmond.

> ■ In attacking a great state, if you can divide your enemy's forces your strength will be more than sufficient.　(XI.52 Mei Yaoch'en)

In a short seven weeks Jackson traveled the length of the valley twice, covered 600 miles, defeated or outmaneuvered three Union armies, threatened Washington, D.C., with capture, and achieved his strategic objective of relieving pressure on Richmond. With only 17,000 men Jackson occupied 50,000 of the enemy, thus epitomizing the use of speed to overcome a lack of resources.[1]

> ■ Come like the wind, go like lightning.　(VI.10 Chang Yü)

Speed Exploits Fleeting Opportunities

Speed is also tightly linked to attacking weakness and exploiting opportunity. One must be bold and aggressive. A commander must not only be able to deal with a fast-changing battle environment, but must desire it, thrive on it, and nourish it.

Mao Zedong, when seeking to reposition China advantageously between its old ally the Soviet Union and its potential ally the United States, once said, "The world is in chaos; the situation is excellent." When his opportunity to shift the balance of power was in his favor, he quickly took it.[2]

> ■ The general must rely on his ability to control the situation to his advantage as opportunity dictates. He is not bound by estab-

lished procedures. A general prizes opportune changes in circumstances.   (VIII.9–10, Chia Lin)

From a military standpoint, if an attack on the enemy's weak point develops slowly, they have more time to counter it. This was the case in World War I with the Allies. Although they were able to achieve a breakthrough in the German trench system several times, because of their lack of mobility they never were capable of moving quickly enough to exploit the opening. German generals were consistently able to close the breach by quickly moving reserves by train to the threatened area and then counterattacking to regain the lost ground. The result was years of bloody trench warfare in which the Allies focused on wearing Germany down through a costly war of attrition.

- Experts in war depend especially on opportunity and expediency. They do not place the burden of accomplishment on their men alone.   (V.21 Ch'ên Hao)

On the other hand, if an attack proceeds with speed, the battle may be over before the enemy can respond. In 1940, Germany was again at war with the Allies. The large, well-equipped French army sat entrenched behind the Maginot Line and most people expected a replay of the trench warfare of World War I. However, a new element of speed had been brought to the battlefield in the form of the tank. Able to use firepower to break through enemy defenses and then move rapidly into vulnerable rear areas to create chaos and confusion, the tank became the signature weapon of the German Army in World War II. This was the new Blitzkrieg paradigm of warfare. Germany's skillful use of it to go around the Maginot Line and hit the weakest part of the French defenses was the key to forcing France to surrender after only a few weeks of fighting.

- He whose advance is irresistible plunges into his enemy's weak positions; he who in withdrawal cannot be pursued moves so swiftly that he cannot be overtaken.   (VI.10)

A little-known fact about the battle for France was that the French Army not only had better tanks than the German Army, but also had more of them. Yet the French still lost the campaign. Why? The reason involved the French method of deploying the tank. French Army doctrine called for tanks to be scattered about in small numbers and tied to slow-moving infantry divisions. These divisions could move only as fast as their feet could carry them.

In contrast, German Army strategy called for motorizing select groups of infantry (putting them in trucks) and attaching them organizationally to the Panzer units so that they could keep up with the fast-moving tanks, support their assaults, and defend their breakthroughs. Furthermore, German doctrine dictated that these tanks be concentrated in large units to apply maximum shock and firepower against the enemy's weaknesses. These panzer divisions were then massed at the point of attack to achieve the breakthrough and supported with tactical air power provided by the German Stuka dive-bomber. Thus, in France, a smaller army based on speed, shock, and concentrated firepower won the day over a larger one composed of widely dispersed tanks tied to slow-moving infantry.

- Strike the enemy as swiftly as a falcon strikes its target. It surely breaks the back of its prey for the reason that it awaits the right moment to strike. Its movement is regulated. Thus the momentum of one skilled in war is overwhelming, and his attack precisely regulated.   (V.14 Tu Yu; 15 Sun Tzu)

Speed Surprises and Shocks the Enemy

Speed is essential in surprising the enemy. By combining deception with quick movement, one can keep the opponent from discerning one's intentions until it is too late. The initial surprise throws them off balance. Then, as one attack quickly follows another, the enemy becomes even more bewildered and unbalanced. Finally, shocked into submission, the enemy ends up paralyzed and unable to respond.

- When campaigning, be swift as the wind; in leisurely march, majestic as the forest; in raiding and plundering, like fire; in standing, firm as the mountains. As unfathomable as the clouds, move like a thunderbolt.   (VII.13)

The German campaign in France was successful largely because of surprise and shock. First was Allied surprise at the place of the German attack; second was the Allied shock at the speed with which the attack was carried out.

The Germans launched their attack in the north, with two dazzling airborne assaults; one in Holland and one in Belgium. These lightning-

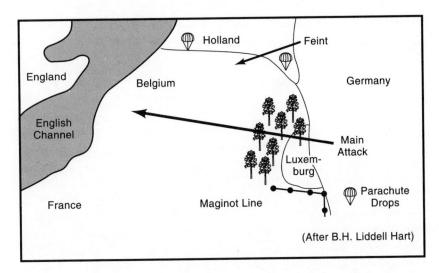

FIGURE 4.2   The German strategy in France: 1940

quick paratrooper landings captured important river crossings, knocked out supposedly impregnable fortifications, and cut critical communications. More important, they drew Allied attention to the north, where the French and British expected the German attack to develop. It was there that the Allies began to move their best, most mobile forces (see Figure 4.2).

However, the real German attack came further south, through the heavily wooded Ardennes. The Allies did not believe the Wehrmacht could mass any sizable force there, especially tanks, given the rough and forested terrain. However, it was here that Germany packed fifty of their 135 divisions, including seven deadly Panzer divisions.

Blasting through the weak French divisions holding the line in the Ardennes (composed mostly of old men with poor equipment), the Wehrmacht's Panzers drove deep into Allied lines. Covering several miles per day, they moved faster than the Allies ever imagined, and in a week the German Panzers reached the English Channel. As the battle for France developed, French and British leaders and soldiers could not comprehend the fast pace of the Blitzkrieg. They were still on the World War I time clock, where attacks lasted months, not hours, and progress was measured in yards, not miles. The speed with which the initial assault came created surprise; the speed with which it continued created shock; and the result was a disorientation from which the Allies could not recover.[3]

- When the thunderclap comes, there is no time to cover the ears. (I.26 Ho Yen-hsi)

Speed Builds Momentum

The final reason speed is critical to success is that it provides the ability to sustain and exploit strategic momentum once a breakthrough has been achieved. German military philosophy in both world wars was to launch simultaneous attacks within the *schwerpunkt* and determine which ones were stalling and which succeeding. Instead of sending reinforcements to attacks that had stalled, the German command sent reinforcements to those that were succeeding. This allowed them to push deeper into enemy territory, cut off areas of resistance, and continue the attack's tempo and momentum. Later, after the enemy had been soundly defeated, the Germans would take the time to mop up the remaining enemy strongholds.

Given the prior discussion on the German Army's proficiency with the tank, you might think that they had invented it. In fact, it was the World War I brainchild of a British war correspondent and Winston Churchill. Churchill, at that time First Lord of the Admiralty, saw Lt. Colonel Ernest Swinton's idea for tracked fighting vehicles as "landships" that could break the trench warfare stalemate and return the war to one of maneuver. Although it was very difficult to convince short-sighted Allied generals that they needed one, the first tank was finally produced in 1916.[4]

To keep the new weapon a secret, it was christened the "tank," whose purported purpose was to carry water to the front lines. After being used haphazardly in minor battles, the tank's first major test came at the battle of Cambrai. In the early morning mist of November 20, 1917, 374 tanks poured from British lines, supported by 1,000 artillery pieces and fourteen squadrons of British aircraft. The goal was to punch a hole in Germany's Hindenburg line and reach the "green fields beyond," where cavalry could exploit the breach and attack the enemy rear areas.

Surprise was complete, as German soldiers fled at the sight of the mechanical monsters. German lines were penetrated to a depth of five miles and a gap six miles wide. Unfortunately, the British generals were as surprised as the Germans. They had no tank reserves to push through the gap and the cavalry reserve was incapable of exploiting this breakthrough. The attack withered, and with it went the one chance the Allies would have to change the course of the war from stalemate to strategic breakthrough. That opportunity would not come again until many more lives were lost.[5]

The Allied approach at Cambrai was exactly the wrong thing to do: one should never launch an attack unless one is ready to reinforce it should it be successful. If one is not prepared but launches an attack anyway, surprise is forfeited, resources are wasted, and the enemy is given the opportunity to learn one's strategy and tactics. It makes no sense to start something that cannot be finished.

- **Now to win battles and take your objectives, but to fail to exploit these achievements is ominous and may be described as "wasteful delay." (XII.15)**

Remember, to be successful at the strategic level one must reinforce successes at the tactical level. Exploit breakthroughs and create unstoppable momentum.

- **When torrential water tosses boulders, it is because of its momentum (V.13)**

The corollary of reinforcing success is that when an attack is failing, drop it like a live grenade. Believing that one's will is strong enough to defeat the reality of the situation will result in throwing more soldiers against a well-entrenched defense; the costs will pile up and one still may not obtain the objective. The key is to reinforce success, starve failure.

After defeating Napoleon at Waterloo and ridding Europe of "the Corsican," the British turned to the New World to settle their scores with the Americans (near the end of the War of 1812). Sending veterans of Waterloo and the Portuguese Peninsula campaigns to punish the fledgling United States and protect her Canadian territories, the British resolved that taking the city of New Orleans would suit her needs well. In British hands, New Orleans would bottle up waterborne trade on the Mississippi River from the interior of America's western territories. New Orleans would also be either a plum for Britain to keep, or an excellent bargaining chip at the future peace table.

The hardened British veterans were led by General Pakenham, an experienced officer and a favorite of Wellington's. Numbering over 14,000 men, the British Army landed its troops downriver from New Orleans in December 1814. Opposing this professional army were 5,700 American troops led by Andrew Jackson. Only 700 of these troops were Army Regulars; the rest were a conglomeration of militia, slaves, and even pirates thrown together at the last moment to save the city.

The Americans were drawn up behind earthworks on both sides of the Mississippi, with the flanks of the works protected by swampy woods. However, the Americans did not opt for a passive defense. As soon as the British landed Jackson launched a night attack that inflicted major casualties on the British and raised American morale. This night attack was followed by a series of night raids by small parties of volunteers, leaving British sentries with their throats cut and their comrades unable to sleep. Long-range sniping during the day added to the frustration and discomfort of the British, while further reinforcing the Americans' belief that they could stop these veterans when the day of decision came.

After having a reconnaissance in force repelled, Pakenham grew impatient. His troops were suffering from the weather and American raids, supply was becoming difficult and the potential for peace arriving before New Orleans could be taken was increasing. Pakenham decided it was time to force the issue. A minor attack on the east side of the river would support two major assaults against the main American line on the west side (see Figure 4.3). These two major attacks would be composed of columns of infantry supported by artillery, a method that had worked time and again in Europe against even stronger fortifications and tougher troops. Scaling ladders would be sent with the lead troops to help them enter the American works.

On January 8, 1815, the British attacks moved forward. Almost immediately the two assault columns on the west bank ran into trouble. The scaling ladders had been lost in the rear and were not available to the front-line troops. Worse, accurate rifle fire from the American lines was dropping British officers and the troops were taking heavy casualties. The British attack was stalled in front of the American earthworks.

To get the attack going again Pakenham ordered his Scottish Highlanders forward, but American rifle and artillery fire blasted holes in their lines. Whereas the Napoleonic wars were fought with muskets, the accuracy and range of the American rifles significantly increased the lethality of the battlefield, especially to officers. Pakenham himself fell. Despite the courage of the British troops the reinforced attacks failed and they were forced to withdraw, giving up hopes of capturing the city. On the field were 2,000 of Britain's finest, sacrificed in repeated attempts to overcome failure. In contrast, the Americans suffered thir-

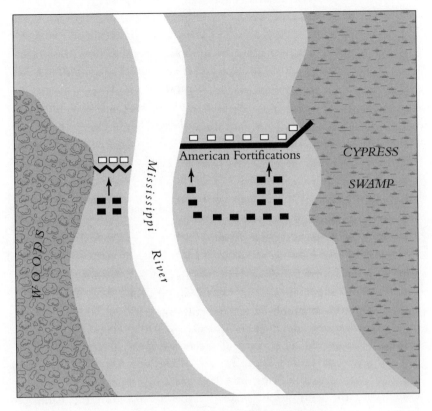

FIGURE 4.3   The Battle of New Orleans

teen casualties, including seven killed. Tragically, the battle came days after peace between Britain and the U.S. had already been signed in Europe.[6]

- If the general is unable to control his impatience and orders his troops to swarm up the wall like ants, one-third of them will be killed without taking the city. Such is the calamity of these attacks.   (III.9)

As the New Orleans example illustrates, directly attacking strong fortifications and reinforcing failed attacks leads to heavy losses. This is exactly the wrong thing to do; instead of reinforcing failure, one must reinforce success and starve failure. When a weak point in the opponent's position has been found and a breakthrough achieved, pour resources through it. Keep the momentum going and turn the enemy's retreat into a rout.

Preparation

It is clear that speed is crucial; the question becomes how to achieve it, both strategically and tactically. To act with great speed requires not frenzied activity, but rather careful preparation matched by a sense of urgency. Only by skillfully planning the campaign ahead of time can one move confidently with blinding swiftness. Only by looking at all the possibilities in advance and then acting with a sense of urgency can one take advantage of fleeting opportunities as they arise. Therefore, plan far in advance of the contest to ensure that victory.

- To rely on rustics and not prepare is the greatest of crimes; to be prepared beforehand for any contingency is the greatest of virtues.   (III.28 Ho Yen-hsi)

The Warring States period in China continued for almost two hundred years, during which the Seven States fought against one another for control of all of China. However, the end to this long and bitter chapter in Chinese history ended rather quickly, with the state of Ch'in defeating the other six states in rapid succession (Han in 230 B.C.; Chao, 228 B.C.; Wei, 225 B.C.; Ch'u, 223 B.C.; Yen, 222 B.C.; and Ch'i, 221 B.C.). In doing so the King of Ch'in became the First Emperor of China, and the name of his state became the basis for the name of China.

The state of Ch'in was able to gain mastery of China due to the preparations it had made over many years. It employed superior weapons, including swords made with advanced metallurgical techniques much better than the simple bronze ones in use by the other states (these swords were so fine that a sword excavated 2,000 years later from the First Emperor's tomb could still split a single hair). Rather than deploying chariots that were the standard in the rest of China, Ch'in built an excellent cavalry army through the breeding of strong horses and tough training.

The government of Ch'in had been ruled by three great dukes prior to the King of Ch'in for 107 years, and the populace was not prone to revolt. Ch'in was a state in which new reforms and ideas were welcome and the rulers recruited far and wide for the most talented of advisors. In doing so the King of Ch'in was able to obtain the services of Li Ssu, who became Ch'in's great strategist. It was Li Ssu who developed many of the strategies that enabled Ch'in's ultimate victory.[7]

The same was true of Alexander the Great. Alexander's army and governmental system were created by his father, Philip of Macedonia. Philip took the Greek phalanx and deepened it from eight ranks to sixteen. He then extended the Greek spear to 21 feet, which became the much-feared Macedonian sarissa. In formation the first ranks spears extended forward and the remaining spears pointed upward to deflect arrows shot by the enemy. To support the phalanx and cover its flanks Philip developed light infantry, composed of peltasts (lightly armored spearmen), archers, darters, slingers, and javelin-throwers.

However, Philip went beyond tinkering with the already-successful phalanx. He built two strong arms that to date had not been fully developed. He created a heavy cavalry (the famous "Companions") and a light cavalry for scouting. He also developed "artillery" in the form of field-mobile ballistas and catapults, the critical parts of which could be carried by troops anywhere (the heavy wooden parts being then made from local trees).

Philip went beyond the creation of three strong combat arms (infantry, cavalry, and artillery) to combining them together and coordinating their actions for maximum advantage in battle. He also had a general staff of older officers who provided counsel and ensured implementation of his orders. The army was put to the test in the battle of Chaeroneia, in which he defeated a larger army of Athenians and Thebans, thus winning mastery of Greece. At that battle the decisive blow was delivered by his eighteen-year-old son Alexander, who lead the Macedonian cavalry in an envelopment against the allied center. After Philip's death by assassination, Alexander would take his army 10,000 miles, winning all of his battles and destroying empires at will.

The Roman Empire depended also on preparation to achieve its success. By building wide and durable roads, Rome was able to extend and control an empire that spanned most of the ancient Western world. In the Second Punic War these enabled Rome to prevent critical assistance from getting through to Hannibal. When Hannibal's brother Hasbrubal crossed the Alps into northern Italy, the Roman armies needed to keep him from joining forces with Hannibal in the south. Luckily for Rome Hasdrubal's messengers was captured, leaving Hannibal unaware that his brother wanted to combine armies. This allowed Nero, the consul charged with watching Hannibal in the south, the opportunity to march 250 miles in seven days to join with the army that was shadowing Hasdrubal. These combined forces destroyed Hasdrubal's army and ended the one opportunity Hannibal had for major reinforcement. This rapid movement was only due to the strategic capability Roman roads provided.[8]

- In planning, never a useless move; in strategy, no step taken in vain.   (IV.12 Chên Hao)

In addition to roads, other means of attaining strategic speed have since been developed. Technologically, one such method is the ship, both for combat and cargo. While the ship allowed strategic movement across seas and oceans in ancient days, transport planes did the same in the twentieth century. The telegraph and now high-speed digital communications networks enable faster communications and strategic direction. Organizationally, the movement from feudal armies to national armies, the formation of the divisional unit in the Napoleonic era and the Blitzkrieg concept of the Second World War, have each contributed to increasing the capacity for speed. Today, the ability to move large units (divisions, corps, armies) swiftly to defend endangered areas or maneuver around the enemy determines success or failure. Large capacity airlift and sea lift capability are crucial to strategic flexibility and a nation's ability to project power quickly.

- Generally, he who occupies the field of battle first and awaits his enemy is at ease; he who comes later to the scene and rushes into the fight is weary.   (VI.1)

Beginning with the horse and the chariot and more recently the tank, truck, motorcycle, and helicopter, many technical innovations have increased speed and mobility on the battlefield at the tactical level. Wireless radio has also enabled instantaneous communications between dispersed units, allowing motorized units to maintain contact with headquarters and their supply lines. Coincident with these technical advances have been organizational changes to match them. Smaller and more flexible units grouped into higher formations have increased battlefield mobility. These units have employed new methods such as Napoleonic columns of attack and stormtrooper tactics, which in turn have improved speed.

On today's battlefield it is critical that both combat and support units have the transport capability to move rapidly. This may take the form of motorized transport, helicopters, or other methods that enable mobility. Furthermore, each unit needs to be motivated and train hard to ensure it can carry its mission out with dispatch and a sense of urgency. Enabling individual soldiers and units to move more quickly than the enemy provides a key advantage on the battlefield.

Beyond preparing for swift tactical movement, it is critical to "prepare the battlefield." German Blitzkrieg doctrine in World War II called for taking up to ten months to prepare for battle: laying out plans, deploying troops, positioning supplies, practicing deception, and gathering intelligence. This long preparation would lead to a very short battle of encirclement and annihilation, as short as six to fifteen days. If success was not achieved in this timeframe then the battle was to be broken off with whatever gains had been achieved.[9]

■ Therefore at first be shy as a maiden. When the enemy gives you an opening be swift as a hare and he will be unable to withstand you. (XI.61)

Critical to supporting the initial Blitzkrieg attack was the artillery plan. Like the German Army's *sturmtruppen* tactics, the artillery methods had their basis in World War I. These artillery tactics were created by Colonel Georg Bruchmuller, whose nickname "Durchbruch" was a combination of a pun and the German word for "breakthrough." Bruchmuller's newly developed tactics were critical to achieving breakthroughs in the enemy's lines.

Bruchmuller was an unlikely candidate to bring a revolution in thinking to artillery tactics. He was medically-retired, little-known, and only a lieutenant-colonel. Yet he was able to take the current state-of-the-art techniques, add his own innovations and then incorporate them into a new system that could flexibly and quickly deliver massive concentrations of fire onto enemy targets. More importantly, he was able to integrate his system with the infantry's maneuver plans to ensure that the artillery support they needed was always readily available. Bruchmuller's methods would become the basis of the tactics used in all modern artillery arms.

Bruchmuller developed his new methods after much experimentation. However, the basis of his concept was the revolutionary idea that artillery should not be used to totally destroy and eliminate any opposition in the trenches, but merely to neutralize it until friendly infantry could either take the position or maneuver around it. Obviously, this is where the close coordination between the two combat arms came into play.

Whereas the current doctrine of the time called for several days of prolonged artillery bombardment, Bruchmuller's new methods depended on a short but violently intense preparation. Lasting only a few hours, these devastating concentrations of fire would daze the defenders and make them incapable of stopping the assault waves of the stormtroopers. Different types of artillery would be tasked to support specific infantry missions, with the right type of guns being used in each instance. To ensure coordination with the infantry Bruchmuller would ensure his staff understood the infantry's plan of attack. The staff would then brief the infantry on the fire plans that had been built to support their attack.

Once artillery plans were in place a great deal of care was made in preparing for the coming battle. Firing positions would be scouted and observation posts and communications put in place. Prior to the guns being deployed each position would be camouflaged, with the quality of the screening being checked by observation balloons. Then the fire direction teams would infiltrate to prepare firing charts and ammunition would be dropped off. The guns themselves would not move into position until hours before the attack, to avoid tipping off the enemy. They would do so at night, with cannon wheels and horse's hooves being wrapped to deaden the sound and limit the raising of dust.

The artillery fire plan itself covered fires before, during, and after the assault. Throughout the battle a mix of shell types were used (gas, high explosive, smoke) to achieve specific effects. Fire plans prior to the assault (*Vorbereitung*, or preparation fires) consisted of three phases. The first phase (*Feueruberfall*, or fire strike) targeted enemy command posts, communications centers, and troop positions. Short and violent (10–30 minutes), the intent was to force the enemy to man their guns. Phase two targeted enemy batteries, with the intent of hitting the gun crews and neutralizing them. This phase lasted an hour and a half to two and a half hours. The final phase of the preparation lasted one to two hours and shifted back to the enemy infantry positions. The third phase ended with a ten-minute barrage using all the guns. Called the *Sturmreifschiessen*, or softening-up fire, the intent was to hit the enemy positions with everything possible. As soon as it lifted the German infantry went forward.

During the attack the Germans employed a creeping barrage ahead of the infantry. This *Feuerwalze* (fire waltz) had been used throughout much of the war. One problem with the *Feuerwalze* was that it went forward according to a strict timetable, regardless of whether the infantry was being held up by an enemy strongpoint. Bruchmuller introduced the ability of junior leaders whose units were stalled to modify the *Feuerwalze*. By signaling back to the artillery command, guns would be taken out of the *Feuerwalze* and used to hit the strongpoint. Once the infantry had taken the position, another signal would be sent and the guns would rejoin the barrage.

After the assault Bruchmuller's plans called for moving guns forward as quickly as possible and reattaching them to their infantry units. The goal of this decentralization was to provide as much support forward as possible, in preparation for the inevitable enemy counterattacks.

Bruchmuller's artillery preparations, built on detailed planning, elaborate deception measures, whirlwind bombardments, and coordination with the infantry scheme of maneuver were instrumental in the success of the 1918 German offensives. His ability to combine preparation with speed laid the groundwork upon which all modern artillery planning would rest.[10]

Speed of Decision-Making

In addition to these obvious requirements for speed is one that is perhaps less obvious. That is the capability to make and implement decisions quickly, at both the tactical and strategic levels. For example, how long does it take for information from the field to get to headquarters? How long does it take for the staff to make battle plans based on the new information? Once the plans have been presented, how quickly does the commander make decisions? Once a decision is made, how quickly is it carried out and turned into action?

If an army is to act with speed the commanders must focus on improving its information–decision–action cycle times. Even if all other execution cycle times are reduced, but the time it takes to make and execute decisions is not shortened, failure will result.

By shortening its decision-making time both a small unit or a large army can increase the speed and tempo of its operations. This in turn throws the enemy off balance, reduces its ability to respond effectively, and increases the possibility of new opportunities surfacing. As noted earlier, this is one of the critical objectives of a commander, creating new opportunities and taking advantage of them.

To shorten the time it takes to implement decisions, it is important to focus on each stage of the information–decision–action cycle. As mentioned in chapter 3, critical information should be gathered quickly by implementing a process that facilitates intelligence, making it rapidly from the field to headquarters. The infrastructure must be set up to enable the quick sharing of intelligence. Barriers that prevent subordinates from coming forward with information and recommendations need to be reduced; too many layers of control, highly formal communications, and overdeveloped egos create problems.

To help one avoid getting bogged down by gathering data and studying a problem until it is too late to do something about it, leaders should consider a rule that General Colin Powell followed. Using zero percent to represent having no information and a hundred percent as having all the information one would ever need to make the decision, make the decision when about sixty percent of the information is available. Making a decision any later risks delaying so long that the opportunity vanishes.[11]

■ What is of the greatest importance in war is extraordinary speed; one cannot afford to neglect opportunity. (I.26 Ho Yen-hsi)

By following these methods a military organization can deal with and capitalize on new opportunities before the enemy and defeat him.

Wargaming

To be successful, one must be able to see and stay several moves ahead of the enemy.

■ If I wish to take advantage of the enemy I must perceive not just the advantage in doing so but must first consider the ways he can harm me if I do. (VIII.13 Tu Mu)

The German Army, which created the first professional staff system, coined the saying "No plan of battle survives first contact with the enemy." Therefore, they created the concept of the *Kriegspiel*, or wargame. They created potential war scenarios by aligning themselves and a set of allies against a set of opponents. They would then develop their battle plans for that scenario and, using rules created to closely simulate actual battle conditions, play out the wargame on huge maps. After playing a scenario several times, the staff would be familiar with all the possibilities and could plan ways of countering the range of moves open to the enemy. When actual battle came and combat was heated, the situations played out earlier would appear and be familiar; there were few, if any, surprises. This gave the German officer a greater sense of confidence in his control over the situation, since he could recall the wargame and determine a proper response. For example, during Germany's invasion of France in May 1940, General Heinz Guderian was able to get his corps across the Meuse River by merely changing the dates on orders issued in a wargame run prior to the war.[12]

■ **He who excels at resolving difficulties does so before they arise. (III.4 Tu Mu)**

By taking into account the favorable factors, he makes his plan feasible; by taking into account the unfavorable, he may resolve the difficulties. (VIII.13)

Wargaming a situation provides experiential learning about the potential battle, campaign, or war. Experiential learning is much stronger than book learning. By playing the role of a different leader, military force, or country one can understand the perspectives of allies or enemies, getting "into their heads" and viewing the struggle from the vantage point. Wargaming also allows one to experiment with different strategies to see which ones work and which may not. It does this in an essentially risk-free environment; no forces are committed, no national prestige is at stake, no destruction has begun. Finally, as the Guderian example shows, a soldier or statesman is prepared for potential changes in the situation, having "experienced" them already in the wargame. However, to profit from wargaming it is critical to learn from the results. When the learnings are ignored the result can be disaster.

One of the key men responsible for what befell America in Viet Nam was Robert McNamara. When McNamara was the head of Ford Motor Company he brought into the company many men from his Air Force statistical analysis team to help run the company. They became known as the "Whiz Kids." When McNamara became the Secretary of Defense he brought in many people from top universities such as Harvard. This new group also became known as the Whiz Kids. The Chief of Staff of the Air Force, Curis LeMay, said that he found the latter-day Whiz Kids to be "the most egotistical people that I ever saw in my life. They had no faith in the military; they had no respect for the military at all. They felt that the Harvard Business School method of solving problems would solve any problem in the world. . . ."

With no military combat or leadership experience but with only corporate background, McNamara and his new team micromanaged U.S. efforts in Southeast Asia in the mid-1960s. His first major strategy to achieve victory was to gradually increase military pressure on North Viet Nam. The Joint Chiefs, America's military leadership, questioned whether it would work, so they commissioned a wargame called Sigma I to test McNamara's strategy.

The results were telling. The wargame showed that North Viet Nam and the Viet Cong would increase their attacks and that the U.S. public would not support the strategy. When McNamara implemented his strategy, the wargame's prophecy turned into reality and the strategy failed.

The next McNamara strategy was to use limited air power to push North Viet Nam to end its support for the Viet Cong insurgency. Another wargame, Sigma II, tested this theory and also found it wanting. The results showed a strengthening of communist resolve and limited military and diplomatic options for the U.S. Again, McNamara ignored the results and the result was a failure of his policies in Viet Nam. Thousands of American soldiers, millions of Vietnamese, and the U.S. suffered due to his arrogance and shortsightedness.[13]

■ For a general unable to estimate his capabilities or comprehend the arts of expediency and flexibility when faced with the opportunity to engage the enemy will advance in a stumbling and hesitant manner, looking anxiously first to his right and then to his left, and be unable to produce a plan. Credulous, he will place confidence in unreliable reports, believing at one moment this and at another that. As timorous as a fox in advancing or retiring, his groups will be scattered about. What is the difference between this and driving innocent people into boiling water or fire? Is this not exactly like driving cows and sheep to feed wolves or tigers? (IV.14 Tu Mu)

Overcoming Friction

Despite all the planning one might do, compounding the problem of achieving speed is something Carl von Clausewitz called "friction." Clausewitz stated that "Everything in war is very simple, but the simplest thing is difficult. The difficulties accumulate and end by producing a kind of friction that is inconceivable unless one has experienced war . . . Countless minor incidents—the kind one can never really foresee—combine to lower the general level of performance, so that one always falls short of the intended goal." Clausewitz goes on to say, "Friction is the only concept that more or less corresponds to the factors that distinguish real war from war on paper."[14]

Examples of friction include orders that never get delivered (or worse, get intercepted), critical equipment not appearing at the right time or place, malfunctioning equipment (such as communications equipment, satellites, and weapons), units getting lost, and commanders misinterpreting or even disobeying orders. Any one of these can, either by itself or in combination, be sufficient to impede progress and cause defeat. To achieve speed and victory, these obstacles must be overcome.

Selection and Training

Overcoming friction and winning conflicts begins with the selection of recruits and the training of military units.

The quality of a nation's forces will be determined by the individual soldier and officer's level of skill, motivation, and psychological makeup. Therefore, selecting the proper individuals to serve is crucial. Skill will be determined by the recruit's education, ability to learn, and training. Motivation will be determined by the recruit's reasons for joining the armed forces and the treatment and rewards received while serving. Actual battle performance will be a result of a combination of these factors and the soldier's psychological makeup and capacity for dealing with the immense difficulties of combat.

Given the current importance of high-technology weapons in modern warfare, it goes without saying that obtaining well-educated and intelligent soldiers and officers is essential. This needs to be a key criteria of selection.

Another criteria is motivation. Greece and Rome early on depended on the citizen soldier as the backbone of the army, making it both an honor and a responsibility to serve. When both armies became overly professionalized, however, their soldiers were motivated not by honor, duty, and country but by war looting. They became attached not to the nation but to their individual leaders, essentially becoming mercenaries. Since that time the dilemma for a nation has been between the need for the expertise of a professional, volunteer force versus the threat it may pose of potential overthrow of the government. History has shown that to achieve the proper balance the armed forces should be composed of individuals motivated not only by sufficient monetary and professional recognition but also by a sense of duty to the nation.

A final criteria should be the psychological capability of the individual to withstand combat pressures and perform their mission. During the twentieth century numerous psychological tests were used to determine which individuals would do well in combat and which should be put in a supporting, noncombat role. Whereas the Western Allies used these test to measure intelligence and thereby channel recruits into different military specialties, the German Army used psychological tests differently. They measured not only intelligence but also overall character, in terms of the man's temperament and social/emotional development. They were looking not just for intelligent men but for "warriors" who could simultaneously be a responsive subordinate yet driven enough to find any means necessary to accomplish the mission. They were seeking something called *Einsatzbereitshaft*—a soldier's willingness to commit himself to achieving his objective, no matter what impediments might stand in the way. The German psychologists believed that endurance and persistence combined with the will and ability to take independent action made for a tough soldier.[15]

The raw recruit who has met the above criteria can be turned into a capable soldier through hard and realistic training. Every army, navy, or air force that has ever been consistently successful over long periods of time was physically tough and well-drilled.

- **If officers are unaccustomed to rigorous drilling they will be worried and hesitant in battle; if generals are not thoroughly trained they will inwardly quail when they face the enemy. (I.12 Tu Yu)**

Rome's military machine depended much on hard training. Before joining the army recruits had to pass physical training in running, jumping, and climbing. After joining the army the soldier was drilled in mock combats and other military matters. According to the historian Polybius, the soldiers were handicapped in the mock battles, forced to use weapons that weighed twice as much as their real ones. Roman soldiers were also trained to dig and build, since on the march all legions would make a fort-like camp wherever they stopped for the evening. To prepare their camps ditches were dug and palisades thrown up to repel potential invaders, while inside the camp the legion's subunits pitched their tents. The layout of the camp was always the same, allowing it to be built quickly and for soldiers to know their battle stations in the dark should the fort be attacked at night.[16]

The need for tough training has been recognized and passed down through the centuries. Prior to Desert Storm the U.S. Army played wargames deep in the Mojave Desert at a place called the National Training Center (NTC). Created as a result of research that showed troops in combat for the first time suffered much higher casualties than veteran units, the NTC provides a place where large-size units (battalion or higher) can practice fighting against specially trained opposing forces (OPFOR). Since the opponents of the U.S. Army are most likely to have been Soviet-trained and equipped, the OPFOR is skilled in former Red Army tactics and equipped with Soviet-style weaponry.

Battalions come to the NTC for roughly a month, where they execute a number of round-the-clock operations against the OPFOR. Enhanced realism is attained by equipping each person and vehicle with sensors that can be "hit" by laser simulators fired by personnel and weapons systems from the other side. When troopers are hit, they become casualties, and fellow soldiers must be assigned to evacuate them to the rear. Therefore, not only do the combat troops receive training, but so do the support troops.

All battles are monitored at the NTC control center, which tracks the movements of the battalion receiving training and the OPFOR. It also tracks all casualties and assigns a winner of each engagement. More important, after each simulated battle, every soldier from the commander on down is briefed on what they did right and what needs improvement.

These briefings, or after-action reports, are crucial to improving the battalion's effectiveness and increasing the probability of success in the next engagement. These reports are a result of a structured discussion on what went right, what went wrong, what the strengths and weaknesses of the unit are, and how the battalion can do better in the next encounter. The findings are then written down for future reference and to track later progress. Thus, through experiencing "combat" and making immediate, honest appraisals of the results, the entire month becomes one excellent learning experience that cannot be replicated.

The NTC is credited as having played a crucial role in the success of Desert Storm by preparing the Army's soldiers for the fast, chaotic tempo of battle, allowing them to be confident and bold in their attacks. The preparation at the NTC also was crucial in significantly reducing the number of casualties suffered by Allied forces during Desert Storm.[17]

- In good order they await a disorderly enemy; in serenity, a clamorous one. This is control of the mental factor. (VII.23)

Furthermore, the U.S. Army was not the only service to utilize this type of training. The U.S. Air Force implemented similar wargaming and simulation training in its "Red Flag" exercises, which pitted pilots trained in Soviet tactics and weaponry against its students, and the Navy did the same with its "Top Gun" program.

Another method for limiting friction is ensuring a clear chain of command. In Viet Nam the American forces had a very tangled command structure, making it difficult to coordinate actions between the different services and implement a consistent strategy. In ancient times, Rome would have two consuls lead its legions on a campaign. Each consul would take his turn at command of the army on alternating days. While the system was effective in limiting the threat to the government by a single general, it could create problems when the two consuls disagreed on strategy. At Rome's greatest defeat, the battle of Cannae, the legions were led to slaughter by the one consul who wanted to attack, as it was his day to command.

- He whose ranks are united in purpose will be victorious. (III.27)

Friction cannot be avoided, but it can be overcome. This can be done through the proper selection of recruits, hard training, and combat simulation. One should also use battle drills, standard operating procedures (SOPs), and clear orders to respond quickly to changes in the situation. Providing clear guidance and simple written orders will speed implementation of decisions. Training commanders and troops to be flexible in responding to new orders and having a simple and streamlined chain of command will also reduce friction. Beyond these actions it is critical to enable lower unit commanders and individual soldiers to exercise initiative and discretion, of which more will be discussed later.

- Generally, management of many is the same as management of few. It is a matter of organization. To manage a host one must first assign responsibilities to the generals and their assistants. (V.1 & V.1 Chang Yü)

Beyond Training: Organizational Learning

Contrary to popular belief, the German Army in both world wars was not an army of mindless automatons, numbingly following orders from above. As compared to the British, French, and American officers, the German officer corps was significantly better educated in the art of war and more innovative in its tactics. There were a number of reasons for this.

One is that in World War I the German Army was very decentralized. This decentralization was possible because the senior officers had a tremendous amount of trust in their junior officers. The junior officers were thereby allowed a great deal of latitude to experiment with tactics, and they readily did so in the front lines. As they found out what worked and what didn't, they informed their fellow officers via army-wide reports. The better ideas also rose to the top where the German high command, eager for new concepts, could institute them in all units. Unlike the Allied armies, the German Army was not an army composed of two groups, the "thinkers" versus the "doers." Instead, it was an army composed solely of "thinker/doers," men who could turn theory into action.

These junior officers were also not as inexperienced as their counterparts in the Allied armies. They stayed at the same rank for several years, commanding the same unit, and were therefore accountable for the long-term improvement of that unit. There they had much time to learn, and their maturity motivated them toward self-education in military art.

All these characteristics were at the other extreme in the Allied armies in World War I. Junior officers were very young, and were switched from unit to unit. The high command was not interested in any new ideas. All tactics were determined in the rear areas, far from the front-line realities. Any serious study of the art of war was looked upon as ludicrous.[18]

The professionalism of World War I continued to serve the German Army in World War II, and it counted in combat.[19] Quantitative studies of sixty World War II battles found that given comparable equipment, the relative combat effectiveness of German soldiers was 2.5 times that of Soviet soldiers and 1.2 times that of American and British soldiers. This superiority was not due to the ridiculous idea that Germans were a "master race," but rather solely the result of a much higher degree of military professionalism and organizational learning.[20]

■ If one ignorant of military matters is sent to participate in the administration of the army, then in every movement there will be disagreement and mutual frustration and the entire army will be hamstrung.   (III.22 Wang Hsi)

Logistics

Supporting any successful strategy is the critical realm of logistics. Without logistical preparation friction will increase and success will be more difficult. For example, in 1854 in Crimea, Britain went to war with Russia over Russia's desire to expand at Turkey's expense. The most famous action in the war was the charge of the Light Brigade, whose reckless attack directly into Russian cannon made no military sense at all (but did make a great poem). Unfortunately for the British, their other planning, especially their logistics, was as bad as their tactics.

As the result of lack of coordination between the army and navy, little understanding of the Crimean climate, a dearth of planning for the requirements of the campaign, and a general disdain by British officers for any type of staff work, the British soldier in the Crimea was woefully ill equipped. Lacking the proper uniforms, food, and medical care, soldiers died by the hundreds of sickness and exposure. Had the Russians been better prepared, the result would have been an even greater disaster for the British. Luckily, however, the warring nations soon tired of the conflict and made peace.[21]

- If we have made no plans we plunge in headlong. By braving the dangers and entering perilous places we face the calamity of being trapped or inundated. Marching as if drunk, we may run into an unexpected fight. When we stop at night we are worried by false alarms; if we hasten along unprepared we fall into ambushes. This is to plunge an army of bears and tigers into the land of death. (VII.11 Ho Yen-hsi)

Contrast the Crimean War fiasco with Desert Storm, a great achievement in logistics and planning. The movement of hundreds of thousands of troops and tons of equipment from all over the world to the Persian Gulf theater of operations in a few months was itself an amazing feat. Keeping these troops supplied with food, fuel, bullets, and bombs was yet another. Coordinating the air war in which airplanes and helicopters from different nations were flying from several dispersed airfields and aircraft carriers to strike targets all the way from Kuwait to Baghdad was still another planning achievement. And lastly, moving troops from several different nations deep into the vast Saudi desert for the lightning quick strike around the Iraqi right flank was the final coup.

Some facts:

1. The U.S. Air Force deployed 46 percent of its U.S. combat force to the Iraqi theater.

2. The Civil Reserve Airfleet, in its first activation, airlifted the equivalent of the entire Berlin Airlift every six weeks.

3. In the first ninety days of the Gulf War, the Coalition put in more communications capability than it had placed in Europe in the prior forty years.

4. The U.S. Military Sealift Command delivered 3.4 million tons of cargo and 6.8 million tons of fuel to the theater, over four times the amount of cargo moved across the English Channel to support the D-Day assault.

5. In the attack, the combat units required 708 tons of food, 34,000 tons of ammo, 804 tons of other supplies, 5 million gallons of fuel, and 1.3 million gallons of water daily.

All this planning and preparation ensured victory within 100 hours of the beginning of the ground war, along with minimal casualties. A major key to such speedy success was superior logistical preparation and planning.[22]

■ **Those adept in waging war do not require a second levy of conscripts nor more than one provisioning.   (II.9)**

Beyond the logistical feats one can best capture the expertise with which the Desert Storm operation was carried out and the preparation it required with this comment by General Fred Franks, VII Corps Commander: "Our . . . victories had not taken eighty-nine hours. They had taken almost twenty years." By this he meant that it had taken all the time between Viet Nam and Desert Storm to rebuild America's armed forces, both physically and morally. Better recruitment, improved recognition and compensation for soldiers, hard training, and new equipment all contributed to the renaissance of the armed forces and led to the eventual victory. The preparation paid off.

A Case in Point: Special Operations

Special operations, those in which a small unit must carry out a specific mission against a larger force or well-defended position, depend even more heavily on speed. These units are specially trained and equipped to attack a certain target, either to destroy it or rescue hostages. Successful completion of the mission will result in military or political results far in excess of the size of the force committed. Missions such as the German attack on the Belgian fort Eben Amael, the British attack on the *Tirpitz*, or the Israeli rescue mission in Entebbe, Uganda, are all examples of special operations.

A close study of special operations shows that success is based on "a simple plan, carefully concealed, repeatedly and realistically rehearsed, and executed with surprise, speed and purpose." Speed is critical because, the longer the small attacking force is in the danger zone, the longer the defenders have to respond to the situation and bring overwhelming force to bear. To achieve speed requires a clear mission based on excellent intelligence, specific tasks assigned to each subunit, a well-defined time table of actions, and numerous rehearsals to work out any problems with the plan and make each soldier know what is expected of him.

The Israeli raid on Entebbe airport to rescue its hostages in 1976 is an excellent example of a well-executed special operation. An Air France flight had been hijacked by terrorists and flown to Uganda, where all Jews and the air crew were separated from the rest of the passengers. There they were being held until the terrorists' demands for the release of other terrorists were met. The Israeli government knew it had to act swiftly to rescue the hostages before the terrorists started executing them, especially since it was the policy of Israel not to negotiate with terrorists.

Armed with intelligence on the whereabouts of the hostages, the airport layout and the fact that the terrorists were being supported by the Ugandan army, the Israelis built a simple plan of attack. Overall command of the rescue mission would belong to Brigadier General Dan Shomron and the attack force was composed of Lt. Colonel Jonathan Netanyahu's Sayeret Matkal Counterterrorist Unit, a paratrooper contingent and soldiers from Israeli's famed Golani Brigade. A mockup airport terminal was made where the rescue force practiced the mission over and over again; problems that surfaced were fixed and minor adjustments made. Finally the rescue unit got the go-ahead from the Israeli government.

It took several hours to fly to Entebbe by C-130s, with much of it at low levels to avoid detection. However, once on the ground the Israeli rescue team moved rapidly. Hitting the runway at 11 P.M. hours one C-130 quickly disgorged the black Mercedes and two Landrovers containing the hostage rescue team. They headed for the terminal, with the Mercedes in the lead, posing as the Ugandan President Idi Amin's car. Told to stop by Ugandan sentries they shot them down and drove full-speed to the terminal.

Once in the terminal they took more fire but dispatched the terrorists and any Ugandan soldiers. One of those hit was Netanyahu, but the assault continued. Clearing the building and rounding up the hostages was the next step, as three more C-130s landed. These other C-130s carried troops to secure the perimeter, forestall any counterattacks by the Ugandans, and destroy the MiG fighters at the airport. Just after midnight, the first C-130 was taking off with the hostages, heading back to Israel. The last plane took off at 4 A.M. Total time on the ground for the entire force was under two hours.

The result of this lightning attack was rescue of the vast majority of the hostages (three died in the crossfire and one was at a local hospital and could not be rescued) and a striking statement to the world that Israel would protect her own. There was a cost, however. Lt. Colonel Jonathan Netanyahu was mortally wounded, giving his life to save others.[23]

Summary

As has been shown, speed is crucial to victory.

- Victory is the main object in war. If this is long delayed, weapons are blunted and morale depressed. When troops attack cities, their strength will be exhausted. When the army engages in protracted campaigns the resources of the state will not suffice. For there has never been a protracted war from which a country has benefited. (II.3–4; 7)

The key is to move with speed and end the battle quickly, before the enemy can react. Use speed to surprise and shock the opponent, make up for scarce resources, exploit fleeting opportunities, and build momentum.

- Hence what is essential in war is victory, not prolonged operations. (II.21)

To move quickly, one must collect and analyze information rapidly, make decisions speedily, and then act with dispatch. A leader must reduce all potential causes of friction as much as possible.

As a base for rapid movement, preparation is essential. Recruit excellent troops and train them hard. Plan first, then act quickly. Develop possible scenarios and then wargame potential enemy responses. Be prepared in advance for their moves and look for short-lived opportunities.

Once one has done so it is possible to plan where to strike, decide how to utilize deception, and think through how forces should be deployed.

- A victory gained before the situation has crystallized is one the common man does not comprehend. Thus its author gains no reputation for sagacity. Before he has bloodied his blade the enemy state has already submitted.   (IV.11 Tu Mu)

It is essential that leaders not get bogged down in a war of attrition. They must plan campaigns to be of short duration and act quickly before the enemy can respond. If they do not, they will either have to pull out and lose the resources already committed, or raise the ante, which forces the commitment of even greater resources than planned.

- For he wins his victories without erring. "Without erring" means that whatever he does ensures his victory; he conquers an enemy already defeated.   (IV.12)

At this point we have covered many ideas: the need to avoid strength and attack weakness, the benefits of deception and foreknowledge, the uses of speed and preparation. It is now time for the consideration of the next principle: putting these many concepts together by "shaping" the enemy and preparing the battlefield, the subject of our next chapter.

5 ▪ Shaping the Enemy
Preparing the Battlefield

- ▪ Therefore, those skilled in war bring the enemy to the field of battle and are not brought there by him.   (VI.2)

To achieve the nation's objectives and defeat the enemy a leader must first make the opponent conform to his strategy, rules, and will. He must seize the advantage and make the enemy meet him at the time and place of his choosing. To master the enemy in this manner is what Sun Tzu means by "shaping."

To shape your enemy one must first put together all that has been learned so far. A leader must know the situation.

- ▪ And as water shapes its flow in accordance with the ground, so an army manages its victory in accordance with the situation of the enemy.   (VI.28)

Then one must be able to deceive the enemy as to one's plans.

- ▪ Subtle and insubstantial, the expert leaves no trace; divinely mysterious, he is inaudible. Thus he is the master of his enemy's fate.   (VI.9)

And all this must be accomplished with blinding speed.

■ **Appear at places to which he must hasten; move swiftly where he does not expect you. (VI.5)**

These principles are the clay the master strategist works with. However, by themselves they are not enough. One must put them all together in a strategy that "shapes" the enemy. One's strategy must attack not only the resources of the opponent, but, more importantly, the minds, thought processes, and wills of its leaders.

To begin, one must gain and hold strategic positions that put the enemy at a disadvantage. To shape the enemy one's strategy must also employ both a direct and an indirect force; these forces work together to first fix the enemy's attention, then surprise and throw them off balance. These forces used in combination make the enemy easier to defeat.

Shaping the enemy is also performed by making nonmilitary strategic moves and sending both overt and covert signals. These moves and signals can either be designed to make the opponent clearly understand one's purpose and comply, or to mislead them in order to put them at a disadvantage.

One must also understand the nature of alliances, how they are formed and maintained, and how to sever those of the enemy. Alliances allow a nation to increase its access to resources and diminish those of the enemy. Used properly, alliances can also limit the enemy's possible moves and strategic options.

■ **When the enemy is at ease, be able to weary him: when well-fed, to starve him, when at rest, to make him move. (VI.4)**

Shaping the enemy consists of all these tactics. Let us discuss how to execute them.

Holding Strategic Positions

One way of shaping the enemy's moves is to hold key strategic positions.

■ **If you are able to hold critical points on his strategic roads the enemy cannot come. Therefore Master Wang said: "When a cat is at the rat hole, ten thousand rats dare not come out; when a**

tiger guards the ford, ten thousand deer cannot cross." (VI.3
Tu Yu)

There are several types of strategic positions that one might capture. There are natural geographic positions such as major rivers, islands, peninsulas, straits, and mountain passes. Thermopylae, the pass in which three hundred Spartans and their Greek allies held off the Persian army of roughly a quarter of a million men, is one such strategic position. The Spartan King Leonidas, leading a Greek army of seven thousand men, used this small mountain pass to limit the Persian Army's mobility and force them into a direct assault. The delay at Thermopylae, at the cost of the lives of all the Spartans, allowed the rest of Greece to muster enough forces to eventually defeat the Persians, helping to save Western democracy and heritage from extinction.[1]

Major rivers provide a significant defensive benefit since the attackers must expose themselves for a significant time to defensive fire. During that time the attacker has limited capability to inflict harm on the defender. On a grander scale, large bodies of water provide the same sort of protection, such as the English Channel for the island of Great Britain or the Pacific and Atlantic oceans for the United States. Conversely, a power can control access to sea lanes either through holding key positions on land (such as the Dardanelles, which have historically kept the Russians out of the Mediterranean) or by covering constricted openings to larger water (such as the North Sea, used by the Western Allies to limit both the German and Soviet navies in the twentieth century).

Beyond natural choke points formed by geography there are man-made strategic positions, such as fortifications, cities, railroads, roads, ports, and air bases. The Great Wall of China, when well-defended and used as a base for offensive operations, served as a useful impediment to incursions from the nomadic tribes of northern China and Mongolia. During the Middle Ages in Europe castles provided the strongholds from which knights would defend their fiefs. Eighteenth-century warfare in Europe to a large extent involved the use of well-designed fortress bases, whose possession was the measure of victory or defeat. As technology advanced further the control of railroads and roads became crucial. During the Battle of the Bulge in World War II the German offensive foundered when they could not capture the crossroads at the town of Bastogne. And since the beginning of naval warfare, the ability to access a port could mean the difference between survival or extinction for a fleet.

- When one man defends a narrow mountain defile which is like sheep's intestines or the door of a dog house, he can withstand one thousand. (V.25 Chang Yü)

Strategic positions are not limited to geographic ones. Raw materials, such as oil, have caused countries to go to war for their possession. Technology or weapons systems (such as nuclear weapons) obviously also provide strategic advantage. There are also strategic diplomatic positions, such as seats on the United Nations Security Council. The veto power conferred by having a position on the Security Council can literally stop the rest of the world from taking concerted action. The Soviet Union realized this painfully during the Korean Conflict. To protest Communist China's exclusion from the UN, the USSR walked out of the United Nations, absenting themselves temporarily from Security Council. Their absence allowed the United States to garner support from the remainder of the United Nations to support South Korea in its war with the North.[2]

Attacking the Enemy's Strategy

- Thus, what is of supreme importance in war is to attack the enemy's strategy. (III.4)

Attacking the opponent's strategy is one of the least resource-intensive means of achieving one's goals, yet it can be a very effective technique when properly executed. That is why Sun Tzu is adamant that "the supreme excellence in war is to attack an enemy's plans."

In the spring of 1943 Nazi Germany was trying to recover from the loss of the Sixth Army at Stalingrad and regain the initiative on the Eastern Front. The mobile fighting after Stalingrad left a major bulge in the front line between the two combatants, with a 160-mile Russian salient around the city of Kursk. This was where Hitler chose to launch his offensive and take the initiative back from the Russians (see Figure 5.1). The offensive, code named Operation Zitadelle (Citadel), had as its goal to pinch the salient off with attacks from both the north and south. If successful, this would cut off 1.3 million Soviet troops in the pocket and tear a huge hole in the Soviet lines. Then the march eastward could resume.

The original target date to launch the attack was to be either February or March, but other battles and lack of tanks delayed Citadel's commencement. At the end of January there were less than 500 German

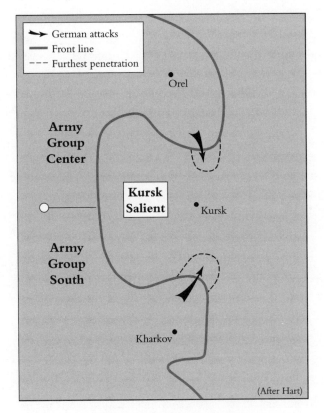

FIGURE 5.1   Operation Citadel

tanks on the field of battle and it took time to rebuild the Panzer forces. German hopes were also pinned on the new tanks, such as the Mark V Panther and the Mark VI Tiger, which could be used to help turn the tide of battle. As a result Citadel would not be launched until July 1943.

During the time of the German buildup the Soviets became privy to the plans for Citadel, most likely through the Western Allies breaking of Germany's Enigma code system. With the knowledge of the German strategy and the additional time between spring and summer, the Soviets were able to prepare. Elaborate and deep defenses were put in place, with the Soviets focusing their efforts at the two places where the assaults would fall. Mines, obstacles, strong points, and antitank guns were set in place. Mobile armored reserves were positioned to destroy any German penetrations that might occur. These efforts culminated in defenses of over one hundred miles in depth to stop the initial thrust and five thousand tanks in reserve for the counterattack.

On July 5, 1943, Operation Citadel began with what was supposed to be a surprise artillery bombardment. However, the Soviets knew when and where the attack would fall. At the end of the first day the northern attack had only penetrated four miles, while the assault in the south made only eight. Already the attack was behind the timetable. A week later found the northern and southern Panzer spearheads still far apart and the intended Blitzkrieg had degraded into a battle of attrition. A reinvigorated push in the south culminated in the largest tank battle in history; a total of one thousand armored vehicles firing at one another at close range. The severe losses suffered by the Germans that day and throughout the offensive, combined with attacks by the Western Allies on other fronts, led to a cessation of Citadel. Soon thereafter the Soviets launched their own offensives, pushing the German Army back towards Berlin.

In the end, knowing the enemy's strategy and attacking it resulted in the successful destruction of German forces at Kursk by the Soviets, allowing them to gain the upper hand along the entire Eastern Front. They would never relinquish it.[3]

Alliances

In the mid 1400s Japan went through a period of warfare among different factions that lasted 150 years. Called the *Sengoku Jidai*, the Age of the Country at War, the Japanese actually took the name for the period from China's Age of the Warring States. During this time samurai warlords fought for control of all Japan, often making alliances with other clans to advance their purpose.

One such warlord was Mori Montonari, a powerful and intelligent leader. Speaking of alliances to his three sons, he told them the "Parable of the Arrows." He gave each an arrow and asked them to break it. After they did he took three more arrows and asked them to break them. When they could not he said, "So it must be with you."[4]

As the parable illustrates, critical to shaping the enemy and making them conform to one's plans is the proper use of alliances. By careful reading of *The Art of War*, one finds six rules to follow in the area of alliances.

Prevent enemies from combining.

If powerful alliances exist, avoid attacking them.

Before attacking, first separate one's main enemy from its alllies.

Make skillful use of allies.

Do not choose the wrong allies.

Know how to maintain an alliance and when to end one.

Prevent Enemies from Combining

To increase the probability of success, it is essential to prevent enemies from combining to oppose one's nation. This can be done by forcing them to consider the consequences of opposition, as in Sun Tzu's example of a king seeking to control all of China.

> ■ Now when a Hegemonic King attacks a powerful state he makes it impossible for the enemy to concentrate. He overawes the enemy and prevents his allies from joining him.   (XI.52)

To illustrate, it is useful to compare two models of alliances from times past: the Romans and the Aztecs. The Romans were able to create and maintain an empire of client states that were very successful for several hundred years. They achieved this through military prowess, sophisticated diplomacy, and by bestowing the benefits of civilization on those they ruled.

Historian Ramon L. Jimenez explains the strength of the Roman system as depending as much on its diplomacy as on its inherent military organizational advantages, such as its warrior culture, well-organized legions, and more flexible tactics:

> The Romans supplemented this slight military advantage over the less organized cities around them with a diplomatic policy that was rare in the ancient world. The usual aftermath of military victory was devastation of the enemy's lands and death or slavery for the conquered people. But the Romans often made alliances of different types with them, and sought to integrate them into their own culture, sometimes incorporating one or more of the defeated peoples' gods into their own pantheon. In other cases, they extended to them trading rights, partial citizenship, or even full citizenship without, or with, voting rights. Roman citizenship, as well as lesser privileges, became coveted rights that each city and tribe negotiated with the Romans, and in return furnished soldiers or warships against the next enemy, and refrained from any further attack. In this way the Romans assimilated dozens of neighboring cities and territories into a monolithic state that gradually became impervious to conquest.[5]

This combination of power and diplomacy served Rome well during its life-and-death struggles with the other Mediterranean power, Carthage. When Hannibal, the Carthaginian general, came marching over the Alps into the Italian peninsula, a key element of his strategy was to turn Rome's allies against her. Hannibal thought that if he could defeat the Roman legions in the field, he would be successful in bringing Rome's allies over to his side.

Hannibal defeated Roman generals numerous times in battle, destroyed several Roman legions, and marched unhindered throughout the peninsula. At the battle of Cannae he defeated a disciplined Roman army of 86,000 men with an army only half its size, composed primarily of mercenaries. Of the 86,000 Romans he fought, 16,000 left the field alive. Hannibal's army suffered only 6,000 casualties, and in military history the Battle of Cannae became synonymous with total and crushing victory.

However, even with victories like Cannae, Hannibal could not convince Rome's allies to turn against her. He was unsuccessful because these allies weighed the balance of benefits Rome could provide against the potential damage she could inflict, and chose to stand by Rome. (It was Hasdrubal, Hannibal's brother, who said to him, "You know how to win victories but not how to use them.") Ultimately, lack of allies led to Hannibal's failure in Italy and, eventually, the defeat and destruction of Carthage.[6]

The Aztec view of alliances was quite different from that of the Romans. When Hernando Cortez arrived in Mexico in 1519, the Aztec empire had existed for hundreds of years. However, the Aztecs maintained power not by a combination of power, diplomacy, and the benefits of an advanced civilization, but by dominating their tribal allies. For example, when the great pyramid temple of Tenochtitlan was dedicated, over 20,000 captives from the subordinated tribes were sacrificed to please the Aztec gods. Obviously, this type of behavior did not endear the Aztecs to their erstwhile allies.

Therefore, when Cortez arrived and demonstrated his prowess in battle, fierce tribes like the Tlaxcalans were only too eager to join him in challenging the Aztecs. Though formerly allies of the Aztecs, these tribes saw an enticing opportunity for retribution. Cortez was just as eager to use them to defeat the Aztecs, and combined with his tribal allies for the final assault on and capture of the Aztec capital of Tenochtitlan in 1521.

Roman policy included exuding power and bestowing benefits, while Aztec policy was to dominate, thereby creating resentment. This resentment led to Aztec allies combining with an outside force to fight against Aztec domination. Thus, while it took several civil wars, numerous barbarian invasions, and hundreds of years for the Roman empire to decline and fall, it took only two years for the Aztec empire to crumble.[7]

In the twentieth century, Germany violated the rule of preventing enemies from combining twice: once in World War I and again in World War II. In WWI Germany's rulers made enemies of both France and Russia, something former Chancellor Otto von Bismarck would never have allowed to happen. Then, instead of reaching out to make Great Britain her ally, the Germans managed to alienate the U.K. by building a strong surface navy that, from a British perspective, threatened Britain's very existence. As it turned out Germany's new navy only sortied out once at the inconclusive Battle of Jutland—providing no return on Germany's huge investment.

In World War II Germany's leadership did execute a deft diplomatic move by signing the Nazi–Soviet Nonaggression Pact, which isolated Poland from the Western allies and removed a threat to Germany from the east. However, Germany then threw that advantage away by attacking the USSR before winning a decisive victory in the West after Japan attacked Pearl Harbor and drew the United States into the war, Germany compounded this mistake by declaring war against the United States in the hope that Japan would then do the same against the Soviet Union. Unfortunately for Germany, Japan remained neutral with regard to the USSR, leaving Germany fighting against three allied powers.[8]

A proper application of this rule occurred during the American Civil War. At the outset of the War between the States the sympathies of many in Great Britain lay with the South, mainly because of the dependency of Britain on Southern cotton and the identification of Britain's aristocracy with that of the South. These sympathies, combined with British imperial interests, created a real possibility that Britain would ally herself with the South. An alliance with Britain would make U.S. President Abraham Lincoln's task of forcing the Confederacy back into the Union difficult, if not impossible. To eliminate this possibility and achieve other aims Lincoln issued the Emancipation Proclamation in September of 1863. The Emancipation Proclamation freed the slaves in all the rebelling states, changing the cause of the war from being solely about restoring the Union to also being about ending slavery. With this proclamation it was no longer morally possible for Great Britain or other European states to side with the South, thus ending the possibility of an alliance for the Confederacy. It also weakened the South economically by freeing slaves wherever Union troops moved, and unified Lincoln's Republican party.[9]

■ (The Hegemonic King) breaks up the alliances of All-under-Heaven and snatches the position of authority. He uses prestige and virtue to attain his ends.   (XI.53 Ts'ao Ts'ao)

If Powerful Alliances Exist, Avoid Attacking

The second rule of alliances is that if one faces an enemy with strong allies, it is best to avoid attacking them until those allies have been removed from their side.

■ It follows that he does not contend against powerful combinations nor does he foster the power of other states.   (XI.53)

In the two world wars, Germany took on almost all the other major powers essentially by herself. In World War I, Germany was opposed by Britain, France, Russia, the United States, and Italy. Furthermore, Germany's major allies were very weak: Austria and Turkey were more of a hindrance than a help. Only in the spring of 1918, when the Allied strength had ebbed (Russia had been knocked out of the war and America had yet to make her presence felt) did Germany come close to winning.

In World War II, Germany was one of the Axis powers, along with Italy and Japan. However, the Axis was not much of a working alliance. In Europe, Italy only attacked France once Mussolini realized that Germany was going to defeat the French Army. In Asia, Germany was never able to coordinate her moves with Japan to any degree. Furthermore, as noted earlier, Germany instead chose to create a new enemy and a stronger enemy alliance by declaring war on the United States immediately after Japan attacked Pearl Harbor. It is critical not to make the same mistake; avoid attacking powerful alliances at all times.

Before Attacking, Separate the Enemy from its Allies

It follows that, before launching an attack, one must find ways to separate the enemy from its allies. As mentioned earlier, Sun Tzu stated that

■ Thus, what is of supreme importance in war is to attack the
  enemy's strategy.   (III.4)

Next best is to disrupt his alliance. Do not allow your enemies
to get together. Look into the matter of his alliances and cause
them to be severed and dissolved. If an enemy has alliances the
problem is grave and the enemy's position is strong; if he has no
alliances the problem is minor and the enemy's position
weak.   (III.5 Sun Tzu, Tu Yu, and Wang Hsi)

When Otto von Bismarck came to power as the chancellor of Prussia, the many princely states of Germany were not united into one
nation. The "Iron Chancellor," as Bismarck came to be known, had
as his primary goal the unification of Germany under Prussia (Bismarck
spoke of the need to unify Germany not by speeches and votes but by
"blood and iron"). To do so he had to first reduce the power of Austria,
the other leading German power. Essential to achieving his aims was
the elimination of support for Austria by the smaller German states or
other European nations while gaining allies for Prussia. He proceeded
to do so through a set of complex yet brilliant maneuvers, culminating
in the Austro–Prussian War of 1866.

First, Bismarck made the Sleswig-Holstein succession question a
primary cause of irritation between Prussia and Austria. The whole
succession question itself was very complicated; as British Lord Pal-
merston said, "Only three men have ever understood it. One was
Prince Albert, who is dead. The second was a German professor, who
became mad. I am the third and I have forgotten all about it." However, Bismarck was able to use this complex issue to force some smaller
German states to fall in line behind Prussia. Simultaneously, Bismarck
made an alliance with the new state of Italy, which thus threatened
Austria from the south. He also ensured that Russia's natural animosity
toward Austria continued. Finally, failing to bring France into an alliance against Austria as well, Bismarck was able to take advantage of
Napoleon II's indecisiveness by moving events so quickly that France
was not a factor in the war.

At midnight on June 15, 1866, Prussian troops went to war against
Austria and the smaller German states that remained her allies. By July
3 the Prussian Army won the critical battle of Koniggratz (or as it is
sometimes known, Sadowa), sealing victory against Austria. While Prussia's victory over Austria could not have been won without an excellent
performance by the Prussian Army under General Helmuth von

Moltke, it was Bismarck's tilting of the balance of power in Prussia's favor that made it possible.[10]

A century later, another great statesmen, Henry Kissinger, was also able to significantly alter the balance of power. During the Cold War he separated an ally from the United States' main opponent, the Soviet Union. This strategic idea was behind the opening of relations between the United States and the People's Republic of China in 1971. By establishing a relationship with China Kissinger was able to create strategic options and move it farther away from its communist counterpart, the USSR. As the relationship between the U.S. and the China grew over time and America became stronger under Ronald Reagan, the difficulty of facing strong foes in Europe and Asia hastened the collapse of the Soviet Union.[11]

- When he is united, divide him.   (I.25 Sun Tzu)

  Sometimes drive a wedge between a sovereign and his ministers; on other occasions separate his allies from him. Make them mutually suspicious so that they drift apart. Then you can plot against them.   (I.25 Sun Tzu and Chang Yu)

Make Skillful Use of Allies

Once an alliance has been created, one must make skillful use of them.

- If one neither covenants for the help of neighbors nor develops plans based on expediency but in furtherance of his personal aims relies only on his own military strength to overawe the enemy country then his own cities can be captured and his own state overthrown.   (XI.53 Tu Mu)

In contrast to the Germans, Great Britain has always sought allies to help her win her wars (perhaps this is why there has not been a successful invasion of Britain since William the Conqueror landed on English soil in 1066). In World War II, Britain first allied with France, the continental counterweight to Germany. When France was knocked out of the war, Britain appealed to the United States for support and received it through the lend–lease program. When Britain learned of Germany's impending invasion of the Soviet Union, it passed the information along to Stalin, along with offers of an alliance. Although Stalin didn't take the British offer at the time, he gladly accepted it when the German Blitzkrieg sliced through Russian defenses and drove toward Moscow.

Also in contrast to Germany and the Axis, the major Allied powers (the United States, Britain, the Soviet Union, France, and China) co-ordinated several times on war policy and strategy. High-level discussions between the very highest political and military leadership, combined with joint operations at the small-unit level, led to a synergistic effort to defeat the Axis.

As the tides of war and peace rise and fall it is often necessary to make allies of former enemies to meet the long term interests of the state. After successfully defeating Germany and Japan in World War II, for example, the United States helped fashion each country into a bulwark against communist expansion.

After World War II the heart of NATO's land forces in Europe were concentrated in West Germany, prepared to stop a Soviet offensive. The lonely outpost of West Berlin, supplied and defended by the U.S. and her NATO allies, was used to gather intelligence from the Eastern Bloc countries. Eventually, West Germany herself was rearmed, adding her manpower and industrial might to protect Western democracy.

Japan was used as a major base of operations to support American efforts to battle communist insurgencies and invasions in Asia. During the outbreak of the Korean Conflict almost immediately after World War II, Japan was indispensable to supplying U.S. naval, air, and land units as they fought the North Korean invasion. Japan played a similar role during the Viet Nam War, and in the interims between armed conflict the strategically situated island nation enabled America to project power far from her shores.

Do Not Choose the Wrong Allies

Although a nation must make allies to survive and prosper, it must not chose poor allies just to have allies. A bad alliance is worse than none at all. Germany's alliance with Italy in World War II led to disastrous consequences for Germany. Mussolini's bungled invasion of Greece, begun without Hitler's knowledge, forced Germany to divert troops to bail out the Italians precisely at the time the German Army should have been preparing for its assault on the Soviet Union. The time it took for Germany to complete its ally's failed attack and conquer Greece set the Russian campaign back two months. This delay made it impossible for the German Army to destroy the Red Army before the Russian winter came, which in turn led to the terrible German defeat and retreat from Moscow in 1941.[12]

Maintaining and Ending Alliances

Choosing the right allies is only the beginning; one must also know how to maintain alliances and how to end them when they are no longer useful.

■ I reward my prospective allies with valuables and silks and bind them with solemn covenants. I abide firmly by the treaties and then my allies will certainly aid me. (XI.19 Chang Yü)

An alliance works when there is trust between the allies: true cooperation, perceived fairness, and, most important, a mutual interest. It is the mutual interest that should be the seed of the alliance. The mutual interest must be strong and lasting. If it is not, the problems of having an ally will quickly overwhelm the benefits and the alliance will fail.

In World War II, the mutual interest of the Soviet Union and the Western Allies in defeating Nazi Germany overcame problems of mistrust, difficulties in long-distance cooperation, and perceptions of unfairness in carrying the load. Given their past histories and relationships, each side had reason to mistrust the other. Coordination and cooperation was difficult because of distance and the differences in language and history. Finally, the Soviet Union felt it unfair that they were carrying the bulk of the burden of the land war with Germany (roughly eighty percent of Germany's land forces were fighting against the Soviets from 1941 on). However, mutual interest, supported by constant discussions and good-faith efforts, kept the alliance intact.

One must also know when to end an alliance. Timing is critical in choosing the specific moment to formally end the alliance, and the reason to end any alliance must be quite clear. An alliance must be ended when the mutual interest that created it no longer exists. If mutual interest fades, yet the alliance is continued, the arrangement will still eventually end—often with acrimony and bitterness.

When considering making and breaking alliances, again, one would do well to follow the example of Great Britain. Britain's overarching aim for hundreds of years was to keep any power from becoming so dominant in continental Europe that they could threaten the British Isles. This led Britain to make a number of alliances, each lasting long enough to defeat the country that was attempting to become dominant.

For example, in the 1820s Britain supported the Greek efforts for independence from the Ottoman Empire, but in the early 1840s allied with the Ottomans against Russia when Russia threatened Britain's interests. However, 1848 found Britain supportive of Russia's efforts to put down a rebellion in Hungary that threatened the status quo. Later in the 1800s, Britain stood by when Prussia defeated Britain's former ally, Austria, because Austria's weakness made her useless as an ally. However, when Prussia threatened to gain primacy in Europe in the early 1900s, Britain allied herself with France and Russia to stop her.[13]

In sum, to shape the enemy one must know the six rules of alliances and follow them. A nation breaks them at its peril.

Cheng and Ch'i: Direct and Indirect Forces

The Western approach, based heavily on science, logic, and mathematics, teaches us that the shortest distance between two points is a straight line. As we have seen, the direct approach is not always the fastest or least resource-intensive means of achieving goals.

The arts of diplomacy and warfare are similar. To be successful in those realms one must not solely rely on the direct approach. An indirect approach is essential to success.

> ■ **The force which confronts the enemy is the normal; "Cheng"; that which goes to his flanks the extraordinary; "Ch'i." No commander of an army can wrest the advantage from the enemy without extraordinary forces.** (V.3 Li Ch'üan)

When one attacks an enemy solely with a direct attack it only strengthens the enemy's resistance, both physically and mentally. Because the attack is landing where it is expected there is no element of surprise. Therefore the enemy is balanced and prepared to receive one's blows. It is not possible to succeed in this fashion.

It is essential to combine both the direct attack and the indirect attack to overcome the enemy. The direct attack is the one the enemy expects, and it focuses the attention of its leaders in the wrong place; the indirect attack then lands, surprising them and throwing them off balance. When off balance, the enemy cannot respond effectively, allowing the exploitation of the situation to achieve total victory.

There is a type of glass shaped like a tadpole and named the "Prince Rupert drop." It is formed by allowing drops of molten glass to fall into a body of water or oil. Named after a seventeenth-century prince who was impressed with its attributes, one can smash these glass pieces on their heads with a hammer and they will not break. However, barely touch their tails and they explode into pieces. In essence, this is the difference between the direct and the indirect approach. One can exert great force directly on the enemy and nothing happens, but hit the right spot indirectly and the result is victory. Remember, the goal of combining the direct and indirect forces is not to nibble away at the enemy's physical strength bit by bit, but to coordinate one's forces most effectively to deliver a series of stunning psychological blows from which the enemy will not recover.

■ **Generally, in battle, use the normal force to engage; use the extraordinary to win. (V.5)**

After Texas gained its independence from Mexico in the mid-1800s, it sought to join the United States. On March 1, 1845, the U.S. Congress invited Texas to do so, which led Mexico to break off relations with the United States. As preparations for war on both sides continued, attempts to negotiate a settlement failed, and a clash between Mexican and American forces on disputed territory marked the opening of hostilities. On May 13, 1846, the U.S. formally declared war on Mexico.

While the modern perception is that this was a war between a powerful United States against a weak Mexico, that was definitely not the view at the time. Many European military observers felt the Mexican Army superior to that of the U.S. Also, the Mexican Army always significantly outnumbered that of America's throughout the war, sometimes by as much as four to one. In addition, the Mexican military was fighting in defense of its homeland, thereby achieving the benefits of knowing the terrain and being motivated to hold it. Finally, U.S. forces had to maintain their offensives over huge distances and difficult terrain with rudimentary logistical means.

The U.S. strategy was twofold: one army was to drive directly south into Mexico from Texas and a second army was to launch a seaborne assault on the Gulf of Mexico coast. This second army was to first secure the port of Vera Cruz, then drive westward across the Mexican highlands in the hope of taking Mexico City, the capitol. In charge of the seaborne effort was Winfield Scott, General in Chief of the U.S. Army, and a strong military strategist and tactician.

Sixty-one years old and standing six foot four, Scott had built a strong reputation in the War of 1812, both as a fighter and a troop trainer. "Old Fuss and Feathers," as Scott was known, got his nickname for his strong belief in military discipline and love for the finery of dress uniforms. However, Scott was also a military theorist and knowledge-able strategist, having spent his own money to study tactics in Europe.

Scott's amphibious assault on Vera Cruz began with a landing out-side the range of the port's defending guns. Mexican cavalry opposing the landing was driven off and a young officer from the Corps of En-gineers, Captain Robert E. Lee, began his work. Lee set troops to work building the siege works that would engage the fortress defending Vera Cruz. Although some impatient American officers wanted to launch an infantry assault directly on the fortress, Scott overruled them. He wanted to spare his men for the remainder of the campaign. Soon three hundred American guns opened fire and the Mexican fortress responded in kind. While the American guns wreaked havoc in the Mexican po-sitions, the guns of the fort were largely ineffective against the American emplacements. After three days of bombardment Vera Cruz fell, at the cost of only nineteen U.S. soldiers killed and eighty-one wounded. On April 8, 1847, Scott turned westward for Mexico City.

Upon reaching the Mexican highlands Scott encountered the Mex-ican Army at a mountain called Cerro Gordo. Commanding the Mex-ican Army was Santa Anna, the Mexican dictator himself. Again rejecting a direct assault, Scott sent Captain Lee to find a means of outflanking the position. Lee found a path that would allow the Amer-ican troops to swing behind the Mexican's left flank. Scott took ad-vantage of Lee's work to turn the Mexican position, breaking free again to move west. The cost was 417 American casualties versus over 1,000 Mexican casualties, with Scott's troops capturing another 3,000 men, 43 guns, and Santa Anna's wooden leg.

After getting reinforced, Scott resumed his march in August. Cut-ting loose from his supply line, Scott hoped to move quickly to take Mexico City and end the war. The famous Duke of Wellington from Britain, viewing this strategy, exclaimed, "Scott is lost! He has been carried away by his successes. He can't take the city and he can't fall back upon his base [Vera Cruz]."

The Battle of Contreras was Scott's next test. Again faced with a fortified position that supposedly could not be flanked, Scott chose to forego a direct assault. Again he sent Lee to scout out another way around the Mexican defense, and Lee did. Lee found a mule path which led around the Mexican right flank. After Lee built the path into a road, Scott used it to send troops around Santa Anna's flank. With this flank attack Scott again was able to drive the Mexican Army out of their defenses. Mexican losses numbered 1,500 men while the Americans suffered 60 casualties.

Scott broke through the final barrier to Mexico City at a place called Churubusco, named for the Aztec god of war. Launching direct attacks on main Mexican defensive position, the imposing Convent of San Pablo, Scott also sent troops around it to cut the only road back to the capitol. Seeing their last means of escape being closed off, the Mexican Army streamed back to the capitol in retreat. American casualties were the highest of the campaign but were still less than a quarter of the four thousand Mexican troops lost.

With the door to the capitol now open, Scott pushed on. After furious fighting around Chapultapec Castle, Mexico City fell to the Americans. Soon thereafter the Treaty of Guadalupe Hidalgo was signed between the United States and Mexico, ending the war. With this victory the U.S. had gained the future states of Texas, New Mexico, Colorado, Utah, Arizona, Nevada, and California.[14]

■ He who wishes to snatch an advantage takes a devious and distant route and makes of it the short way. He turns misfortune to his advantage. He deceives and fools the enemy to make him dilatory and lax, and then marches on speedily. (VII.3 Tu Mu)

The key to successfully using a combination of the direct and indirect approaches is to take the line of attack the enemy least expects. After North Korea invaded the Republic of Korea without a declaration of war on June 25, 1950, the North Korean People's Army achieved immediate success. Taking advantage of strategic surprise and the initially poor quality of the South Korean and U.S. troops (the latter having gotten soft on garrison duty in Japan), the NKPA pushed rapidly down the peninsula. The only toehold that remained to the U.S. and ROK forces (now fighting under the United Nations' flag) became known as the "Pusan Perimeter" for the port city in the southeast corner of the peninsula through which the UN forces brought in supplies and troops.

The new UN commander, General Douglas MacArthur, planned to defeat the North Koreans by emulating the amphibious strategy he had used in the Pacific theater of World War II. To defeat the Japanese MacArthur had executed an island-hopping strategy, using amphibious assaults to take critical enemy island strongholds while bypassing other Japanese-held islands. The bypassed islands, now isolated and unable to be resupplied, essentially "withered on the vine" and became irrelevant to the outcome of the war. Fighting now on a peninsula surrounded on three sides by water, MacArthur believed an amphibious strategy could work again.

Once an amphibious strategy had been decided upon the question now became where to best launch the assault. Although his advisors warned him against choosing the South Korean port of Inchon, with its dangerous currents, difficult navigation, fortified defenses, and high seawall, MacArthur stated, "We shall land at Inchon and I shall crush them."

Given only three weeks to plan the details, the United States Navy and Marine staff developed a plan. Shortly thereafter, Joint Task Force 7 slipped out of Japan and made its way to Inchon. Supported by naval bombardment and tactical air attacks, U.S. Marines landed at Inchon on September 15, 1950, achieving complete surprise (see Figure 5.2). Securing the port city in two days, the Marines quickly pushed inland towards Seoul, the enemy-held capital of South Korea.

Simultaneously, the UN forces in Pusan launched an offensive against the NKPA, attempting a breakout. Caught between the direct attack from Pusan in the south and the indirect assault on Inchon in the north, the North Korean forces disintegrated. The UN forces joined up a week later in Seoul, and MacArthur was able to present South Korean President Syngman Rhee the keys to his capitol.[15]

- He who knows the art of the direct; "Cheng;" and the indirect; "Ch'i;" approach will be victorious. Such is the art of manuevering   (VII.16)

Throughout the early years of the American Civil War, Abraham Lincoln sought earnestly for a Union general who would fight and win. Union generals McClellan, Hooker, and Burnside each failed to defeat General Robert E. Lee and the Army of Northern Virginia. So when General Ulysses S. Grant won several victories in the Western theater, Lincoln brought him east to put him in charge of all the Union armies.

Grant's original plan to defeat the South combined the direct and indirect approaches. He planned to remove 60,000 men from the defense of Washington, D.C., and invade North Carolina via a seaborne invasion. Once those forces landed on the Carolina coast they would drive west to Raleigh, cutting off the eastern rebel armies from their chief source of supply. This indirect assault would have created a new

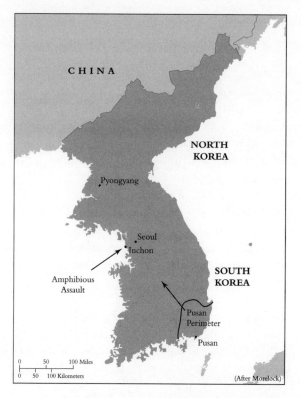

FIGURE 5.2   Inchon landing, 1950

front for the Confederates to defend while the Union armies in Virginia and Tennessee put direct pressure against the Rebel armies facing them. However, Lincoln felt this plan was too risky and vetoed it.

Thus the plan Grant eventually put in place was less daring, but combined the direct and indirect approaches (see Figure 5.3). Grant's strategy was to continue pressure in the West while coordinating the actions of the two Eastern armies of Meade (Army of the Potomac) and William Tecumseh Sherman (Army of the Tennessee). Meade's army would put continuous pressure on Lee in Virginia (the direct approach) while Sherman cut loose of his supply lines to ravage Tennessee, Georgia, and the Carolinas (the indirect approach). As executed, the constant pressure by Meade in Virginia made it impossible for Lee to take advantage of breaks in the action to reinforce the Confederate army in Tennessee. Simultaneously, Sherman's "march to the sea" destroyed the infrastructure and supplies the Southern armies depended on to survive and fight. In the end this strategy led to the end of the Civil War.[16]

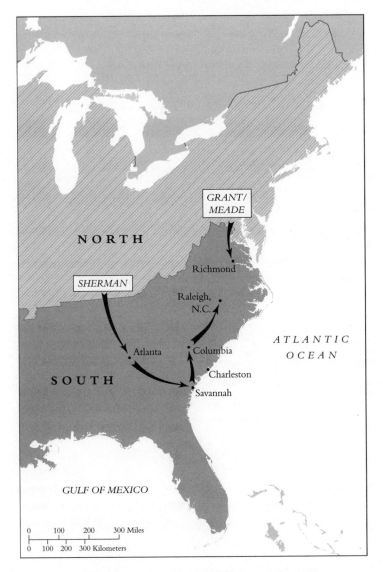

FIGURE 5.3 Defeating the South, Eastern Campaign

- In battle there are only the normal and extraordinary forces, but their combinations are limitless; none can comprehend them all. (V.11)

What if the indirect approach fails to surprise the enemy and its leadership correctly perceives the indirect attack as the main blow?

Move swiftly to change the weight and focus of the attack, turning Ch'i into Cheng.

■ I make the enemy conceive my normal force to be the extraordinary and my extraordinary to be the normal. Moreover, the normal may become the extraordinary and vice versa.   (V.3 Ho Yen-hsi)

If the indirect attack is failing yet the direct assault has met with success, resources must be put behind the direct one. Reinforce success and starve failure. By combining direct and indirect forces, the enemy is left with no good options and will be forced to submit.

■ For these two forces are mutually reproductive: their interaction as endless as that of interlocked rings. Who can determine where one ends and the other begins?   (V.12)

By utilizing Cheng and Ch'i interchangeably, one will be able to shape the enemy and successfully destroy its ability to oppose one's plans.

■ Now the resources of those skilled in the use of extraordinary forces are as infinite as the heavens and earth; as inexhaustible as the flow of the great rivers.   (V.6)

Psychological Attacks

■ Anger his general and confuse him. If the general is obstinate and prone to anger, insult and enrage him, so that he will be irritated and confused, and without a plan will recklessly advance against you.   (I.22 Sun Tzu and Chang Yü)

All leaders of state and commanders of armies share one quality: they are human. Given their human emotions they may be vulnerable to well-planned psychological operations.

One of the commentators in *The Art of War*, Tu Mu, provides an example mentioned earlier. He relates the story of the Sung general Tsang Chih defending the city of Yu T'ai. Before the battle Tsang Chih's opponent, the Emperor T'ai Wu, requested the customary gift of wine from Tsang Chih. Rather than sending wine, Tsang Chih sent the Emperor a pot of urine. In a fit of rage the Emperor ordered his troops to attack the city walls, day after day, for thirty days. After losing half his force in these vain attacks the Emperor was force to retreat.[17]

> ■ A sovereign cannot raise an army because he is enraged, nor can a general fight because he is resentful. For while an angered man may again be happy, and a resentful man again be pleased, a state that has perished cannot be restored, nor can the dead be brought back to life. Therefore, the enlightened ruler is prudent and the good general is warned against rash action. Thus the state is kept secure and the army preserved.   (XII.18.19)

Angering an enemy general is but one method of psychological operations. After World War II the French attempted to regain their colonies in what was then called French Indochina (modern Viet Nam, Laos, and Cambodia). However, French efforts to reassert control were severely hampered by Vietnamese communist insurgents, the Viet Minh. Led politically by Ho Chi Minh and militarily by General Vo Nguyen Giap, the Viet Minh used guerilla tactics to deny the French the countryside. Utilizing hit and run tactics, avoiding battle when outnumbered, and wiping out isolated French outposts, the Viet Minh created an aura of success, reduced support for the war among the French populace, and frustrated the French Army.

This frustration led the new French commander, General Henri Navarre, to develop a strategy to lure the Viet Minh into a western-style set piece battle. Navarre was convinced that by doing so the French forces could come to grips with the Viet Minh and utilize superior firepower to destroy them. Navarre planned to fight his battle at a place called Dien Bien Phu.

Dien Bien Phu was chosen because of its location (see Figure 5.4). It sat astride one of the major Viet Minh supply routes yet was remote enough that Navarre believed it would be very difficult for the Viet Minh to bring in any heavy weapons to support an attack against it. Thus, to open their supply route the Viet Minh would be forced to attack Dien Bien Phu, but (according to French expectations) could do so only using infantry unsupported by artillery. Dien Bien Phu was a hamlet in the middle of a three-mile-wide by ten-mile-long valley. While the valley had some small hills the position itself was surrounded by mountains that were as high as 3,000 feet. In addition, the valley was often covered by fog or drenched in heavy rain, both of which would factor heavily in the coming battle.

Operation Castor, the occupation of the valley of Dien Bien Phu,

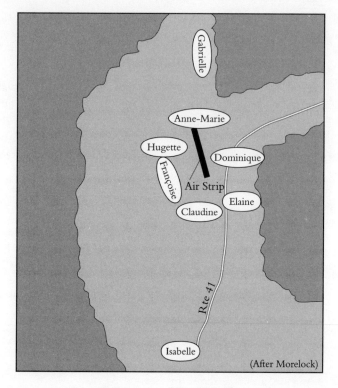

(After Morelock)

FIGURE 5.4   Dien Bien Phu

began on November 20, 1953, with the dropping of two paratroop battalions. Soon reinforced by other units, the French began to build an interlocking set of heavily fortified battle positions and an airstrip. The airfield in the middle of the valley would enable the outpost to be supplied. With this base Navarre expected to create a target "sufficiently tempting for the Viet Minh to pounce at, but sufficiently strong to resist the onslaught." Navarre put the roughly 11,000 troops defending Dien Bien Phu under the command of Colonel Christian de Castries, a flamboyant and brave leader who named each battle position after his current and past mistresses. Using these troops, supported by air power, sixty artillery pieces and ten tanks, de Castries planned to destroy the human wave attacks he believed the Viet Minh would launch against his base. In fact, the French artillery commander, Colonel Piroth, stated that his guns would destroy any Viet Minh artillery piece that dared fire.

General Giap, however, refused to play into the French strategy.

Rather than launch human wave assaults at the outset of the battle, Giap intended to slowly surround and then strangle the French fire base. To do so he used 100,000 peasants to bring in mortars, artillery, and supplies and to dig trenches and emplacements surrounding Dien Bien Phu. He then brought in 50,000 combat troops to the valley, as well as 200 artillery pieces and several antiaircraft weapons. The artillery and antiaircraft weapons he placed on the mountains surrounding the French-occupied valley.

On March 13, 1954, General Giap launched his attack, overrunning firebases Beatrice and Gabrielle, which until their capture had provided the bulk of the French artillery support. Lacking effective artillery counter-battery fire, there was nothing the French could do when Viet Minh artillery closed in to shell the airfield, Dien Bien Phu's sole source of resupply. Unable to provide the artillery support he promised, Colonel Piroth put a live grenade to his chest and blew himself up. Soon the only supplies that could arrive had to be parachuted in, as the French positions were pounded by 130,000 communist artillery rounds. These resupply efforts in turn were hampered by the fog and monsoon rains for which the area was known.

Between March 30 and April 4 Giap launched another series of assaults. Digging trenches closer and closer to the French positions, the Viet Minh took parts of Dominique, Elaine, and the airstrip. Realizing the precariousness of Dien Bien Phu's defenders, Navarra dropped 850 Foreign Legionaires onto the outpost on April 11. Due to the closeness of the lines almost half the Legionaires fell onto Viet Minh positions, where they were either killed or captured. In addition Navarre launched a relief operation called Condor, to try and lift the Viet Minh siege. It too was unsuccessful.

Between May 1 and May 7 Viet Minh infantry attacked the remaining French positions without artillery preparation, as by now the opposing trench lines were only yards apart. Hand-to-hand fighting followed, as one by one Huguette, Claudine, and Elaine fell. By May 8, 1954, it was all over. Colonel Castries led 6,500 French officers and soldiers into captivity, having lost 2,200 men and another 10,000 wounded or missing. Giap's casualties were roughly 23,000 in total, but his victory ended the French control of Indochina.[18]

> ■ Heart is that by which the general masters. Now order and confusion, bravery and cowardice, are qualities dominated by the heart. Therefore the expert at controlling his enemy frustrates him and then moves against him. He aggravates him to confuse

him and harasses him to make him fearful. Thus he robs his enemy of his heart and of his ability to plan.   (VII.20 Chang Yü)

Using Bait to Shape the Enemy

Another way to shape the enemy is to entice its leadership with bait.

■ Thus, those skilled at making the enemy move do so by creating a situation to which he must conform; they entice him with something he is certain to take, and with lures of ostensible profit they await him in strength.   (V.20)

In 1866, soldiers of the U.S. Army were in the process of building and defending a lonely outpost in Wyoming Territory named Fort Phil Kearny. In the midst of hostile Sioux, Cheyenne, and Arapaho warriors, the soldiers did their best to build and provision the fort. The detachment that went out to gather wood was often the target of attacks and the troopers who manned it were frustrated. They were being picked off one by one and the relief party was unable to retaliate effectively.

So it was with great glee on December 21 that the relief party from the fort saw a chance to get revenge. Hearing gunfire from the wood train and seeing ten of the enemy within reach, eighty-one troopers vied with each other to catch them. The ten warriors did their best to stay only a little way ahead of the cavalrymen, stopping when necessary to let them catch up.

When the soldiers crossed Peno Creek, the trap was sprung. Two thousand warriors under the command of the great Sioux leader Crazy Horse attacked the troopers. In bitter hand-to-hand fighting, not a single soldier was left alive. The Fetterman Massacre, named after the leader of the detachment, became history.[19]

■ One able to make the enemy come of his own accord does so by offering him some advantage.   (VI.3)

Thus, march by an indirect route and divert the enemy by enticing him with a bait. So doing, you may set out after he does and arrive before him. One able to do this understands the strategy of the direct and the indirect.   (VII.3)

Sending Signals

At times it is important to send clear signals to allies and enemies about one's intentions. This is especially critical when a nation is outlining national priorities for which it is willing to go to war.

We have discussed many of the key aspects of the Korean War in the 1950s. One essential aspect concerns how the war came about. In laying out the American policy of containment of communism, Secretary of State Dean Acheson defined the U.S. defensive perimeter, those countries considered vital to its national interests and for which it was willing to go to war. During a speech before the National Press Club on January 12, 1950, Acheson put South Korea outside of the perimeter and refused to guarantee the security of any Asian mainland country. Therefore, most historians take the position that neither North Korea nor the Soviet Union expected the United States to come to South Korea's defense once North Korea invaded. Failing to signal the United States's eventual position to the communist aggressors significantly contributed to the outbreak of the Korean War.[20]

- When I wish to avoid battle I may defend myself simply by drawing a line on the ground; the enemy will be unable to attack me because I divert him from going where he wishes. (VI.12)

Leaving a Way Out

A final consideration in shaping the enemy is to consider leaving them an easy way out to save face and avoid further conflict.

- Do not press an enemy at bay. Prince Fu Ch'ai said: "Wild beasts, when at bay, fight desperately. How much more is this true of men! If they know there is no alternative they will fight to the death. (VII.32 Sun Tzu and Tu Yü)

In January 1943, at the Casablanca Conference in Africa, Winston Churchill and Franklin D. Roosevelt, the leaders of the two strongest Western powers, declared an unconditional surrender policy against Nazi Germany. This policy stated that no agreement short of total and complete surrender by the Germans was acceptable. While this declaration was very well-received by the public, it is questionable whether it was good strategy.

Many prominent historians, supported by insights gained after World War II, have stated that the Allies' unconditional surrender policy made the Germany Army continue to fight for two and a half years longer than necessary. This is because the German Army saw no chance of negotiating a surrender that would allow Germany an honorable peace.

Had the Allies provided an offer that allowed more favorable terms, it is quite possible that the German Army may have overthrown Hitler and the Nazis in hopes of achieving better peace terms. This would have ended the war much earlier, with a great deal less death and destruction on all sides. Just as important, it would have avoided the projection of Soviet power into Central Europe, which resulted in the domination and subjection of those small countries by communism for fifty long years.[21]

Therefore, before launching any attack, one must consider this thought as well. Is the total defeat of the enemy necessary or even desirable? Is it not logical that the enemy will instinctively fight harder if its leaders know they are fighting for survival versus a limited objective. The alternatives must be thought through carefully.

- To a surrounded enemy you must leave a way of escape. When Ts'ao Ts'ao surrounded Hu Kuan he issued an order: "When the city is taken, the defenders will be buried." For month after month it did not fall. Ts'ao Jen said: "When a city is surrounded it is essential to show the besieged that there is a way to survival. Now, Sir, as you have told them they must fight to the death everyone will fight to save his own skin. The city is strong and has a plentiful supply of food. If we attack them, many officers and men will be wounded. If we persevere in this it will take many days. To encamp under the walls of a strong city and attack rebels determined to fight to the death is not a good plan!" Ts'ao Ts'ao followed this advice, and the city submitted.   (VII.31 Sun Tzu and Ho Yen-hsi)

Avoid Being Shaped

We have talked much about shaping the enemy. It is also critical to avoid being shaped by the enemy.

- The ultimate in disposing one's troops is to be without ascertainable shape. Then the most penetrating spies cannot pry in nor can the wise lay plans against you.   (VI.24)

To avoid being shaped by the enemy one must avoid using the same tactic twice in succession and developing patterns in one's actions. Using the same methods twice in a row is a cardinal sin in small-unit tactics. For example, when a patrol is sent out into enemy territory to scout, it should never come back to friendly lines using the same path; it should return a different way. It should also avoid patrolling an area using the same route at the same time every day. If it does either, the enemy will discern the pattern from observing its movements and execute an ambush with deadly results.

The lesson to learn from this is to not develop repetitive patterns in one's strategy or tactics. As the first implementer of the revolutionary "nation-in-arms" concept of war (in which all male citizens of military age are conscripted to protect the nation, versus the earlier use of royal standing armies composed of an aristocratic officer corps and enlisted men dragooned from the lower classes), France won many victories over its European enemies. However, over time France's enemies learned from those victories and modeled their armies to replicate or take advantage of France's tactics. Similarly, with the Blitzkrieg concept Germany had a major strategic advantage in the first years of the war. Over time, first the Russians and then the British and Americans learned the secrets of the new method of warfare. As the war continued the Allies improved on the German methods by significantly increasing the contribution of tactical air power. Lack of effort to stay ahead of their enemies with new tactics left both France and Germany vulnerable when those same enemies adjusted and improved.

- **Therefore, when I have won a victory I do not repeat my tactics but respond to circumstances in an infinite variety of ways. (VI.26)**

A key part of not allowing the enemy to shape one's forces is tied to the earlier-discussed topic of deception. Denying the enemy the ability to track one's forces and using deception to keep the enemy off balance all limit the likelihood of being shaped by the enemy.

Summary

To shape the enemy one's strategy must utilize both the direct and indirect approaches, make the proper use of alliances, limit the scope of the opponent's moves, and take advantage of their leaders' emotions. One must also guard against being shaped.

By combining direct and indirect approaches it is possible to misdirect the attention of the enemy leaders, take them by surprise, put them off balance, and then exploit the resulting advantage. One must be very creative and take the route least expected.

One can limit the enemy's movements and make them conform to one's desires by holding strategic positions or enticing the enemy with bait. These moves, performed properly, will play off the emotions of the enemy's leaders, leading them to make mistakes.

By properly utilizing alliances, one can increase strength while decreasing that of the enemy. Sever or disable the enemy's alliances, court their allies, choose the right allies, and then maintain those alliances. Avoid attacking enemies who have strong alliances until those alliances are broken. To enter into battle with poor allies against a strong array of foes is folly.

To ensure success, one must avoid being shaped. Never use the same tactic repetitively. Avoid getting into routines or patterns with strategy and tactics.

- **The flavors are only five in number but their blends are so various that one cannot taste them all.** (V.10)

All of these actions requires leadership, which is the subject of the next chapter.

6 ■ Character-based Leadership
Leading by Example

The principle that the leader is responsible for everything that happens under his command is a well-entrenched rule in armies throughout the world. This is as it should be, especially in Western armies, in which the commander has the authority and responsibility to carry out his mission and to ask for support if the resources at hand are insufficient for the task. Finally, it is a tradition (indeed the duty) for a commander to resign if he believes the mission and/or strategy are incorrect or the goal unattainable. This responsibility for one's command increases as the level of the command increases. Obviously, the decisions of commanders of armies, fleets, and air forces in battle will determine the fate of the nation.

> ■ Now the general is the protector of the state. If this protection
> is all-embracing, the state will surely be strong; if defective, the
> state will certainly be weak.   (III.18)

Military historian and theorist Colonel Trevor N. Dupuy is well-known for his studies of past battles, including the interviewing of officers and men to understand the reality of armed conflict. In a study spanning two centuries of warfare, the purpose of which was to determine the reasons an army was defeated, Dupuy came to the following conclusions about leadership.

While there were some reasons for defeat essentially beyond the commander's control, such as overwhelming odds, inferior technology or simply bad luck, there was much for which the defeated commander was responsible. Many of these reasons are subjects which have already been discussed and of which Sun Tzu warns, such as lack of preparation, being surprised, inadequate intelligence, poor planning, and insufficient logistics. However, there are other reasons that determine success or failure in battle, including inferior leadership (confused mission, weakness of will, self-delusion), poor morale, inadequate control, and inferior doctrine and/or tactics. These subjects, the essence of leadership, are now our topics of discussion.[1]

To defend the nation, achieve its objectives, and win wars Sun Tzu states that a leader must have many qualities. A successful leader must have the right character, be able to motivate others, provide clear direction, have a sense of military and diplomatic genius, and work to make the nation stronger.

- **And therefore the general who in advancing does not seek personal fame, and in withdrawing is not concerned with avoiding punishment, but whose only purpose is to protect the people and promote the best interests of his sovereign, is the precious jewel of the state. Such a general has no personal interest. Few such are to be had. (X.19 Sun Tzu, Li Chi'üan, Tu Mu)**

Truly, leaders of this caliber are unique and hard to find. As the passage suggests, they are desirable because of their willingness to put the needs of the nation before their own; they have strong, well-developed characters. To become such a leader, to put others before self, is not an easy task. It demands sacrifice.

Build Character, Not Just Image

The Art of War recognizes that successful military leadership is based on character, that to lead and command properly, one must have certain character traits and virtues.

- **By command I mean the general's qualities of wisdom, sincerity, humanity, courage and strictness.**

If wise, a commander is able to recognize changing circumstances and to act expediently. If sincere, his men will have no doubt of the certainty of rewards and punishments. If humane, he loves mankind, sympathizes with others, and appreciates their industry and toil. If courageous, he gains victory by seizing opportunity without hesitation. If strict, his troops are disciplined because they are in awe of him and are afraid of punishment.   (I.7 Sun Tzu and Tu Mu)

In warfare there are many unknowns. Therefore, wisdom is important, for it allows a leader to clearly divine the situation and craft a strategy. Courage is essential because without it, a leader cannot take advantage of wisdom with bold action when the situation requires it. Sincerity and humanity are crucial because leading soldiers requires their trust. Discipline is necessary, for it is required to keep order and ensure that strategy is executed successfully. All these traits are a manifestation of a strong, positive, and well-developed character.

Just as it is important to be sincere and humane, leaders must appear to be in control of the situation, exuding confidence and assurance. This appearance of confidence cannot be a facade, but must be based on true confidence built on wisdom, sincerity, humanity, and courage. If the leader has even one doubt, his soldiers will have several.

General Dwight D. Eisenhower recognized the importance of showing confidence to encourage his men. In a draft of his memoirs (never published), Eisenhower wrote, "optimism and pessimism are infectious and they spread more rapidly from the head downward than in any other direction." Beyond the fact that stressing optimism to others helped him maintain a positive attitude himself, he realized that a leader's positive attitude "has a most extraordinary effect upon all with whom he comes in contact. With this clear realization, I firmly determined that my mannerisms and speech in public would always reflect the cheerful certainty of victory."[2]

■ Shen Pao-hsu said: "If a general is not courageous he will be unable to conquer doubts or to create great plans."   (I.7 Tu Mu)

It is the business of a general to be serene and inscrutable, impartial and self-controlled. If serene, he is not vexed; if inscrutable, unfathomable; if upright, not improper; if self-controlled, not confused.   (XI.42 Sun Tzu and Wang Hsi)

Integrity	Maturity
Will	Self-discipline
Flexibility	Confidence
Endurance	Decisiveness
Coolness under stress	Initiative
Justice	Self-improvement
Assertiveness	Empathy
Sense of humor	Creativity
Bearing	Humility
Tact	

TABLE 6.1

After the leadership problems it experienced in Viet Nam, the U.S. Army regained interest in creating leaders with character. Field Manual 22–100, titled *Military Leadership*, was written specifically to communicate to the ranks what leadership is and how one becomes a leader. Chapter five of the manual discusses character traits desirable in a leader and developed a list somewhat longer, but very similar to that of Sun Tzu's (see Table 6.1).

What nation would not want its generals and admirals to possess these traits? An army peopled with leaders who have these abilities and military acumen, combined with the right doctrine and weaponry, can be assured of success.

Before he gained renown as leader of the Afrika Korps in World War II, Field Marshal Erwin Rommel learned combat first hand as a small unit leader in the First World War. In battle after battle Rommel pushed himself and his men hard, found creative ways of bringing combat power to bear against the enemy, yet was always chivalrous to his opponent. This accounts for his numerous WWI successes in France, Rumania, and especially Italy, which were rewarded with several decorations, including the coveted *Pour le Merite*. David Fraser, in his biography of Rommel, sums up those early years well:

> Wherever Rommel appears in those early encounters of his fighting life there is a sense of a man endowed with extraordinary powers of rapid decision, remarkable self-confidence and courage, both moral and physical, in following decision with action. Young Rommel, to a degree which must often have infuriated slower or more senior heads, made up his own mind, saw and decided in an instant,

and then grabbed the nearest troops . . . and moved like lighting to inflict maximum damage on the enemy. His nose for an opponent's vulnerability was like the scenting of a thoroughbred hound, while his lethal rapacity in striking at that vulnerability became legendary, and so remained. His was indeed, as Sun Tzu described the quality of decision, like the swoop of a falcon.[3]

While there are many qualities a commander may possess that help him lead his troops to victory, there are also many character traits a commander may have which will bring defeat.

■ **There are five qualities which are dangerous in the character of a general.**

If reckless, he can be killed; A general who is stupid and courageous is a calamity.

If cowardly, captured; One who esteems life above all will be overcome with hesitancy. Hesitancy in a general is a great calamity.

If quick-tempered you can make a fool of him: An impulsive man can be provoked to rage and brought to his death. One easily angered is irascible, obstinate, and hasty. He does not consider difficulties.

If he has too delicate a sense of honour you can calumniate him; One anxious to defend his reputation pays no regard to anything else.

If he is of compassionate nature you can harass him; He who is humanitarian and compassionate and fears only casualties cannot give up temporary advantage for a longterm gain and is unable to let go this in order to seize that. (VIII.17–22, including Sun Tzu, Tu Mu, Ho Yen-hsi, Tu Yu, and Mei Yao-ch'en)

At the beginning of the American Civil War many regimental officers were elected by their units and several generals obtained commissions due to their political connections. This led in numerous instances to commanders being appointed who lacked the necessary mettle to lead troops in battle and was a problem particularly prevalent in the Union armies. However, even some of the best-trained officers from America's military academies failed to have the character to win battles and achieve victory.

One such commander was that of the Union Army of the Potomac, General George Brinton McClellan. Although an excellent officer in many ways (McClellan won two brevets for gallantry during the Mexican–American War) McClellan soon proved that he lacked the qualities necessary to defeat the Confederacy.

After the Union defeat at the First Battle of Bull Run in 1861, McClellan was appointed to command the Army of the Potomac. This appointment was due in large part to credit for two small victories (Rich Mountain and Carrick's Ford) for which he was not even entirely responsible.

Upon taking command in July of 1861, McClellan began to impose discipline on the Army of the Potomac, training it hard. He was also very popular with the troops and the public, in large part because he cut a dashing figure and was quite eloquent. In time, McClellan was given not only command of the Army of the Potomac but overall command of all the Union forces. However, Lincoln's patience—and the nation's—began to wear thin as McClellan continued to train his men and refused to take the Army south. As Lincoln put it, "He's got the slows." Compounding this frustration was McClellan's egocentric view of reality, in which he saw himself as the sole savior of the Union. Too many of his statements started with "I," such as "I shall carry this thing *en grand*, and crush the rebels in one campaign." Also, rather than living with his men, McClellan chose to live in a large house in downtown Washington. There he threw frequent dinner parties, dressing his guard in finery and attended by his huge staff, which included European princes of royal blood and American princes of business.

Holding McClellan back were his fears of the Confederate forces. Privately he wrote, "I have scarcely slept one moment for the last three nights, knowing well that the enemy intend some movement and fully recognizing my own weakness. . . . I am here in a terrible place. The enemy have from three to four times my force." This last statement was definitely not true but had been put in McClellan's mind by his intelligence source, Allan Pinkerton. McClellan, relying solely on this one source of information, did not use his cavalry or other means to test his enemy's defenses and check Pinkerton's estimates.

McClellan finally moved south in force the spring of 1862, foregoing an overland attack for a naval landing on the York Peninsula. This approach put McClellan's 53,000 troops behind the main Confederate army under General Joseph Eggleston Johnston. It also put Mc-

Clellan closer to Richmond, where only 15,000 Rebels faced him in static defenses. On April 4, 1862, McClellan ordered his troops forward, only to cancel the order the next day. McClellan had been misled by the Southern commander, John Bankhead Magruder, who had marched his 15,000 soldiers around to make his force look bigger. Taking counsel of his fears, McClellan told his men to dig in and begin siege warfare. On May 4, Union shells began to fall on the Confederate line, but they had no effect. Johnston, the overall Southern commander, had taken advantage of the month delay to combine his army with Magruder's and withdraw it closer to Richmond the night before the Union shelling began. McClellan followed, but too slowly to catch the Confederate forces in a decisive battle.

Now reinforced to a strength of 105,000 men, McClellan found himself only a few miles from Richmond. Johnston had only 60,000 men but McClellan continued to believe Pinkerton, who said the Rebels had 250,000–300,000 troops. Perhaps this is why McClellan allowed Johnston to take the initiative on May 31, 1862, when Southern troops attacked a Union bridgehead at Fair Oaks. Although inconclusive, the battle put the Union troops on the defensive. It also had another, much more major, effect. In the battle Joe Johnston was severely wounded and had to be relieved of command; his replacement was General Robert E. Lee.

Lee continued to keep McClellan on the defensive. After dispatching Stonewall Jackson to the Shenandoah Valley to draw away potential reserves from McClellan, Lee again attacked. Assaults at Mechanicsville and Gaine's Mill, while costly in manpower to Lee, convinced McClellan he had no option but to retreat.

Many of McClellan's generals, convinced of Confederate weakness, were enraged by his order to fall back. One of them, General Philip Kearny, stated to his officers, "I say to you all, such an order can only be prompted by cowardice or treason." Lincoln, on coming to the Peninsula himself to observe the situation, decided a few days later to replace McClellan with his subordinate, General Henry Halleck. Although McClellan would take the field again, he would suffer further defeats or inconclusive actions (including a sixteen-hour delay at the Battle of Antietam, when McClellan intercepted Lee's orders to his men and could have defeated Lee in detail). Ultimately, McClellan would again lose command of the Army of the Potomac, ending his military career in ignominy.

McClellan, although he looked and acted the part of the leader, was guilty of having many of the negative traits Sun Tzu calls out. His hesitancy in battle, refusal to discern the actual size of the enemy forces opposing him, aversion to risk, and concern for his reputation all led to his defeats.[4]

> ■ Now these five traits of character are serious faults in a general and in military operations are calamitous. The ruin of the army and the death of the general are inevitable results of these short-comings. They must be deeply pondered.   (VIII.23–24)

Motivate the Troops

Sun Tzu discussed several ways to motivate and lead troops in battle, including leading by example, sharing the common soldier's lot, improving morale and delegating authority.

Lead by Example

> ■ Thus, such troops need no encouragement to be vigilant. Without extorting their support the general obtains it; without inviting their affection he gains it; without demanding their trust he wins it.   (XI.34)

The best way to prove one is a leader—to show character—is not to talk about it, but set the example. Leading by example means to lead not primarily with words but by action. Strategies, missions, and orders are important, yet they must be followed and supported by actions that are consistent for orders to be meaningful. Nothing sends a truer, clearer message to soldiers about a leader than his behavior.

Erwin Rommel, both as a small-unit leader and as a field marshal, always led in this manner. As a platoon and company commander he would often lead the advance element of his troops, taking a few men with him to scout the enemy defenses and making the initial penetration of their lines. His greatest feat as a small-unit commander in WWI occurred on the Italian front. In the battle of Mount Matajur, Rommel led 150 men to capture the Italian defensive position. In the short space of fifty-two hours Rommel captured his objective and took nine thousand men prisoner, while only suffering thirty-six casualties.[5]

> ■ Because such a general regards his men as infants they will march with him into the deepest valleys. He treats them as his own beloved sons and they will die with him.   (X.20)

Share Soldiers' Trials

- The general must be the first in the toils and fatigues of the army. In the heat of summer he does not spread his parasol nor in the cold of winter don thick clothing. In dangerous places he must dismount and walk. He waits until the army's wells have been dug and only then drinks; until the army's food is cooked before he eats; until the army's fortifications have been completed, to shelter himself.   (X.20 Chang Yü)

A leader "must be first in the toils and fatigues of the army," sharing not only the army's triumphs but also its tribulations. In this manner the leader establishes a bond with the troops that increases their morale and makes them stronger in the face of war's many adversities.

In warfare, one of the most compelling stories of a leader sharing the trials and struggles of his followers is that of Admiral Matome Ugaki. Ugaki was the naval commander of the Japanese kamikaze force in World War II, Japan's last–ditch attempt to prevent the total defeat of their nation. After having supervised the effort that sent so many young Japanese men to their fate, Ugaki felt he owed it to them to join them. On hearing of the surrender of Japan to the Allies, he flew out on the last day of the war to attack American ships and pay his debt to his men. Enroute he was shot down and killed. This is a very extreme example of a leader sharing the fate of his men, yet it shows the depth of the bond good leaders form with their followers.[6]

- During the Warring States period, when Wu Ch'i was a general he took the same food and wore the same clothes as the lowliest of his troops. On his bed there was no mat; on the march he did not mount his horse; he himself carried his reserve rations. He shared exhaustion and bitter toil with his troops.   (X.20 Tu Mu)

Contrast the above devotion to the troops with the scene found by General H. Norman Schwartzkopf when he reported to the headquarters of the Americal division at Chu Lai in Viet Nam to serve as a battalion commander:

The place was almost worthy of a Club Med, a spacious building with screened porches and low tropical eaves, nestled on a hilltop with a gorgeous view of the South China Sea. We were seated at a long, U-shaped table with white tablecloth, china and wineglasses—

Major General Lloyd B. Ramsey, his deputy commanders, his staff, and me—as soldiers waited on us. At the end of the meal came what I was told was the nightly ritual: a staff officer stood and recited a poem he'd written about the day's events at headquarters. Everybody laughed and applauded. Then another officer stood and with a lot of joking asides announced the movie for the evening. I was heartsick. We had men—about eighteen thousand men—out in the mud and the jungle, maybe fighting the enemy, maybe dying at that moment, while their senior officers ate off fine china and recited cutesy little poems.[7]

Leadership starts at the top and both good and poor examples of leadership trickle all the way down the chain of command. It is interesting to note that a unit from the American division had been responsible for the My Lai incident two years earlier.

In addition to the individual soldier's fighting capability, the soldier's welfare must always be one of the leader's major concerns. Late in the year 1777, General George Washington led his American army to Valley Forge for the winter. He chose Valley Forge over more comfortable quarters in order to stay closer to the British army in Philadelphia and prevent the British from foraging in the rich Valley Forge area. In American history the words "Valley Forge" bring to mind the great sacrifices and tribulations that Washington's troops suffered, including lack of clothing and food, illness, and difficult winter weather.

Washington did his best to improve the conditions for his men, allowing foraging to bring in food and other supplies. Washington also stayed in Valley Forge with his troops, sharing their trials. Furthermore, Washington brought in a Prussian, Friedrich von Steuben, to train the troops. Von Steuben's hard drilling focused the men on their task, improved the discipline and combat power of the army, and increased morale. As spring of 1778 came, the increase in the food supply brought in new recruits, all of whom von Steuben introduced to soldiering. The new army that came out of Valley Forge would form the hard steel core of the forces that would eventually drive the British out of the colonies.[8]

A leader must do his best to ensure his troops are well-fed, well-armed, and hard trained. He should meet with small-unit commanders, noncommissioned officers, and individual soldiers to learn their concerns and needs. In this manner a leader will know his unit's true capabilities, take measures to improve them and strengthen the unit's morale.

- Pay heed to nourishing the troops; do not unnecessarily fatigue them. Unite them in spirit; conserve their strength.   (XI.32)

One final comment: ensuring troops are taken care of must not be misconstrued. Troops should not be spoiled or softened with luxury items or excessive time off.

- If a general indulges his troops but is unable to employ them; if he loves them but cannot enforce his commands; if the troops are disorderly and he is unable to control them, they may be compared to spoiled children, and are useless.   (X.21)

Rather, leaders must take care that their soldiers have the necessities to make war and have the discipline and training to take the battle to the enemy. Any more and one runs the risk of making the troops soft.

Morale and Motivation

- The responsibility for a martial host of a million lies in one man. He is the trigger of its spirit.   (VII.20 Ho Yen-hsi)

To defeat the enemy, the morale of one's unit must be excellent. Therefore, an essential part of leadership is motivation, for the morale of any organization begins at the top.

- When the general is contemptuous of his enemy and his officers love to fight, their ambitions soaring as high as the azure clouds and their spirits as fierce as hurricanes, this is the situation with respect to morale.   (V.25 Chang Yü)

If the leaders of the army have low morale, if they are fearful or hesitant, how can the soldiers be expected to respond? For the first three years of the Civil War the Army of the Potomac had never been able to win a clear victory over Lee's Confederate Army of Northern Virginia. In fact, most campaigns ended in defeat for the Union army. It wasn't until the Battle of Gettysburg in 1863 that the North could truly claim a victory. Yet even then the Army of the Potomac's commander, General George Gordon Meade, refused to pursue Lee's army and destroy him before Lee reached sanctuary. All the Yankee soldiers in the Army needed was a general with a strong enough will to lead them.

That is exactly what happened when General Grant took overall control of the Union forces in 1864. While directing all the Union armies in every theater, Grant traveled with the Army of the Potomac, making his influence felt directly by his presence. After taking control, Grant's first move in the east was to fight Lee in an area called the Wilderness. After severe fighting at the Battle of the Wilderness, Union casualties were roughly double those of the Rebels. As they were ordered to form up and march, the men of the Army of the Potomac wondered whether Grant would retreat back north as all the prior generals of their army had.

The answer came at a crossroads; if they turned left the marching troops would know they were retreating. If they turned right it meant they were heading south to continue the fight. They turned right . . . and a huge cheer went up among the soldiers. They had finally found a commander who would lead them to victory.[9]

- Now when troops gain a favorable situation the coward is brave; if it be lost, the brave become cowards. (V.19 Li Ch'üan)

Success in battle is crucial to making soldiers believe in themselves. Belief in a cause and patriotism are also essential motivations. Finally, the leader must also recognize that personal glory can be a strong motivator as well. Medals, ribbons, special uniforms, and other means of recognizing soldiers are crucial to morale (obviously, this special recognition must be earned; if awards are given when not earned they are meaningless to both the recipient and others).

- One who confronts his enemy for many years in order to struggle for victory in a decisive battle yet who, because he begrudges rank, honors, and a few hundred pieces of gold, remains ignorant of his enemy's situation, is completely devoid of humanity. Such a man is no general; no support to his sovereign; no master of victory. (XIII.2)

Delegation of Authority and Commander's Intent

To be successful on the field of battle it is important to develop subordinate leaders, and to increase morale a leader must delegate authority and responsibility.

- A sovereign of high character and intelligence must be able to know the right man, should place the responsibility on him, and expect results. (III.29 Wang Hsi)

The need to drive authority and responsibility down the chain of command is essential to keep pace with the dynamics of combat and the battlefield. Sun Tzu recognized this. The philosophy is consistent with current military doctrine in the Marine Corps. Marine doctrine states that the procurement or use of any equipment that allows a commander to over-control sub-unit commanders in battle is unjustifiable and forbidden. This thinking is the direct result of generals in Viet Nam directing the movement of platoons on the ground while cruising the battlefield in a helicopter overhead.[10]

- Now in war there may be one hundred changes in each step. When one sees he can, he advances; when he sees that things are difficult, he retires. To say that a general must await commands of the sovereign in such circumstances is like informing a superior that you wish to put out a fire. Before the order to do so arrives the ashes are cold. And it is said one must consult the Army Supervisor in these matters! This is as if in building a house beside the road one took advice from those who pass by. Of course the work would never be completed. (III.29 Ho Yen-hsi)

In the U.S. Army this is called understanding the "commander's intent." The basic idea behind commander's intent is that a subordinate commander does not follow orders from a superior exactly to the letter, but instead uses personal initiative and a solid understanding of the situation to carry out the mission and achieve what the leader intended to accomplish.

The eventual goal to be achieved over time is for subordinates to know the commander's mind and each others' so well that actual time spent communicating is reduced, while the leaderships' shared understanding increases. Officers and enlisted men who have worked together closely for an extended period of time, who have built a wealth of trust, and operate with a consistent strategic and tactical philosophy, will learn to "read each others' minds." They will be able to anticipate how their leader and team members respond in certain situations and then act accordingly. This is the ultimate attainment of commander's intent.

In the First World War, the German Army had a concept very similar to that of commander's intent, called *Weisungsfuhrung*. Translated as "leadership guidance," the Weisungsfuhrung concept materialized in parallel with the creation of the stormtrooper concept. As you'll recall, the idea of the stormtrooper arose from the effort to break out of the trench warfare of World War I, in which long lines of foot soldiers advanced directly into strong defenses bolstered by machine-gun fire, artillery shells, and barbed wire. Gaining a few yards of ground at tremendous cost became unaffordable and unpalatable, not to mention ineffective.

In response to the stalemate, the German Army formed the elite *Sturmtruppen* units, small groups of highly trained, highly motivated soldiers who were very capable of acting independently and combined a mix of skills in different weapons systems—essentially a self-contained, combined arms team.[11] Individual initiative was highly prized, as the soldiers advanced not in long lines, but independently in dispersed fashion. Their mission was to avoid enemy strong points and attack the rear areas, where they were the weakest. In this highly dynamic and fluid situation, when it might not be possible to stay in contact with one's leader, following the exact orders of a commander made no sense; hence the Weisungsfuhrung concept. This demanded the type of soldier who could think for himself, interpret the intent of his leader, and then take the necessary steps to make that intent a reality. The combination of the Weisungsfuhrung and stormtrooper concepts formed the foundation for the new tactics that provided the breakthroughs Germany had sought and allowed Germany to come within a hairsbreadth of winning the war.[12]

In a sense, the Weisungsfuhrung and stormtrooper concepts of World War I proved to be the precursors for World War II and the modern-day soldier. Today's soldier must be highly skilled, highly motivated, and able to interpret the leader's intent in order to survive and carry out the unit's mission in today's more dynamic battlefield.

Therefore, leaders must supply their subordinates not with orders to be carried out to the letter, but with strategic objectives to be met, and the means and maneuvering room to achieve the intent as they see fit. The payoff is to instill boldness of action to enable dramatic breakthroughs. To harness this power and obtain the payoff, a leader must be able to say to the troops:

- When you see the correct course, act; do not wait for orders. (VIII.8 Chang Yü)

Discussed in chapter five was Grant's plan at the end of the American Civil War to keep Lee fixed in the east while General Sherman cut loose from his base and destroyed the infrastructure of the Confederacy. These are Grant's orders to Sherman, which show how a great commander provides direction to a trusted subordinate:

> You I propose to move against Johnston's army, to break it up and to get into the interior of the enemy's country as far as you can, inflicting all the damage you can against their war resources. *I do not propose to lay down for you a plan of campaign, but simply to lay down the work it is desirable to have done, and leave you free to execute in your own way.* [emphasis mine].

- **To put a rein on an able general while at the same time asking him to suppress a cunning enemy is like tying up the Black Hound of Han and then ordering him to catch elusive hares. What is the difference?   (III.29 Ho Yen-hsi)**

Since one must find the right person and "place responsibility on him and expect results," there must be both positive and negative consequences for behaviors and results. Leaders hold heavy responsibility for the success of the army and the fate of its soldiers and the nation are dependent on it. If one finds a commander who cannot take the proper action, then he must be replaced. Success must be rapidly followed by reward, while failure must be first understood, then addressed.

- **Good commanders are both loved and feared.   (X.21 Chang Yü)**

When taking over a new command, a leader must be especially careful to set the correct tone right away. Be sure not to overstep. Take time to learn each subordinate's character, intelligence, strengths, and weaknesses before taking action.

- **If troops are punished before their loyalty is secured they will be disobedient. If not obedient, it is difficult to employ them. If troops are loyal, but punishments are not enforced, you cannot employ them.   (IX.47)**

A leader must be both fair and consistent, all the while using Sun Tzu's principles to build toward success.

- Thus, command them with civility and imbue them uniformly with martial ardor and it may be said that victory is certain. (IX.48)

One will know soon enough if what one is doing is working or not working.

- When the troops continually gather together in small groups and whisper together the general has lost the confidence of the army. (IX.41)

In the end, it comes down to truly caring for people, trusting them to carry out the strategy, and providing both positive and negative incentives for behavior and results.

- Too frequent rewards indicate that the general is at the end of his resources; too frequent punishments that he is in acute distress. (IX.42)

(A good general) administers rewards and punishments in a more enlightened manner. Neither should be excessive. (I.13 Tu Mu)

Desperate Situations

There is one final way to motivate soldiers, as Sun Tzu indicates.

- Throw the troops into a position from which there is no escape and even when faced with death they will not flee. In a desperate situation they fear nothing; when there is no way out they stand firm. Deep in a hostile land they are bound together and there, where there is no alternative, they will engage the enemy in hand-to-hand combat. (XI.33)

There may be times when the fate of the nation hangs in the balance and a unit must sacrifice itself for the greater sake of the whole. One such instance was faced by the Greeks in 480 B.C.

Since his father's defeat at Marathon in the prior decade, the Persian King Xerxes wanted to avenge himself against the Greeks and conquer them once and for all. Crossing from Asia into Europe at the Hellespont with 250,000 men, Xerxes brought with him the power of an empire against the small collection of independent Greek city-states.

To stop the Persians and give the Greek city-states time to combine forces, King Leonidas of Sparta led a small detachment of Spartans and Greek allies to the pass at Thermopylae. If Leonidas and his men could hold this pass and delay the advance of the Persians, the Greeks might have a chance to mobilize their combined armies and navies to defeat the Persians.

Leonidas formed his phalanx of 7,000 men to defend the pass in depth, facing the huge Persian army. The ancient Greek historian Herodotus tells of the attitude of the Greek forces:

> Although extraordinary valor was displayed by the entire corps of Spartans and Thespians, yet bravest of all was declared the Spartan Dienekes. It is said that on the eve of battle, he was told by a native of Trachis that the Persian archers were so numerous that, when they fired their volleys, the mass of arrows blocked out the sun. Dienekes, however, quite undaunted by this prospect, remarked with a laugh, "Good. Then we'll have our battle in the shade."

As King Leonidas stood and fought with his men the Persian King Xerxes sat atop the mountain with his retainers to watch the battle. For three days the armies fought and still the Greeks held the pass. It was only after a deserter showed the Persians a path around the pass that the situation became untenable.

Sending his allies back to join forces with the main Greek army, Leonidas stayed with his 300 Spartans. Fighting to the last man they delayed the Persians another day. The Greeks would use the time well to unite their forces, eventually stopping the Persians by destroying their navy at the Battle of Salamis and their army at Platea.[13] King Leonidas and his men would go down in history, their monument at Thermopylae stating simply

> Go tell the Spartans, stranger passing by,
> That here obedient to their laws we lie.

■ **In death ground I could make it evident that there is no chance of survival. For it is the nature of soldiers to resist when surrounded; to fight to the death when there is no alternative, and when desperate to follow commands implicitly. (XI.23)**

Provide Clear Direction

■ He whose ranks are united in purpose will be victorious. (III.27)

To carry out their mission subordinate leaders need to know the commander's intent and strategy. To perform effectively, soldiers must first understand how their efforts fit into the overall picture.

■ If the army is confused and suspicious, neighboring rulers will cause trouble. This is what is meant by the saying, "A confused army leads to another's victory." (III.23)

This is why it's important for a commander not only to have a commander's intent but ensure it is shared.

■ When orders are consistently trustworthy and observed, the relationship of a commander with his troops is satisfactory. (IX.50)

To ensure orders are observed, one must have a clear chain of command.

■ Generally, management of many is the same as management of few. It is a matter of organization. To manage a host one must first assign responsibilities to the generals and their assistants, and establish the strengths of ranks and files. (V.1 Sun Tzu and Chang Yü)

During the Viet Nam War the United States had no clear mission and the chain of command was extremely confused. Pulled bit by bit into the war in Southeast Asia, the government's overall goal was to contain the spread of communism. However, this greater objective had no viable strategy to achieve it. Eventually, management of the war degenerated from attempting to build a democratic bulwark against communist expansion down to merely trying to increase the body counts of Viet Cong soldiers. Compounding the lack of a winning strategy was a fragmented execution system. Much of the air war was directed from Washington, with targets being prioritized by officials up to the President. However, the Navy and Air Force air assets were run by different commands. The ground war was also run by independent commands, the Army in one area and the Marines in another. Finally, various intelligence agencies ran their own intelligence gathering and covert operations.

Contrast this to the Persian Gulf War, in which the mission was clear: push Iraq out of Kuwait. And although the American-led Coalition forces were composed of not only European units but Arab units as well, the chain of command was clear. Air assets from all the nations were coordinated, and often tasked to fly missions together. Ground units from different nations and services were also enabled to work together effectively. All this was due to a clear mission and chain of command.

Beyond ensuring the clear direction, another major part of leadership is the proper staffing and organization of one's unit. Crucial to success is selecting the right leadership team, composed of the best people available. Getting the best people is essential, for they will carry out the strategy and greatly influence one's soldiers.

- The difficulties in the appointment of a commander are the same today as they were in ancient times.   (11.21 Ho Yen-hsi)

  . . . Therefore Master Wang said: "To make appointments is the province of the sovereign; to decide on battle, that of the general."   (III.29 Tu Yu)

  He selects his men and they exploit the situation.   (V.22)

A leader must find out their soldiers' special abilities and use them. One must take time to learn about each subordinate, their strengths and their weaknesses, their desires and their fears, what they do well and what they do poorly. In this way a leader can use them to the best of their ability.

- Now the valiant can fight, the cautious defend, and the wise counsel. Thus there is none whose talent is wasted.   (V.22 Li Ch'üan)

In battle it will be the qualities of those who stand with the leader that will make the difference.

- The Grand Duke said: "A sovereign who obtains the right person prospers. One who fails to do so will be ruined."   (III.18 Chang Yü)

Military and Diplomatic Genius: Character Is Not Enough

■ It is according to the shapes that I lay the plans for victory, but the multitude does not comprehend this. Although everyone can see the outward aspects, none understands the way in which I have created victory.   (VI.25)

Throughout time there have been new tactics and new weapons that have changed how battles on land, sea, and air are fought. Most of this dynamic interplay between advances in weaponry and tactics has lead to incremental improvements and often has taken many years. For example, as the use of gunpowder weapons became more widespread in the late fifteenth century, commanders deployed musketeers protected by pikeman. Eventually the two types of infantry were combined into one when the "socket" bayonet provided the musketeer pike-like protection when his weapon was empty or he was charging. Unfortunately, it took three hundred years for this evolution to take place.[14]

However, there exist points in time when a military visionary—a man with a brilliant view—will look at the latest advances and see the potential for a revolutionary change in the nature of warfare. One such visionary was Oda Nobunaga, the first of the three great samurai leaders who fought to consolidate power in Japan and end the Sengoku Jidai. Oda Nobunaga came from a simple background and rose to power in the sixteenth century because of his military ability. He displayed this ability at the Battle of Nagashino between the Oda clan and their enemies, the Takeda clan.

At Nagashino Oda Nobunaga faced the feared Takeda clan cavalry, 15,000-strong arrayed against him. However, he had on hand a new weapon, the arquebus (the early precursor of the musket, brought to Japan by European traders) and 10,000 men to use it. Oda Nobunaga took 3,000 of his most effective arquebusiers and stationed them in three ranks behind a wooden palisade. Using essentially the same tactic the British would eventually make famous, Oda had the first rank fire when the Takeda cavalry attacked. They would then retire to reload, while the second rank fired. The same process would be then followed by the third rank.

The combination of this new weapon and improved means of deploying it led to the devastation of the Takeda cavalry, with two-thirds of them laying dead or dying on the field of battle. Oda Nobunaga would go on from this success to others, laying the groundwork for the eventual unification of Japan under his heirs.[15]

- Thus, one able to gain the victory by modifying his tactics in accordance with the enemy situation may be said to be divine. (VI.30)

In today's military parlance a sea-change in tactics and weaponry as noted above is called a Revolution in Military Affairs (RMA). Numerous RMAs have been driven by visionary leaders. Other examples include the Theban improvements of the traditional phalanx by Epaminondas, the maniple legion of the Romans, and King Edward III's deployment of English bowmen at Crecy. More recent instances of RMAs are Napoleon's exploitation of conscription and German General Heinz Guderian's development of the Blitzkrieg. In each situation a leader with military genius saw the potential capabilities and speedily took advantage it. General Rommel summed up the need to seek out RMAs: "However praiseworthy it may be to uphold tradition in the field of soldierly ethics, it is to be resisted in the field of military command. For today it is not only the business of commanders to think up new techniques which will destroy the value of the old; the potentialities of warfare are themselves being continually changed by technical advance. Thus, the modern army commander . . . must be able to turn the whole structure of his thinking inside out." Furthermore, as an instructor of troops Rommel was fond of telling his officers, "Don't tell me what Clausewitz thought. Tell me what you think."[16]

Currently, opportunities for new RMAs include (but are not limited to) network warfare, space warfare, undersea warfare, nontraditional warfare, and biological, chemical, or genetic warfare. Given how quickly new technologies are evolving, the only limit to potential new methods of warfare is creativity.

- The musical notes are only five in number but their melodies are so numerous that one cannot hear them all. The primary colors are only five in number but their blends are so various that one cannot visualize them all. (V.8–V.9)

Just as important as having military commanders who posses genius is to avoid having political leaders or others who have no understanding of military affairs.

- Now there are three ways in which a ruler can bring misfortune upon his army.

> When ignorant that the army should not advance, to order an advance or ignorant that it should not retire, to order a retirement. This is described as "hobbling the army."

> When ignorant of military affairs, to participate in their administration. This causes the officers to be perplexed.

> When ignorant of command problems to share in the exercise of responsibilities. This engenders doubts in the minds of the officers. (III.19–22)

These problems that Sun Tzu foresaw in ancient China came into play during the Viet Nam War 2,500 years later. During the Johnson Administration one of the critical American decision-makers directing the war was Secretary of Defense Robert S. McNamara. Chosen initially by President John F. Kennedy for his academic qualifications, his business background, and his use of statistical methods in the U.S. Air Force in World War II, Kennedy was impressed with McNamara's numerical and management skills. It was McNamara's strong belief as Secretary of Defense that the U.S. military should be managed using statistics.

McNamara's insistence on managing via statistics instead of leading by example resulted in over-control of the war from Washington, D.C. This in turn led to a lack of initiative by lower unit commanders, the reporting of false statistics to provide the appearance of progress in pacification of the countryside, and the general corruption of the officer corps. The latter made itself visible as generals (up to and including the Joint Chiefs of Staff) made decisions that would please their superiors and protect their careers instead of winning the war. The conduct of the Viet Nam war made it clear that over-control, management by numbers versus inspired leadership, and ignorance of military matters results in disaster.[17]

> ■ In recent times court officials have been used as Supervisors of the Army and this is precisely what is wrong. (III.22 Chang Yü)

Genius must not be limited to the military realm, but must be evident in the diplomatic arena as well. This means that a soldier requires a grasp of not only military affairs but international and domestic affairs as well. An aspiring commander would do well to study the methods of leading diplomats such as Metternich, Bismarck, Kissinger, and others. A soldier following Sun Tzu's principles must know how to avoid wars as well as fight them.

Make the State Stronger

- When one treats people with benevolence, justice and righteousness, and reposes confidence in them, the army will be united in mind and all will be happy to serve their leaders.   (I.4 Chang Yü)

In the year 627 A.D. a new emperor came to power in China, T'ang T'ai-tsung. He immediately smashed his enemies, the Eastern Turks, which led to a fifty-year-long peace. Next he destroyed the Western Turks, opening up a trade route to India and Persia. Soon all the nomadic tribes paid tribute to China and its emperor.

T'ang T'ai-tsung not only pacified his borders; he made his kingdom stronger. He made advisors of the wisest men in the empire, regardless of their birth, employment, or their support for former enemies. Rather than choosing officials by their clan allegiance he had them chosen by public examination and used inspectors to rove the provinces, ensuring that the officials chosen were serving the people and not corrupt. T'ang T'ai-tsung created ministries to develop the country economically and enrich its citizens. Furthermore, the law was fairly applied and taxes were low (and lowered more during bad harvests); even so, the government's revenues multiplied. T'ang T'ai-tsung realized that it was the nation and its people that made him and the empire strong, stating, "For if the emperor is a boat, then the people are the waters of the river. And while the waters can bear the boat, they can also sink it."[18]

For a nation to be strong and prosper its leadership must put in place policies and practices that develop the economy, leverage the creativity of the people, and strengthen the national character. If these steps are taken one can achieve the nation's objectives.

- Those who excel in war first cultivate their own humanity and justice and maintain their laws and institutions. By these means they make their governments invincible.   (IV.15 Tu Mu)

Although a nation may be strong, that does not mean it can implement any type of strategy in order to win. A leader's strategy must fit the national character. National character is composed of the qualities, virtues, and values of the people of the nation. This includes their martial spirit, desire for victory, national psychology, and form of government.

For example, during the Punic Wars the strategy of avoiding battle with Hannibal employed by Fabius Verrucosus (*Cunctator*, the Delayer) was successful in denying Hannibal victories and allies. However, the Roman people's national character could not tolerate this strategy. Instead they choose to fight Hannibal at Cannae which, as discussed earlier, was a major Roman defeat. So even while the Fabian strategy worked in the short term, it was ultimately unsuccessful.

The same was true during the Peloponnesian War between Athens and Sparta. The great Athenian general, leader, and "first citizen" Pericles was known for wisdom, honesty, patriotism, and his speaking ability. He led the Athenian democracy and developed its strategy to defeat Sparta. Pericles hoped not to totally defeat Sparta, but convince its leaders that both Athens and Sparta could respect one another and coexist within their own spheres of influence. With this in mind Pericles' strategy was to avoid battle on land (where Sparta was superior), instead defending Athens' walls and using her navy to attack Sparta where the latter was vulnerable. Unfortunately, this left Athens' countryside open to Spartan pillaging, which the Athenians had to watch from behind their walls. Since most Athenians had land holdings which were being devastated and because the Greek philosophy of warfare was to fight a decisive battle and end the fighting, Pericles' strategy (no matter how brilliant) was not given time to work. As the Greek historian Thucydides recorded of the Athenian populace:

> Naturally, it seemed to them terrible to see their land ravaged in full view. The young men had never seen such a thing, and the older men not since the Persian War. It was the general opinion, and especially among the younger men, that they should not stand about and watch but go out and put a stop to it. . . . The city was irritated in every way, and they were angry with Pericles. They completely forgot the warnings he had given them in advance, abused him for being a cowardly general who would not lead them out to battle, and held him responsible for all their troubles.

While Pericles was able to maintain his plans for a while, his untimely death allowed his successors to undo his strategy. Like the Romans several centuries later, the new Athenian leaders chose to strike directly at their enemies, likewise suffering disastrous result. An Athenian expedition to Sicily was destroyed (Athens lost 40,000 men and expended 20 million drachmas in defeat) and, by war's end, Athens was left exhausted.[19]

The lesson to learn from both the Fabius and Pericles examples is that no matter how intellectually superior a strategy may be, it must fit with the character of the nation. Otherwise, it will ultimately be unsuccessful.

- Those skilled in war cultivate the Tao and preserve the laws and are therefore able to formulate victorious policies. The Tao is the way of humanity and justice; "laws" are regulations and institutions.   (IV.15 Sun Tzu and Tu Mu)

Summary

The leader is responsible for everything that happens, whether to the nation or his command. If there are problems, the leader must first look within himself to see if there is something that he has done incorrectly, then look at the officers who report directly to him, then look further down the chain of command. The last place one should look to find the root cause of any problem is at the individual soldier, for the strengths and weaknesses of any organization flow from the top down.

- Now when troops flee, are insubordinate, distressed, collapse in disorder or are routed, it is the fault of the general. None of these disasters can be attributed to natural causes.   (X.9)

Therefore a leader must have a strong character, otherwise disaster will be the result.

- When the general is morally weak and his discipline not strict, when his instructions and guidance are not enlightened, when there are no consistent rules to guide the officers and men and when the formations are slovenly, the army is in disorder.   (X.14)

Thus it is essential to improve one's own character. A leader should read widely on many subjects, listen well to others and seek their counsel, and take time to think in order to increase his wisdom. He must realize that having courage means not only taking risks but also having the courage to do what is militarily or ethically right. A leader must be sincere and humane in his dealings with subordinates, and when he must enforce discipline it should be done in a manner that is consistent and fair.

> ■ Now, the supreme requirements of generalship are a clear perception, the harmony of his host, a profound strategy coupled with far-reaching plans, an understanding of the seasons, and an ability to examine the human factors.   (IV.14 Tu Mu)

To create a strong military force one must lead by example. A good leader must know his people and share in their tough times as well as the good. A leader should also say what is important and then follow through.

Communicating strategy effectively is important so that the troops will be able to carry it out even in the leader's absence, by knowing his intent. To help them operate, one must assign clear and distinct missions, then select the right people to achieve those missions. Empower them within limits so that they can respond as circumstances dictate. As one gets to know his troops, one will find the best ways to motivate them and will learn to use each according to their abilities.

> ■ He whose generals are able and not interfered with by the sovereign will be victorious.   (III. 29)

Finally, leaders must implement policies to make the nation stronger. If one does so the people will gladly follow. Sun Tzu calls this "moral influence."

> ■ By moral influence I mean that which causes people to be in harmony with their leaders, so that they will accompany them in life and unto death without fear of mortal peril.   (I.4)

Now that we have discussed leadership, the capstone of the six principles, we move to the summary of all we have learned.

7 ■ The Changing Character of War
Ancient Principles for Future Battlefields

"Here begins our tale. The empire, long divided, must unite; long united, must divide. Thus it has ever been." So begins *Three Kingdoms*, the ancient historical Chinese novel. It tells the story of three warring kingdoms that fought each other during the civil war at the end of the Han dynasty. The situation *Three Kingdoms* speaks of, a world of ever-changing political situations and continual conflict between states, has been true throughout history and rings true even today.

After the end of the Cold War some wrote of "the end of history"—a world in which further military conflict would not occur, a world that would live primarily in peace. Unfortunately, that hoped-for dream has not become reality. Instead, small nations continue to fight one another, factions within nations battle in civil wars, and large nations exert influence and flex their muscles to gain strategic advantage. A count of conflicts within and between nations at the turn of the twenty-first century by the National Defense Council Foundation listed sixty-eight conflicts throughout the world. This was much higher than the thirty-five conflicts occurring at the end of the Cold War. While many of these struggles are being fought with conventional weapons, many nations are also deploying increasingly powerful weapons, including weapons of mass destruction (WMD). Examples at the time of this writing run the gamut from "rogue states" such as North Korea, Iran and Iraq to emerging superpowers such as China and India. Further, there exist countries that currently are not regional or superpowers but have that capability and potential should they choose to achieve it, such as Japan and Germany. According to the current CIA's Global Trends 2015 assessment, it is expected that the continued transfer of technology will enable many nations to either achieve WMD capability or expand their WMD arsenal's size and reach. For example, the CIA assessment expects China to be able to deploy both ICBMs targeted at the U.S. as well as hundreds of shorter range missiles for regional use; North Korea may have several nuclear missiles by 2005; Iran may have cruise missile capability by 2004; and Iraq could have a nuclear ICBM with the range to hit the U.S. by 2015.[1]

Geoffrey Blainey's classic study of the causes of war since 1700 shows that nations, in attempting to achieve their respective goals, fight because they disagree on their relative strength and ability to impose their will upon their rival. In choosing war each nation's leaders believe it is powerful enough to defeat the enemy, but reason and history tell us that in the end, only one nation's leaders will be proved correct.[2] As new powers such as China emerge and others like Russia decline, and as alliances dissolve while new ones form, the potential for disagreements on relative strengths increases. The only clear method of resolving differing beliefs on relative strengths is to go to war, which many leaders may prove willing to do. This leads to the conclusion that future wars, at varying levels of intensity, are extremely likely to occur.

Given the above, the question for the diplomatic and military leaders of these nations becomes how they can best use Sun Tzu's principles to achieve their goals. A nation may start by spreading the knowledge of Sun Tzu's concepts throughout both its military and its diplomatic institutions. As mentioned earlier, China's strategic approach is already heavily influenced by Sun Tzu and other ancient Chinese strategists. In the United States, Sun Tzu's influence is growing as more military leaders at the highest levels of the armed services propagate his ideas throughout the ranks. However, for the United States and its Western allies it is not only necessary to accept and understand Sun Tzu but also to analyze, compare, debate, and finally come to grips with the military theories of Sun Tzu versus those of Carl von Clausewitz, the West's leading military theorist.

East Meets West: Clausewitz vs. Sun Tzu

Let us look first at the major areas in which Clausewitz was correct, based on the writings in his treatise *On War*. One crucial point that

Clausewitz makes is that war is an extension of national policy and that military goals should aim to achieve and be subordinate to the nation's goals. The most famous quotation of Clausewitz is that "war is merely the continuation of policy by other means." Clausewitz elaborates on this, stating that "the political object is the goal, war is the means of reaching it, and means can never be considered in isolation from their purpose."

Sun Tzu's principles are consistent with Clausewitz in this respect. He realized that the national objectives should determine the wisdom of employing military power and then direct and guide its use once the decision has been made to go to war.

- ■ Normally, when the army is employed, the general first receives his commands from the sovereign. He assembles the troops and mobilizes the people. He blends the army into a harmonious entity and encamps it.   (VII.1)

Clausewitz was also correct in his understanding on the need for military "genius" in warfare, devoting an entire chapter early on in his book on the subject. He states that "genius refers to a very highly developed mental aptitude for a particular occupation"; given the arena we are discussing, a highly developed mental aptitude for conducting war. As elaborated in the chapter on leadership, Sun Tzu also recognizes the need for military genius.

Finally, Clausewitz coined the term "friction." He developed the viewpoint that friction in combat made what should be simple, difficult; therefore, it was critical to plan for and prepare hard to overcome friction. This is another example of consistency between the two military theorists.

However, there are a number of concepts Clausewitz puts forth that clearly differ from Sun Tzu and have had a negative effect on Western warfare. Many are interwoven and are derived first and foremost from Clausewitz's preference for "total warfare." Heavily influenced by the success of the French Revolution's mobilization of France's entire populace to fight, Clausewitz believed that a nation must mobilize all its resources (military, economic, diplomatic, social, etc.) to defeat its enemies. Clausewitz then stated that the primary aim of a country's military leadership was to launch a major attack in which the nation's main army would fight against the enemy's main forces in a "decisive battle" that would end the war favorably. The goal in fighting this decisive battle is the destruction of the enemy's army, preferably through a Cannae-like battle in which heavy fighting would win the day and friendly casualties were of little consequence. To quote Clausewitz in his second chapter, titled "Purpose and Means in War":

> Our discussion has shown that while in war many different roads can lead to the goal, to the attainment of the political object, fighting is the only possible means. Everything is governed by the supreme law, the *decision by force of arms*. . . . To sum up: of all the possible aims in war, the destruction of the enemy's armed forces always appears as the highest.

And to reiterate Clausewitz from his chapter "The Battle—Continued: The Use of Battle":

> No matter how a particular war is conducted and what aspects of its conduct we subsequently recognize as being essential, the very concept of war will permit us to make the following unequivocal statements:
>
> 1. Destruction of the enemy forces is the overriding principle of war, and, so far as positive action is concerned, the principal way to achieve our object.
> 2. Such destruction of forces can *usually* be accomplished only by fighting.
> 3. Only major engagements involving all forces lead to major success.
> 4. The greatest successes are obtained where all engagements coalesce into one great battle.
> 5. Only in a great battle does the commander in chief control operations in person; it is only natural that he should prefer to entrust the direction of the battle to himself.[3]

It is in these views that Clausewitz and Sun Tzu differ greatly, and it is Sun Tzu that history proves correct. First, while it is true that when warfare comes a nation must mobilize its resources to prevail, it is not necessarily the case that a country should seek "total war" in which the complete destruction of the enemy is the objective and the survival of one's own nation is put at risk. It was the desire for total war that led to the millions of casualties in the twentieth century's two world wars. In World War II the idea of total war between "races" led to inhuman warfare on the Eastern front and the enslavement and annihilation of millions of civilians.

Sun Tzu would argue that "limited" wars to achieve specific national objectives are preferable over unleashing the destructive and often uncontrollable forces of total war. Furthermore, even when engaged in a total war, it is important abide by humanitarian rules that limit human suffering and physical destruction.

The view that one should seek a decisive battle by engaging the main enemy force has also not been born out by history. Despite the clear victory by Hannibal against the main Roman army at Cannae, the battle was not decisive. If fact, the Carthaginian winners of the battle eventually lost the war. Gettysburg, Stalingrad, Midway, and other major battles have been major turning points in various wars but were not in themselves decisive in terms of leading to an immediate suing for peace by the loser. It was the search for a decisive battle in Southeast Asia that led the French to Dien Bien Phu and the Americans to Khe Sanh, neither of which led to ultimate success. Indeed, Clausewitz' writings, whether interpreted correctly or not, have led generals to direct attacks on enemy strengths, which in turn have led to huge casualties and limited success. Thus it is imperative that Western leaders not allow themselves to be misled by Clausewitz and instead look to Sun Tzu for guidance in this arena.

Employing Sun Tzu's Principles

In addition to studying and understanding Sun Tzu's concepts, future leaders must employ them both to achieve the nation's aims without war and, should conflict be unavoidable, during wartime itself.

Prior to military conflict it is critical to use Sun Tzu's principles to position the nation favorably to achieve its goals through either diplomacy or warfare. From a diplomatic standpoint one must employ Sun Tzu's guidance by forming strong alliances, breaking up the alliances of adversarial states, and obtaining strong strategic positions (diplomatic, geographic, industrial, etc.). From an intelligence viewpoint investments must be made to gather information on the enemy's national policy, strategies, military capabilities, and overall strengths and weaknesses. Intercepting and breaking the codes of adversaries is an important aim, given that knowing the enemy's thoughts is valuable in both peace and war.

Militarily, Sun Tzu's principles should influence both doctrine and training in preparing for a potential war. Doctrine that stresses the indirect approach over the direct, maneuver versus attrition, attacking weakness versus strength, and leadership over management is crucial.

Training must be hard and as close to real combat as possible, with emphasis on individual initiative, battle simulation, live fire exercises, and wargaming. Finally, potential revolutions in military affairs (RMAs) in areas such as network, space, and undersea warfare must be sought out, explored, debated, and incorporated where appropriate.

During Peacetime ("Between Wars")

Based on Sun Tzu's writings and the principles I've developed from them, prior to war there are five "deadly sins" a leader can commit. These are:

1. Blundering into conflict, either by not using military strength and diplomatic skills to achieve goals and/or fighting without understanding the implications of going to war.

2. Not knowing or misreading a potential adversary's intentions and capabilities.

3. Allowing potential adversaries to ally with one another and, conversely, failing to multiply one's strength through strong alliances.

4. Allowing potential adversaries to gain control of key strategic positions or resources and, conversely, failing to gain control of key strategic positions or resources for oneself.

5. Allowing military capabilities to deteriorate.

Let us examine each one, from the perspective of the current leading Western power, the United States, looking to the future.

Blundering into Conflict

■ War is a grave matter; one is apprehensive lest men embark upon it without due reflection. (I.1 Li Ch'uan)

A potential future opponent of the United States is the People's Republic of China. The most likely trouble spot in which their interests conflict is Taiwan, the island nation off the coast of China. The potential for conflict is the result of the end of China's civil war between the communists under Mao and the Nationalists led by Chiang Kai-shek. After Chiang lost the war he retreated to Taiwan, planning to continue the war from there. Protected by the American navy, Taiwan was safe from invasion by the communist forces. Although Chiang was never able to make good his threat to return to the mainland, both he and the communists have maintained that Taiwan is part of China.

While the international status of Taiwan changed after the recognition of the communist government, it has recently made moves towards claiming independence from China. As the PRC has become stronger and other former parts of China have been recovered (e.g., Hong Kong), the Communist government has striven to reclaim Taiwan. In the process the PRC has not ruled out the use of armed force. Simultaneously, the U.S. administration in power from 1992 to 2000 has moved to limit arms sales to Taiwan and improve its relationship with the PRC, viewing it not as a potential adversary but as a "strategic partner." These moves have raised doubts about whether the U.S. would maintain its traditional promise to come to Taiwan's aid should it be attacked by the Communists.

As discussed earlier, wars start because nations either misread their enemy's resolve and intent or they predict that they are relatively stronger than their potential opponent should warfare result. The doubts about the resolve of the United States to protect Taiwan and the PRC's view of the U.S. as a declining power (discussed in chapter 3) raise considerably the chances of conflict breaking out between the United States and mainland China. Thus it is important that the U.S. use its military strength to protect Taiwan and use its diplomatic skills to clearly communicate to the PRC that this is its policy.

Not Knowing or Misreading a Potential Adversary's Intentions and Capabilities

■ Therefore I say, "Know the enemy and know yourself; in a hundred battles you will never be in peril. When you are ignorant of the enemy but know yourself, your chances of winning or losing are equal. If ignorant both of your enemy and yourself, you are certain in every battle to be in peril." (III.31–33)

The United States faces many potential adversaries, both in the form of nation states and terrorist organizations. Each day, as technology progresses, the ability of these adversaries to inflict harm on U.S. military units, national infrastructure, or civilians increases. To protect itself and achieve its national objectives, the United States must first understand the objectives, intentions, world view, policies, strategies, and plans of these potential adversaries. For this task human intelligence, communications intercepts, and code-breaking assets are critical, as they allow insights into the minds and plans of these potential enemies. The U.S. must also use its technical capabilities, such as satellite photos, combined with the information garnered above, to determine the capabilities of adversaries. Knowledge of both intentions and capabilities are crucial because it is important to know not only what the enemy can do, but what they will do.

Allowing Potential Adversaries to Ally with One Another and Failing to Multiply One's Strength through Strong Alliances

- One ignorant of the plans of neighboring states cannot prepare alliances in good time; if ignorant of the conditions of mountains, forests, dangerous defiles, swamps and marshes he cannot conduct the march of an army; if he fails to make use of native guides he cannot gain the advantages of the ground. A general ignorant of even one of these three matters is unfit to command the armies of a Hegemonic King. (XI.51)

Currently, given that it is the only remaining superpower and that it benefits from a strong set of alliances in place (such as NATO), the United States may feel relatively secure. However, the thawing of the international situation after the Cold War has freed nations' policies and relationships, allowing new alliances to form and old ones to decay.

China may choose to assert a more prominent role through alliances with various nations. An emerging relationship began in the late 1990s between China and Russia, with one aim being to challenge the United States. China has also been seeking influence through arms and technology sales to American adversaries such as Iran and North Korea. And, ties have been strengthened with U.S. Cold War adversaries such as Cuba, a nation that could potentially play the same role as client state as China did with the former Soviet Union.

As Europe continues to become more integrated through further political and economic agreements there is movement to build a pan-European military structure beyond NATO, which potentially would exclude the United States. In Asia, Japan and India are major players. Japan will watch closely as the U.S. and China dynamic plays out. Its relationship with the United States will evolve based on how much its leadership believes Japan can depend on the U.S. in time of need and how it defines its national interests. India, a nuclear power whose government is no longer ruled solely by the Congress Party as in the past, will also be seeking to assert its strength.

The United States must pre-empt moves by potential adversaries to combine in alliances that would threaten her interests. At the same time the U.S. must maintain its ties with traditional European and Asian allies while looking for new ones to tilt the balance of power in its favor.

Allowing Potential Adversaries to Gain Control of Key Strategic Positions or Resources and Failing to Gain Control of Key Strategic Positions or Resources for Oneself

- **When one man defends a narrow mountain defile which is like sheep's intestines or the door of a dog house, he can withstand one thousand. (V.25 Chang Yü)**

The loss of military and technological secrets to China during the 1990s was one area in which the United States suffered the loss of key strategic information. Future Chinese access to key technology and strategic resources must be denied. The control of the operation of the Panama Canal to Chinese companies, while appearing unimportant, does provide China the potential ability to prevent or delay access to the canal to the United States Navy through sabotage of the vulnerable locks. The U.S. needs to determine the extent of this threat and develop methods to deal with it. Other vital sea lanes through which much of America's commerce and oil supplies reach the U.S. are also strategic positions that must be guarded. Control of strategic positions and resources such as these will enable the United States to achieve its goals without resorting to warfare; or, should war break out, allow the U.S. to achieve military victory.

Allowing Military Capabilities to Deteriorate

- **It is a doctrine of war not to assume the enemy will not come, but rather to rely on one's readiness to meet him; not to presume that he will not attack, but rather to make one's self invincible. (VIII.16)**

After the Cold War and the Persian Gulf War the United States dramatically decreased the size of its armed forces. While a diminished threat made this decrease possible and even tolerable strategically, the impact of the reduction in force was compounded by numerous other policies that have led to a deterioration in the capabilities of U.S. forces. Smaller budgets in the 1990s led to poor pay for service people, reduction in training time, lack of equipment, and delay in the implementation of potential RMAs. Extended deployment of forces in a "policing role" in areas of dubious national interest (e.g., Haiti) overextended the armed forces and made the personal lives of service people more difficult. A focus on extending the inclusiveness of the military (for example, women and homosexuals), while understandable in a democratic society, complicated the military's main task: winning the next war. All the above factors contributed to an exodus by critical officers and NCOs from the services and the inability to make recruiting quotas for new soldiers and sailors.

As history has shown (including a rapid demobilization following World War II that arguably tempted the Soviet Union into challenging the U.S. and resulted in the Cold War), the damage done to military force by its government can take years to repair. To retain its superpower status and its stated strategy of being able to fight and win two major wars simultaneously, the United States must maintain a military capability that will keep in place the doctrine, training regimen, weaponry, and force structure to defend U.S. interests. This needs to include a missile defense system designed to protect the United States and its allies (even if its ability to shoot down incoming missiles is not one hundred percent it will introduce a huge element of uncertainty in the minds of enemy leaders), causing them to refrain from threats clearly articulated to allies and potential foes alike as a purely defensive weapon. Only by maintaining its military can the United States ensure that it has a credible force that can be deployed to protect U.S. interests, either to add support to its diplomatic moves or, should those fail, through armed combat.

During War

As there are a number of deadly sins a leader can commit prior to warfare, there are also errors a leader can commit once a nation goes to war (see Table 7.1).

Many of the above "sins" should be obvious by now and do not require further illumination. A better topic for discussion is how leaders can implement Sun Tzu's approach to strategy in wartime planning and

1. Attacking strength
2. Not knowing the enemy
3. Not knowing one's own strengths and weaknesses
4. Not knowing the environment
5. Moving too slowly
6. Failing to practice deception
7. Following an attrition-only strategy
8. Using only the direct approach
9. Poor leadership
10. Protracted warfare

TABLE 7.1   Ten Deadly Sins during Wartime

operations. This process, outlined below, has six steps that flow naturally from the six principles. Although parts of each of the six principles may apply to more than one step, for simplicity's sake I have made them correspond directly. This process can be implemented for strategy at either a global, theater, army, or corps level.

1. **Win All Without Fighting: Prioritize Threats and Determine Strategic Focus**
   Once engaged in war, the first step the national leadership must take is to determine which enemy threats pose the highest threats or provide the best opportunity to achieve the nation's objectives if successfully attacked. The end result of this step is a prioritization of enemies, theaters of war, or military threats, leading in turn to a prioritization of resources for each one.

2. **Avoid Strength, Attack Weakness: Develop Attacks Against the Enemy's Weakness**
   Once a priority has been established and resources allocated, the next focus must be to determine that chosen enemy's strengths and weaknesses, as well as understanding one's own. Prioritization of the enemy's weaknesses can then be done by elevating in importance those weaknesses that, if attacked successfully, would severely unbalance and degrade that adversary's ability to fight. Next, the enemy's three to five most critical weaknesses should be studied and two to three potential attacks developed for each.

3. Deception and Foreknowledge: Wargame and Plan for Surprise

Each potential attack developed above must now be wargamed, using the knowledge of the enemy to play out the moves and countermoves that could occur. It is especially important to forecast how the enemy might leverage its strengths in counterattacks. As part of the wargaming exercise it is critical to think through how surprise might be achieved against the enemy by disguising the attacks with deceptive moves.

4. Shape the Enemy: Integrate Best Attacks to Defeat the Enemy

This is the point to select the enemy's one or two key weaknesses to exploit. The results of the wargaming will provide the insight to do so and will also assist in deciding which set of attacks to utilize, and how they can best be integrated for maximum impact on the enemy. This becomes of the overall strategy.

5. Speed and Preparation: Ready Attacks and Release Them

To support the strategy, preparations (orders, logistical support, troop deployments) are required for successfully executing the integrated set of attacks. Then the attacks must be executed with speed, shock, and firepower.

6. Leadership: Reinforce Success, Starve Failure

Once the attacks have been launched, the leadership must support the strategy with prompt action, determining quickly which attacks are succeeding and which are not. Leaders must ruthlessly reinforce success and starve failure.

These are the essential steps in this strategy process; each step is discussed in greater detail below. While there is obviously no exact recipe for strategic success, this process provides the structure for creating a strategy based on Sun Tzu's principles. Keys to successful use of this approach are the integration of the principles (using them together to reinforce one another), simplicity, and creativity. In the end it is the leader's knowledge of the principles, military genius, and character that will ultimately determine success or failure.

1. Win All Without Fighting: Prioritize Threats and Determine Strategic Focus

The first decision to be made after the outbreak of conflict is to prioritize enemy threats. Factors to consider are the importance of different theaters (based on alliances, resources, strategic positions, etc.), the danger posed by the different threats to the nation's survival, and opportunities for achieving the nation's objectives.

One strategy is to target the most dangerous threat as the one that should receive the highest priority. During World War II the United States and the British Empire agreed that Germany was a more dangerous threat than Japan, and built a strategy based on allocating the majority of their joint resources to defeat Germany first. The rationale for this approach was the need to keep the Soviet Union in the war, destroy Germany's industrial strength, strangle its technical capability to produce new weaponry (rockets, jets, advanced submarines), and end attacks on the United Kingdom from German-occupied territory.

This strategic approach has the advantage of dealing directly with the primary threat. Although attacking the strongest enemy appears to be a less subtle and more direct approach, as long as one attacks that enemy's weaknesses with an indirect approach, success can be achieved.

Another strategic option is to target one or two of the weaker enemies in an alliance with the goal of eliminating them from the conflict. This approach has the advantage of knocking away support from the primary enemy and of leveraging one's strength against the weaker enemies. This was Churchill's preferred approach in World War I, in which he hoped to knock German allies such as Turkey out of the war by using Britain's advantage in naval mobility.

Obviously, in this first step intelligence about the capabilities of all the nation's enemies is crucial. The collection, augmentation, and analysis of this intelligence is essential to truly divine the correct enemy to concentrate against. The end result of this step is a prioritization of enemies, theaters of war, or military threats, leading in turn to a prioritization of resources for each one.

2. Avoid Strength, Attack Weakness: Develop Attacks Against the Enemy's Weakness

Now that a enemy target has been selected to focus on, the next step is to determine its strengths and weaknesses. One should look at its military forces: are there weaknesses in its command and control infra-structure or weaponry? In a particular branch of their services (naval, air, armor)? Have their codes been broken and read? Does their in-dustrial base have any potential bottlenecks that could be targeted, or can access to critical resources such as energy be cut off? Is there any internal opposition that can be supported to create unrest, perform sab-otage, or provide intelligence?

All potential areas must be examined for weaknesses and detailed. The weaknesses should then be prioritized based on their vulnerability to attack and ability to wreak significant damage upon the enemy.

Next, it is important to determine the enemy's strengths and list the main ones. Then complete this step by listing the strengths and weaknesses of one's own nation and forces. This will show where strengths might be leveraged against enemy weaknesses, which strengths the enemy might employ against friendly forces, and friendly weak-nesses that need to be improved.

The final step for each of the major enemy weakness is to develop two to three attacks that would be effective against it.

3. Deception and Foreknowledge: Wargame and Plan for Surprise

At this point there should be roughly five weaknesses and three attacks for each weakness—essentially fifteen attacks to wargame. This may seem like too many; however, if these attacks are wargamed thoroughly much strategic ground can be covered, many new options illuminated, and potential enemy attacks uncovered. This effort will provide great knowledge and insights about potential paths the conflict may take.

As the wargaming is conducted it is important to think creatively about how the direct and indirect approaches that could be used to surprise and deceive the enemy. One should also determine if there is something the enemy's leadership views as important that could be seized, thereby controlling their emotions and actions. Also, it is essen-tial to think through, as countermove follows countermove, how alli-ances might be affected. As you think through the enemy's potential responses remember to take into account the enemy's strengths, since it will likely rely heavily on these to repel your assaults or launch its own. Wargaming is to be continued until it is determined which attacks would be most successful.

4. Shape the Enemy: Integrate Best Attacks to Defeat the Enemy

After wargaming, the next step is to take the six or seven best outcomes, and pick the three or four attacks that, when used in synergy, will yield the best *integrated* strategy. It is important to look for attacks that build on one another, make good use of available resources, cause confusion in the enemy leadership, and can be used as combinations of the direct and indirect approach. Once combined appropriately, these attacks become the overall strategy; used together they shape the adversary.

5. Speed and Preparation: Ready Attacks and Release Them

With an overall, integrated strategy in place, it is now necessary to fill in the details so that it can be implemented. Specific details of each attack must be put on a timeline and methods to coordinate them must be laid out. Orders need to be relayed to lower commands, logistics put in place, and coordination with supporting arms carried out.

Finally, a contingency plan must be developed in case the strategy does not bear its expected fruit. The wargaming should provide ample information to build a credible contingency plan. Now the strategy must be executed with speed and shock, released in a timed series of moves, with blow following blow. The enemy must not be allowed to regain balance once the attacks have started; assault must follow assault in rapid succession to keep the enemy off balance.

6. Leadership: Reinforce Success, Starve Failure

Soon after the initial attacks have been launched it will become clear as to which ones are working or which are failing. Assuming the proper intelligence network is in place, information will rapidly become available that illuminates how the enemy is reacting, where attacks have been successful, and where forward progress has been stymied. This is the time when strong leadership must be exercised.

The commander must not fall into the trap of ignoring successful attacks by trying to prop up failing ones or lose nerve as the situation develops. The commander must keep a clear head and reinforce successful attacks by funneling resources to them. Those successful ones will pay off many times over.

At the same time the commander must stop allocating reinforcements to attacks that are failing. One must not be deluded into thinking that a failing attack can be rescued. Once an attack is launched and is proving unsuccessful, the element of surprise is gone. The resources that must be committed to revive an attack once surprise and momentum are lost are huge, and must be weighed against the small probability of success.

Postwar

Sun Tzu's principles apply not only before and during conflict; their use is essential when planning for the postwar balance of power and the global environment. Postwar planning is important because it is not enough to militarily "win" the war. The end objective is to achieve greater security and a more favorable global situation in which the nation can survive and prosper.

Planning for the postwar world must at a minimum begin coincident with the commencement of hostilities—but preferably, planning will begin even before conflict breaks out. Then the hoped-for postwar view can become the basis for wartime strategies, ensuring that those strategies implemented enable the achievement of postwar goals.

For example, while the United States made a mistake in World War II by following a policy of unconditional surrender (which, as discussed earlier, may have prolonged the war and enabled the Soviet Union to extend its power), it also did many things right. One of these was the creation of the United Nations during the war. Another was the postwar Marshall Plan, which rejuvenated Europe. And in Asia, General MacArthur instituted a new constitution for Japan after it was subjugated. All of these efforts to build a new world contributed to greater security for the United States and laid the base for greater prosperity in the Western world.

Beyond postwar planning, there must be an effort during the war to limit its damage by following internationally accepted rules of conduct toward soldiers and noncombatants. Not only is this the humane thing to do—making the war less brutal—but it also makes peace easier to attain and will reduce the destruction that must be repaired once the war is over. Admittedly, this is more difficult in a total war versus a limited one, or in a war of competing ideologies versus one between countries that share similar perspectives or governmental types. However, doing so will avoid the barbarities such as that experienced on the Eastern Front in World War II, in which differing ideologies led to cruelties, death, and destruction on a scale never before seen.

Summary

■ If a general who heeds my strategy is employed he is certain to win. Retain him! When one who refuses to listen to my strategy is employed, he is certain to be defeated. Dismiss him! (I.15)

While in this book we have discussed many examples of the brilliance of Germany's armed forces in the twentieth century, one must recall that Germany was also instrumental in starting (and then losing) two World Wars. A major reason for these errors was poor strategy and ignoring the fundamental principles of Sun Tzu.

Blinded by paranoia and consciously avoiding efforts to diplomatically break up the allies arrayed against her, Germany entered the First World War with a strategy that had two major flaws. The first was that it depended on a single decisive battle at the beginning of the war to defeat France and Britain. Winning that battle would in turn leave Germany free to redeploy those force in the East to destroy Russia. No strategy or contingency plan existed if victory was not achieved in the first battle in the West.

The second strategic error Germany's generals made was ignoring the lack of military resources necessary for winning the decisive battle. Prior wargaming had concluded that the German Army required thirteen corps to achieve victory in the decisive attack on the Allies' left flank. However, in reality, nowhere near that many troops were available. The German general staff's excellent strategic plan was based completely on soldiers who did not exist.

After Germany failed to achieve success in the first battle and the war dragged on, its leaders' focus turned to operational excellence, encapsulated in the stormtrooper concept. In fact, General Ludendorff, the leader of the German Army, forbade the use of the term "strategy" at headquarters, and only allowed his staff to discuss and use the word "tactics." In the end, excellent operational execution failed to achieve a favorable strategic outcome.

World War II again found Germany favoring operational excellence over strategy. In their haste to rearm Germany's forces with the latest in weaponry, military leaders focused on tactical, not strategic requirements. As a result, they did not select the proper arms to match Germany's political goals, they did not coordinate weapons selection between the navy, army, and air force, and their rapid buildup of Germany's military might created enemies of countries that were initially supportive of Germany, such as Britain.

Next, even though Germany's main political goal was living space in the East, German diplomacy failed at keeping the Western powers from entering the war against her. Once the war began, the German Luftwaffe was unable to defeat Britain because its aircraft had not been designed for that task. Instead of finishing off Britain, Germany attacked the Soviet Union, forcing herself into fighting a two-front war where the resources to win were lacking. Another diplomatic folly was Germany's choice to declare war on the United States after Pearl Harbor, recklessly adding to the list of enemies arrayed against her. Finally, as the war turned against Germany and she went on the defensive, Hitler's policy of defending every inch of ground rather than using the mobility of German forces to hit an overextended enemy led to huge losses at Stalingrad, in Africa, in Normandy, and numerous other battles.

In the end, the operational and tactical excellence of Germany's armed forces, exemplified by the prowess of the Wehrmacht's armored divisions, the Luftwaffe's jet fighter planes and rockets, and the Kriegsmarine's technologically advanced submarines was insufficient for victory. It only extended the length of the war and increased the human and physical destruction endured by all. Germany in the twentieth century failed to emulate the brilliant diplomacy of the kind Bismarck had practiced, believing instead that military considerations superseded diplomacy and politics once "the iron dice rolled." It proved to be Germany's undoing.[4]

Thus two things are clear. First, neither strategic nor tactical excellence is sufficient by itself; the two must accompany one another for decisive victory. If a nation has the right strategy but executes it poorly, it will not be successful. Similarly, a nation that executes a poor strategy with excellence will also fail in war. To achieve victory a nation must have a creative, powerful strategy and carry it out with will, dispatch, and force.

Secondly, it is necessary to have a set of principles to guide the nation's strategy. I believe those principles are the ones outlined in this book. By integrating these principles into a strategy, being creative and disciplined in their application, and practicing simplicity in execution, a commander can be victorious. Through integration of the six principles one will achieve the maximum synergistic effect. To integrate these principles effectively a leader must be both creative and disciplined, open to new ideas yet able to ruthlessly pare those ideas down to a simple strategy and execute it, able to logically assess the environment and the strategy and yet have the heart, will, and sense of urgency to motivate his forces to implement that strategy expeditiously.

- ■ Therefore when those experienced in war move they make no mistakes; when they act, their resources are limitless.   (X.25)

National leaders ignore Sun Tzu's principles at their peril, for they have a huge responsibility for the people and their actions must be considered and thoughtful. By using these principles wisely a leader can achieve the nation's goals and ensure its continued survival and prosperity. There is no greater burden one can carry.

- ■ And therefore the general who understands war is the Minister of the people's fate and arbiter of the nation's destiny.   (II.21)

In the next and last chapter we will look at the unique character of the war on terrorism and find principles of Sun Tzu that can provide powerful strategic and tactical methods of combatting this unconventional form of warfare.

8 ■ The War on Terrorism
Applying Sun Tzu's Principles

■ And therefore the general who understands war is the minister
of the people's fate and arbiter of the nation's destiny. (II.21)

I completed the previous chapter in early 2001 with the above quotation and submitted the manuscript that would become this book before
the events of September 11, 2001. Once the terrorist attacks occurred
and their magnitude became apparent, it was clear that a chapter ad-
dressing the application of Sun Tzu's principles to the war on terrorism
was needed. The significance and meaning of the above quotation became even more important and twenty-five centuries later Sun Tzu's
words still ring true: how U.S. leaders carry out the war on terrorism
will, to a large extent, determine America's fate and Western civilization's destiny.

Sun Tzu's Principles Used against the West?

Unfortunately for the United States, the terrorist attacks on the World
Trade Center in New York and the Pentagon in Washington, D.C.
were effected by many of Sun Tzu's principles. Whether or not the
perpetrators of the attack, the al-Qaeda (The Base) leadership, had studied *The Art of War* is unknown; on the tactical level, however, the

methods employed in the attacks and the damage inflicted were consistent with Sun Tzu's concepts.[1]

For example, the terrorists avoided strength and attacked weakness. Rather than hit a militarily hardened target such as a front-line base or operational unit, al-Qaeda decided to hit an exposed civilian target (the World Trade Center) and a military headquarters (the Pentagon). The White House itself was also a potential target for the third plane that was brought down by civilians over Pennsylvania. The high concentration of people in these buildings, their lack of defense against a suicidal airplane attack, and their symbolic importance made them attractive, vulnerable targets from a terrorist viewpoint. In accordance with this principle, al-Qaeda terrorists took advantage of poor airline security, bringing onboard "weapons" (knives and box cutters) that were insufficient to raise concern but sufficient to gain control of the airplanes. Finally, the choice of airplanes itself was consistent with this principle. Civilian planes were highly vulnerable to takeover and yet their characteristics (long range, high speed, and explosive potential when filled with highlyflammable jet fuel) made up for the lack of a powerful weapon.

Deception was also employed. Although the planning for the attack was complex and took several years to develop and deploy, al-Qaeda was able to maintain operational security over that time. While U.S. intelligence agencies did have many clues and signs available to them they were not able to put the pieces together until after the attacks. This was due in part to the use of sophisticated communications methods by al-Qaeda operatives, including the use of coded and hidden Internet messages. The final pieces of deception took place during the operation itself; the terrorists did not dress in a manner that would draw attention to themselves, but instead dressed like Western businessmen. Last, they deceived both the pilots and passengers until it was too late for any of them to take action (at least on the first two planes), telling them that if they cooperated no one would get hurt.

Preparation for the attacks was considerable. Using their Taliban allies al-Qaeda had a secure base in Afghanistan from which to plan their operations, recruit and train terrorists. Over a long period of time U.S. targets were scoped out and selected, safe houses set up in Europe and America, money flowed to support the operation, and terrorist pilots were trained in Florida. Once the operation was in process speed was employed; the attacks happened so fast that the U.S. government could not effectively respond. As we know, only those heroes on

United Airlines Flight 93, the third airplane, could do something in time.

An Important Principle Overlooked

While tactically the operation was a success, the 9/11 attacks at this point appear to be much like the Japanese attack on Pearl Harbor; a tactical victory but a strategic mistake. The killing of innocent civilians, the surprise nature of the attack, and the fact that it took place on American soil assured a massive response by the United States. In this manner the terrorists ignored Sun Tzu's first principle: win-all-without-fighting. They have thus brought the military power, resources, and intelligence of the American people to bear against them. While in the future al-Qaeda and other terrorists may achieve some success, as of this writing the terrorists have suffered serious reverses. Those will be discussed shortly. In the interim, how could the terrorists miscalculate the ability and willingness of the United States to respond?

To answer this we must go back to Geoffrey Blainey's analysis (see Chapter Seven) of why warfare occurs in the first place. Nations (or in this case, terrorist organizations in league with nations) fight because they disagree on their relative strength and ability to impose their will upon the enemy and thus achieve their goals.[2] In the case of al-Qaeda, their primary tactical goals seem to be to push the United States and the West out of Islamic territories (especially the "holy land" of Saudi Arabia) and eliminate U.S. support of Israel (thus allowing that nation to be eradicated). Ultimately, the goal may be to create a pan-Islamic "Caliphate" that could challenge the West militarily and politically. The terrorists' targeting of the West in general and the United States in particular is based, in my opinion, on several things: a perceived "un-godliness" of Western culture, resentment of its military, economic, diplomatic, and cultural power, a fanatical religious belief in Islam, and the call for jihad (holy war) against nonbelievers.

While it is difficult to believe al-Qaeda underestimated the military power of the United States (given its relatively recent display during the Gulf War against an Arab state) it is highly probable that the terrorist organization believed the U.S. lacked the will to respond. That belief, combined with fanatical religious belief in the rightness and ultimate success of their cause, are key factors that led to the initiation of the 9/11 attacks.

Given recent history and prior U.S. responses to terrorist attacks it is not totally surprising that the al-Qaeda leadership believed that America lacked the will to respond effectively. For while many view the war with Islamic terrorism as starting on 9/11, in truth it has been going on for many years. In 1979, militant Islamic students in Iran took over the U.S. embassy and held 66 Americans hostage; this was most likely the first shot in this war. Although the hostages were eventually returned after 444 days, the humbling of the United States was instrumental in illustrating to nations and to terrorists alike that terrorism could be successful. Three elements contributed to the increased oc-curence of terrorist attacks: first it would be impossible to engage the United States in direct, conventional military conflict and win (reinforced by the defeat of Iraq, one of the most powerful Islamic nations, in the Gulf War). Second, terrorist acts are a relatively inexpensive means of achieving political aims compared to conventional and even guerilla warfare. Third, the United States was often unwilling or unable to respond effectively.

In April 1983, the U.S. embassy in Beirut, Lebanon was bombed, leaving 63 people dead. Later that same year the U.S. Marine barracks in Beirut were bombed, with 241 dead. The year 1985 saw two high-jackings: TWA Flight 847 from Athens, Greece, and the Italian cruise ship *Achille Lauro* off the Egyptian coast, both of which led to the killing of Americans. In December, 1988, Pan Am Flight 103 was blown up by a bomb over Lockerbie, Scotland, with 270 dead. In 1993 the first attack on the World Trade Center by Islamic terrorists occurred, followed in 1998 by bombings at Khobar Towers in Saudi Arabia, U.S. embassies in Kenya and Tanzania, and the attack on the U.S. Navy destroyer *USS Cole* in 2000. The United States did make some military effort to respond. President Carter attempted but failed to rescue the Iranian hostages at Desert One; President Reagan bombed Libya in 1986; the Achille Lauro hijackers were captured, and cruise missiles were launched at Osama bin Laden during the Clinton administration. Many times the terrorist attacks were treated more as crimes than political acts. Neither the limited military actions nor attempts to catch terrorists with criminal methods were particularly effective in preventing further attacks.[3]

Contributing to the belief that the United States lacked the will to engage and defeat terrorism were the series of events that occurred in Somalia in 1993. U.S. Rangers and the elite Delta Force were in Somalia, a country suffering from famine due to an ongoing civil war between rival clans. The U.S. forces' overall mission had evolved from a focus on humanitarian aid and minimizing the impact of the famine (implemented by the U.S. Marine Corps, who left once their mission was completed) to an engagment in the civil war. Drawn into the conflict to stop the suffering and impose order, the Rangers and Delta Force soldiers were involved in capturing leaders of clans involved in the fighting. On October 3, the mission of the joint Special Forces team was to capture two key lieutenants of Mohamed Farrah Aidid, leader of the Habr Gidr clan. As those who have read the book or seen the movie *Black Hawk Down* know, the mission was transformed from a quick and bloodless capture and extraction to a bloody and prolonged fire-fight in the middle of the city of Mogadishu.

The cause of this transformation has many layers. While there was excellent intelligence on the target and the units involved were well-trained, there was a lack of preparation and a gap in the knowledge about Habr Gidr's capabilities. The capture mission, including a helicopter insertion of the Delta Force unit to capture the leaders, and the Ranger team to provide force protection, went smoothly. However, the situation deteriorated quickly from there. Aidid's men were able to congregate much more rapidly then expected, surrounding the raiding force. As this was happening the extraction force got lost in the maze of Mogadishu's streets. As American helicopters hovered overhead to provide directions and fire support, Aidid's men began launching rocket-propelled grenades (RPGs). This was quite unexpected, as the U.S. forces believed that the hot back blast from an RPG made it impossible to fire them upward without the blast scalding the firer. However, Aidid's men overcame this obstacle by digging holes that would contain the blast, allowing them to shoot down first one Black Hawk helicopter, then another. The lack of an on-call extraction team for downed helicopters was another oversight, forcing the raiding and extraction forces to move through the streets on foot to reach the downed choppers. Lack of coordination between the Delta Force operatives and their supporting force of Rangers magnified problems, leading to small units being cut off from one another and surrounded by Habr Gidr clansmen. Now that the raiding force was in trouble, the lack of coordination with the other U.N. peacekeepers in the area (who had tanks and personnel carriers) meant that it was hours before a new force could be put together to extract all the surrounded men. The need to coordinate with a non-U.S. team was due to the lack of a strong U S. extraction force in Somalia. Shortly before the raid, U.S. Secretary of Defense Les Aspin had turned down a request for an

AC-130 Specter gunship for air support as well as armored tanks and personnel carriers. This most likely led to higher casualties among the Special Forces team.

Militarily the mission was accomplished; the two leaders were captured and huge casualties were inflicted on the Habr Gidr clan's forces. However, in the process eighteen American soldiers were killed, one captured, many more wounded, and four helicopters lost. These losses and the television images of Somalis dragging the bodies of American soldiers provoked the immediate pull-out of American forces. This immediate pull-out formed and reinforced America's enemies view that she lacked staying power, the will to engage in conflicts, and would retreat over even small losses. In his book *Black Hawk Down*, Bowden states in the Afterword, "The lesson our retreat taught the world's terrorists and despots is that killing a few American soldiers, even at the cost of more than five hundred of your own fighters, is enough to spook Uncle Sam." He goes on to state in the same paragraph, "Military credibility is not just a matter of national pride. It lessens the chances of war because enemies are less inclined to challenge America. This principle is especially important in a world with only one military superpower. The eight-hundred pound gorilla's only weakness is his will. Routing Aidid would have, in the long run, saved American lives."[4] Although written in November of 1999, almost two years before 9/11, Bowden's words are eerily prophetic, especially given that there is evidence that al-Qaeda operatives were aiding and assisting the Habr Gidr clan during the Somalian conflict.

But it isclear that the United States' attack on Afghanistan, in concert with her Allies, wasnot expected by al-Qaeda. Though the terrorist organization may have implicitly employed some of Sun Tzu's principles, it failed to "win-all-without-fighting."

Conventional Warfare vs. Unconventional Warfare

After World War II, the two major superpowers fielded large armies in Europe to protect their spheres of influence. The NATO forces of the West faced those of the Soviet Warsaw Pact. Both were composed of "conventional" forces: tanks, artillery, planes, and mechanized infantry. Each force was designed to defeat the other but the NATO forces also played another role, that of a nuclear "tripwire" that would unleash American nuclear missiles and bombs against the Warsaw Pact forces should a NATO defeat look probable.

To avoid the chance the tripwire might be activated it was important that NATO forces have the conventional strength to also serve as a deterrent to attack. This was particularly important since it was not a certainty (at least in European minds) that Washington would risk a nuclear attack on the U.S. by launching one against the Soviet forces in Europe. Conventional forces were critical as they served as protection for Europe (and indirectly, the United States), both against Soviet conventional forces and the chance that a conventional war would escalate and "go nuclear".

The fact that neither the United States nor the Soviet Union wanted to risk the chance of direct conflict becoming a nuclear exchange led to limited wars fought by "proxy" nations. These wars often had the characteristics of "unconventional" war. For example, the Korean War started with a conventional attack by massed North Korean divisions styled on the tank and artillery-heavy Soviet model. Once destroyed by United States conventional forces, the unconventional strategy and tactics of the Chinese armies turned the tide back in the Communists' favor. As we saw in Chapter three, the Chinese were able to infiltrate stealthily North Korea with huge infantry armies; they avoided detection by U.N. forces with tactics they had learned from their guerilla victories in China itself—a war in which Mao Tse-tung carefully studied his copy of The Art of War. When those armies launched a surprise attack on U.S. and U.N. forces the latter were sent reeling back south.

The war in Viet Nam was next; guerilla tactics were utilized to wear down the will of the United States to continue the conflict. American arming and support of the anti-Soviet Mujahadeen in Afghanistan is another example. Other guerilla conflicts in South America, Asia and Africa also sprouted, making unconventional and guerilla warfare a hallmark of the Cold War.

With the end of the Cold War, the discrediting of Communism as a philosophy worth fighting for, and the emergence of the United States as the only superpower, the scene changed. The Persian Gulf War was the first major war of the new era. The devastating defeat of Iraq by the United States and the Coalition made manifest the power of U.S. conventional forces. Interestingly enough, General Norman Schwartzkopf, was himself a student of Sun Tzu and employed tactics from The Art of War to win his victory. The defeat of Iraq by the United States with minimal casualties made it apparent to all that fighting the United States toe-to-toe was a serious strategic mistake.

For some Islamic states and terrorist organizations the lessons of the Gulf War reinforced those learned in wars against America's ally, Israel.

Conventional wars with Israel, especially the Six-Day War in 1967, always ended in defeat for Islamic forces. However, the use of guerilla warfare, such as that against Israel in Lebanon in the early 1980s, and the use of terror tactics, employed by the Arabs starting in the late 1960s, could be used to achieve one's objectives.

Conventional wars require significant resources: tanks, artillery, planes, armored vehicles, trucks, et cetera. These forces are expensive to build and require a high level of technological skill to operate and to maintain. If destroyed, they represent a huge loss and waste of precious resources. They must be replaced to achieve the nation's prior level of strength. Guerilla and terrorist forces, however, are less expensive to create and require less technological skill to maintain, thus they are often the weapon of choice for those with fewer resources. Both less sophisticated and cheaper, terrorist forces can be sustained over a long time period, wearing down the enemy in a protracted war. The stealth and secrecy inherent in fielding these forces can make them harder to destroy than conventional forces and allow nation-states to disassociate themselves from their attacks, providing a cover behind which that nation-state can hide. Whereas conventional forces tend to be composed of professional troops the guerilla/terrorist is often ideologically driven. Because they are at a military disadvantage when fighting conventional forces guerillas and terrorists focus on weak targets; in the case of guerillas they might target isolated military units or poorly-defended bases. Terrorists may also focus on military targets when the target is attractive enough yet insecure (e.g. the U.S. Marine barracks in Lebanon) but are more likely to attack police units and civilian targets. Lastly, while conventional forces often destroy the physical ability of the enemy to fight by massive attacks that incur significant destruction, unconventional forces tend to target the psychological will to resist through pin-pointed attacks on softer targets that may also have political or social significance.

The Limitations of Unconventional Wars

Historically, however, the problem with unconventional warfare is that it typically cannot achieve victory on its own. The war that Spanish irregulars fought against Napoleon's troops gave the name to "guerilla" warfare (little war). While their attacks wore down the French it was the conventional British forces under Wellington that succeeded in defeating Napoleon's troops in Spain. During the Chinese civil war in the

1930s and 1940s Mao's forces began as a guerilla force, launching attacks on isolated Nationalist units in the hinterlands. As they grew stronger the Chinese Communists fielded large and more conventional armies which took the Nationalist cities. While the war in South Viet Nam did feature Viet Cong guerillas ultimately it was the conventional forces of the North Vietnamese Army (NVA) that conquered South Viet Nam. If one were to look back at the pictures of the fall of Saigon one would see NVA tanks hurtling down the boulevards and crashing through the gates of government buildings.

The 9/11 attacks changed this equation. The destructiveness of the terrorist attack was massive in comparison to any that came before; thousands were killed on U.S. soil. Massive infrastructure damage was inflicted as well. Not only were the two huge World Trade towers brought down and the Pentagon damaged, but air flights were cancelled for days. The stock market was affected. New security procedures were put in place that not only were expensive in and of themselves but these added "hidden" costs such as millions of formerly productive man hours now wasted waiting in airport security lines.

The 9/11 attacks also served as harbingers of potential attacks of even greater magnitude; those using weapons of mass destruction. Scenarios involving terrorist use of nuclear, biological, and chemical weapons that could kill hundreds of thousands or even perhaps millions moved from being Hollywood fantasy to a potential reality. These attacks moved terrorist warfare from a low-level threat to a major threat, on par with an attack by a sovereign state.

America's Response to 9/11: The Intelligence Failure

How is it that the United States intelligence agencies could miss an operation of the magnitude of the 9/11 attacks?

- An army without secret agents is exactly is like a man without eyes or ears. (XIII.23 Chia Lin)

Lack of human intelligence is one key reason the United States did not foresee and preempt the 9/11 attacks. There were other reasons as well, many of which were violations of Sun Tzu's principle of Foreknowledge.

A July 2002 Congressional report by the House Permanent Select

Committee on Intelligence detailed several failures of intelligence.[5] To quote from the executive summary,

> The terrorist attacks perpetrated on September 11th, 2001 constituted a significant strategic surprise for the United States. The failure of the Intelligence Community (IC) to provide adequate forewarning was affected by resource constraints and a series of questionable management decisions related to funding priorities. Prophetically, IC leadership concluded at a high-level offsite meeting on *September 11, 1998* that 'failure to improve operations management, resource allocation and other key issues within the (IC), including making substantial and sweeping changes in the way the nation collects, analyzes, and produces intelligence, will likely *result in a catastrophic systemic intelligence failure*' *(author's emphasis).*

The blame for the "systemic intelligence failure" was shared between the three primary U.S. intelligence agencies; the CIA, the FBI, and the NSA. The CIA's primary shortcoming was its lack of "humint" (human intelligence). The lack of human agents deep inside the al-Qaeda terror organization left the U.S. "without eyes or ears." This lack of "humint" capability was due to reduced funding based on the perception that the threat to America had diminished significantly. It was also driven by a set of guidelines that made it very difficult to recruit agents with "dirty hands"; people who might themselves be terrorists, involved in crime or other unsavory activities. This was the case despite the fact that it would likely be these very types of people who might have access to the intelligence the United States needed. One other key CIA problem was information overload; the fact that the CIA provided so much information of limited value combined with constant warnings of potential but vague threats.

- And therefore only the enlightened sovereign and the worthy general who are able to use the most intelligent people as agents are certain to achieve great things. (XIII.23)

The FBI's primary shortcoming was a lack of focus on preventing terrorism. For example, in July 2001, the Phoenix FBI office found evidence that a large number of suspected terrorists were taking flying lessons and asking about airport security. This evidence, however, was ignored by FBI Headquarters, which was preoccupied with other priorities, concerned about perceived racial profiling.

This shortcoming was compounded by an inability to share critical terrorist intelligence information internally and with other organizations. In August 2001 agents in Minneapolis captured Zacarias Moussaoui, who is currently thought to be linked to the 9/11 hijackings.. However, the Minneapolis FBI agents never learned of the Phoenix report and its findings. This was due to the FBI's policy of decentralizing its investigations, which made the sharing of intelligence problematic. Furthermore, the security of FBI communications was such that they could not send encrypted emails to the CIA to make them aware of other intelligence the latter organization would have found useful.[6]

The NSA's main shortfall was its passive gathering of intelligence. Rather than prioritizing its collection priorities based on threats, the NSA should have been more pro-active in targeting terrorist communications. The NSA also lacked the capabilities to tap into new communications methods terrorists might be using (the Internet and cell phones), follow those communications across different types of networks and integrate that data into actionable intelligence. Finally, within the NSA (as well as the CIA and FBI) a lack of foreign language specialists were a crucial shortcoming; key intercepts that may have provided warning of the attacks were lest untranslated and unanalyzed. This includes messages intercepted on September 10, stating: "The match begins tomorrow," and "Tomorrow is zero hour."

Another key shortcoming found was that each agency within the U.S. Government involved in counter-terrorism had a different definition of terrorism. These differing definitions made an unified view and method of dealing with terrorism, as well as inter-agency coordination, problematic.

Furthermore, key agencies such as the FBI focused on treating terrorism as a crime instead of an act of war. The FBI's definition of terrorism prior to 9/11 reads "Terrorism is the *unlawful* (author's emphasis) use of force or violence against persons or property to intimidate or coerce a government, the civilian population, or any segment thereof, in furtherance of political or social objectives." The tendency to see terrorism as a crime instead of (to quote Clausewitz when he discussed warfare) "a continuation of politics by other means" leads to ineffective means of countering it. Rather than attacking the source of the problem (terrorist organizations and the nation states that support them) with military might and other methods, the FBI focused on solving the "crime" and going after individuals.

These shortcomings all enabled the successful al-Qaeda attacks and obviously need to be addressed to prevent future attacks.

■ To rely on rustics and not prepare is the greatest of crimes; to be prepared beforehand for any contingency is the greatest of virtues. (III.28 Ho Yen-his)

America's History with Unconventional Warfare

It is common for those unfamiliar with American military history to assume the United States is not adept at unconventional warfare. This is especially true of those who grew up during the Vietnam era and view that conflict as proof positive of America's inability to fight guerillas and their descendants, the terrorists. As author Max Boot illustrates in his book *The Savage Wars of Peace,* however, the United States has a fought many "small wars" and achieved many successes.

Soon after its birth as a nation U.S. merchant traders were being captured by Barbary pirates off the coast of North Africa and its captured citizens turned into slaves. The American government first tried to buy off the pirates but when the total amount of tribute grew to the comprise one-sixth of the federal budget it was decided that military action was a more prudent course than appeasement. The fledgling Navy was expanded and sent to protect U.S. shipping in the Mediterranean. Early unfortunate reverses were soon followed by significant successes, including a march on Tripoli (still remembered in the Marine Corps Hymn) and naval bombardments of Barbary ports. These efforts ended in the defeat of the Barbary pirates in 1815.

Between 1800 and 1934 U.S. Marines staged 180 landings abroad, sometimes staying only a few days to protect U.S. citizens and interests or many years to help a nation ensure a fair election and a more stable government. The Marines became so adept at these missions that they wrote a book called *The Small Wars Manual,* which became the manifesto that codified how to achieve U.S. objectives in these unconventional wars.

After taking possession of the Philippines from Spain in the Spanish-American war the United States had to fight a native insurgency. Using a combination of military action to defeat the guerillas and governmental efforts, such as building schools and holding local elections, America was eventually successful in pacifying the islands' population. The major guerilla resistance was eliminated in a daring raid. A few Americans, led by one General Frederick Funston, posed as prisoners of Philippinos who were actually American scouts. Taken to the guerilla hideout, Funston and his scouts surprised and captured Emilio Aguinaldo, the guerilla leader. The United States pacified the Philippino insurgency in four short years at the cost of roughly seven thousand casualties.[7]

Of course, the United States used unconventional warfare in its efforts against the Native Americans. Many tribes, such as the Apaches, were the ultimate guerilla warriors. So it is clear that, when one looks beyond Vietnam, the United States has had a wealth of experience in unconventional warfare and could apply these lessons to its fight on terrorism.

What Would Sun Tzu Advise?

Immediately after the 9/11 attacks I spent time thinking about what Sun Tzu's advice to the United States to defeat the terrorists would be. I felt his first piece of advice would be:

- **Your aim must be to take All-under-Heaven intact. Thus your troops are not worn out and your gains will be complete. This is the art of offensive strategy. (III.11)**

Strategically, this would mean that, prior to taking precipitate action, the U.S. government would need to look at its end game objectives: What would be the preferred outcome be if the U.S. actions were successful?. Of course, the destruction of the radical Islamic terrorist organizations and the eradication of those governments that supported them (or at least the ending of their support for terrorists) are the basic goals. Equally important, however, is the question, how would these objectives be achieved? Creating more terrorists, disrupting the international order, hobbling the U.S. economy or failing to protect U.S. allies and interests in other theaters would all be counter-productive. It would not be helpful for U.S. long term interests if, in the process of destroying the terrorist threat, a nuclear war was triggered between India and Pakistan; China took advantage of American preoccupation with terrorism to attack Taiwan; Israeli security was threatened; the U.S. economy fell apart. Aside from avoiding the pitfalls noted above, the United States also needs to look at the opportunities this situation might present, perhaps the potential to spread democracy, or eliminate possible threats to U.S. security. To achieve any of these goals, the end game objectives would have to be put in place and precise actions (favored by good luck!) implemented.

Sun Tzu would also offer the following advice:

- For to win one hundred victories in one hundred battles is not the acme of skill. To subdue the enemy without fighting is the acme of skill. (III.3)

While Sun Tzu would be the first to recognize that battles would have to be fought and the terrorist organizations destroyed, he would also advise that battles and attacks in themselves are not the end goal. Achieving the end-game objectives while maintaining international order, keeping the economy strong, and thwarting additional terrorist attacks is the goal. Thus a multi-faceted strategy combining economic, diplomatic, intelligence and military efforts would all play a role. Part of the diplomatic effort would be garnering the support of allies.

- If one neither covenants for the help of neighbors nor develops plans based on expediency but in furtherance of his personal aims relies only on his own military strength to overawe the enemy country then his own cities can be captured and his own state overthrown. (XI.53 Tu Mu)

Despite the fact that the United States has the requisite military means necessary to destroy the terrorist groups by herself, Allied help would be instrumental to success. This help could take many forms: logistical support, intelligence on terrorist whereabouts, the capture of terrorists in the allied countries themselves, overflight capabilities, military assets, access to bases, votes in the United Nations, and moral support. Together, these additional assets could avoid future terrorist attacks, decrease U.S. casualties, and shorten the war.

Sun Tzu would most likely also advise that of all these assets probably the most important one would be intelligence, or as he called it, foreknowledge:

- Now the reason the enlightened prince and the wise general conquer the enemy wherever they move and their achievements surpass those of ordinary men is foreknowledge. (XIII.3)

In any unconventional conflict, guerilla or terrorist, the actual destruction of the enemy is not the major problem, *finding them* is. U.S. satellites, listening devices, and other technological capabilities will be helpful but even more critical will be human intelligence.

- We select men who are clever, talented, wise and able to gain access to those of the enemy who are intimate with the sovereign and members of the nobility. Thus they are able to observe the enemy's movements and to learn of his doings and his plans. Having learned the true state of affairs they return and tell us. (XIII.11 Tu Yu)

As the House Committee report made clear U.S. human intelligence capabilities need significant improvement through the recruitment of spies and others with inside knowledge of the terrorist plans. To defeat the terrorists their organizations must be infiltrated and no limits should be put on the use of any source of reliable information.

- When he is united, divide him. (I.25)

Sun Tzu would also say that it is crucial to split the terrorist from his sources of support, financial resources, bases to train and equipment to use.

- Sometimes drive a wedge between a sovereign and his ministers; on other occasions separate his allies from him. Make them mutually suspicious so that they drift apart. Then you can plot against them. (I.25 Chang Yu)

Attacking or threatening to attack nation states that provide al-Qaeda safe harbor and support would be a strategy Sun Tzu would condone. But beyond states other organizations and individuals that assist the terrorists must be targeted and stopped from providing this assistance, either through diplomatic, police or financial methods.

- Now an army may be likened to water, for just as flowing water avoids heights and hastens to the lowlands, so an army avoids strengths and attacks weakness. (I.27)

Obviously, Sun Tzu would recommend seeking out and concentrating U.S. attacks on the terrorist organization's weaknesses. These weaknesses include communications that can be intercepted, members that may be less sophisticated and may be turned to the U.S. cause, high visibility to detection when operating in the West, and sources of support that may are concerned with being targeted by the United States.

- Therefore, when I have won a victory I do not repeat my tactics but respond to circumstances in an infinite variety of ways.

Attacking these weaknesses would require the employment by the United States of creative strategies and tactics. U.S. advantages in technology will lead to the creation of new weapons to fight terrorism, however, historically the possession of new weapons alone are not sufficient for victory. Again, creativity in battling terrorism is critical not only to military efforts but diplomatic, economic, and others as well.

American Actions-to-Date versus Sun Tzu's Principles: A Pre-emptive Strike?

So how would Sun Tzu analyze American actions as of August 2002? We will analyze these actions in terms of U.S. objectives, diplomatic efforts, economic and financial actions, military actions, and the security and defense of the "homeland."

After 9/11 the U.S. response to terrorism was to tolerate it no longer. The focus became, as President Bush stated, to find and destroy anti-U.S. terrorist organizations and the nation states that support them. Furthermore, the policy claims the prerogative to launch strikes to preempt terrorist attacks. The U.S. policy also appears to go so far as to take advantage of the war on terror to eliminate threats from nations acquiring weapons of mass destruction, such as Iraq, even though the link between these countries and terrorists has been a matter of debate. What would Sun Tzu say to this?

- 'Weapons are tools of ill omen.' War is a grave matter; one is apprehensive lest men embark upon it without due reflection. (I.1 Li Ch'uan)

The United States was forced into war and has enjoyed significant successes militarily. However, Sun Tzu would advise care before expanding the war without careful study and analysis:

- With many calculations, one can win; with few calculations one cannot. How much less chance of victory has one who makes not at all! By this means I examine the situation and the outcome will be clearly apparent. (I.28)

- Such calculations should include not only military strategy and tactics, but also diplomatic relations with U.S. allies and nation-states in the region. Finally, public opinion and Congressional support will be a crucial factor in any decision to pre-emptively attack another country. If you say which ruler possesses moral influence, which commander is the more able, which army obtains the advantages of nature and the terrain, in which regulations and instructions are better carried out, which troops are stronger; which has the better trained officers and men; and which administers rewards and punishments in a more enlightened manner; I will be able to forecast which side will be victorious and which defeated. (I.11–I.14)

Assuming the "calculations" made by the U.S. government and military showed an extreme threat to the United States, and its calculations included diplomacy and public opinion, and predicted a solid probability of success, Sun Tzu would recommend achieving U.S. objectives as quickly as possible.

- Victory is the main object in war. If this is long delayed, weapons are blunted and morale depressed. When troops attack cities, their strength will be exhausted. When the army engages in protracted campaigns the resources of the state will not suffice. (II.3–II.4)

The reasons for ending the war quickly include not only those above but also to avoid potential enemies from taking advantage of U.S. engagement in the war on terrorism in order to achieve their own objectives. China attacking Taiwan would be one example.

- When your weapons are dulled and ardor damped, your strength exhausted and treasure spent, neighboring rulers will take advantage of your distress to act. And even though you have wise counselors, none will be able to lay good plans for the future. (II.5)

Diplomatically, the United States has been fairly successful to date in building a coalition of states to support the attainment of its objectives. The United States has rebuilt its relationship with Pakistan and created new ones with former Soviet states in southwest Asia to provide bases to support its attack on Afghanistan. Russia has been very helpful as well. NATO has moved forces to replace American units so that the latter could be used to defeat the Taliban and al-Qaeda. And as always, Great Britain has proven a stalwart ally, sending troops and other forces to work closely with American units in Afghanistan. Arab states, especially those surrounding Iraq as we have pointed out, are natural allies but they are concerned about an attack on another Islamic nation and caught up in the Israeli-Palestinian conflict. As a result, they have been less enthusiastic in their support and need to be brought into the planning in a way that will gain their support.

In addition to military support U.S. allies have also been helpful in providing intelligence, shutting down terrorist access to financial support and tracking down terrorists in their own countries. Given the complexity of global relationships, Sun Tzu would most likely applaud U.S. diplomatic efforts.

Militarily, Sun Tzu would probably also be impressed with the speed and the apparent success the United States employed in driving al-Qaeda and its Taliban supporters out of Afghanistan. The United States definitely employed many of Sun Tzu's principles in achieving its success in that theater.

For example, highly-trained Special Forces units were inserted to establish links with anti–Taliban forces such as the Northern Alliance. These men, experienced in small unit operations and well-versed in understanding local cultures, won the trust of the Taliban's enemies on the ground. This was done through meetings and discussions but more importantly, by the Special Forces troops calling in precision air attacks on Taliban positions. The small Special Forces units delivered devastating airpower that weakened the Taliban forces so much that they either deserted before the ensuing Northern Alliance offensive or fell apart quickly in the subsequent attacks. While many predicted a never-ending guerilla war in Afghanistan (in essence, another Viet Nam) this blend of elite small units on the ground directing sophisticated airpower from above routed the Taliban in a few short months. This showed the far-sightedness of U.S. military strategists in creating flexible weaponry and tactics that could defeat a spectrum of enemy forces.

Many of the weapons used were created for the Cold War. For example, the B-52 bomber, designed, and tested in the late 1940s and early 1950s for the Cold War, was used effectively to destroy Taliban troops, materiél and morale (the youngest B-52 still flying came on line in 1962, four decades ago). Tried and true weaponry was combined with new technologies such as the Predator unmanned aircraft, which could loiter above Taliban positions and gather intelligence. Some

Predators were later armed and attacked targets on their own. And making this technological wizardry effective were soldiers, sailors and airmen who were highly-trained specialists. Due to prior strategic planning (despite being a process messy at times due to bureaucratic infighting and political influences from Congress) the United States had a portfolio of military forces trained to attack terrorism.

- A victory gained before the situation has crystallized is one the common man does not comprehend. Thus its author gains no reputation for sagacity. Before he has bloodied his blade the enemy state has already submitted. (IV.11 Tu Mu)

Subsequent to the victory in Afghanistan, a new government has been installed. Whether it survives and leads the Afghan nation to prosperity remains to be seen. Whether the United States will capture more key leaders of al-Qaeda (such as Osama bin Laden himself) is yet to be seen. In the short term, however, a key objective of the United States has been achieved. Afghanistan is no longer a haven in which terrorists can train openly for attacks on America.

- Thus, those skilled in war subdue the enemy's army without battle. They capture his cities without assaulting them and overthrow his state without protracted operations. They conquer by strategy. (III.10 Sun Tzu and Li Ch'uan)

Homeland defense efforts have been more problematic, yet they are in some ways more crucial than U.S. offensive actions. As Sun Tzu said,

- Invincibility lies in the defense; the possibility of victory in the attack. (IV.5)

The military and diplomatic strength of the United States rests on its economy, which in turn rests on trust and belief that the United States is a safe-haven in a world of that is often chaotic and uncertain. Ongoing terrorist attacks, especially if they employ weapons of mass destruction, will wreak not only physical damage but psychic damage that would be deeper and last longer. While the United States and its people are resilient, the 9/11 attacks had a severe impact; its repercussions are still being felt economically and psychologically. Thus the protection of the "Homeland" is critical.

Despite this critical need for national safety, airline security is still ineffective, American borders are still porous, stocks of vaccines against potential biological attacks remain low, and many potential targets remain insecure. This is not totally surprising; in World War II it was months before the U.S. shipping industry found ways to make their ships less vulnerable to German submarine attacks. Ships were still sailing with their lights on and getting sunk within sight of the Eastern seaboard. The formation of the Office of Homeland Security may improve coordination between agencies but it alone is not the answer. The change required is one of attitude; we must be serious about the threat and willing to take real action that will protect U.S. citizens and property. To date, it is more likely that the ferocity of the American response to the attacks of 9/11 is responsible for the prevention of another major attack, rather than U.S. homeland defense efforts.

Where the war on terrorism will go from here is open to speculation. However, two things appear clear at the time of this writing. The United States must continue to find terrorists wherever they are and eliminate them. Second, an opportunity exists at this time to eliminate the threat of potential rogue Islamic nations that may be seeking weapons of mass destruction, namely Iraq and even potentially Iran. This can be done either through direct attacks or the use of surrogate forces. Reaching for this opportunity entails risk, but the risk of not acting may indeed be greater.

- **When troops are raised to chastise transgressors, the temple council first considers the adequacy of the rulers' benevolence and the confidence of their peoples; next, the appropriateness of nature's seasons, and finally the difficulties of the topography. After thorough deliberation of these three matters, a general is appointed to launch the attack. (I.3 Chang Yu)**

Lessons Learned

What, then, are the lessons we can learn for the future?

1. **The United States must be prepared for war—in all its forms**

   "The story of the human race is war." So spoke Winston Churchill. The events of 9/11 prove the enduring wisdom of this quotation. Although there have been many efforts in the twentieth century to eliminate war as a scourge of mankind (including trying to pass international laws against it!) warfare will always be something for which a nation must be prepared. Many thought World War I was the "War to end all wars." World War II proved that an illusion. The creation of the United Nations after World War II was supposed to end conflict. Instead war continued (albeit of lower intensity) between the West and Communism, between India and Pakistan, between Israel and the Arabs, and even between those belonging to the same belief systems, between Iran and Iraq, and skirmishes between China and the U.S.S.R. After the Cold War many thought warfare might end; however, the Persian Gulf War, vicious battles in the Balkans and Africa, and 9/11 all proved that an empty dream. Instead, new threats arose. In addition to the threat of terrorism, the continued existence of rogue states run by dictators, willing to utilize weapons of mass destruction, threaten the United States. And on the horizon an ever-stronger China is the next possible superpower.

Therefore it is crucial that the United States have a portfolio of military capabilities that enables it to fight and win across the spectrum of potential conflicts; terrorist, guerilla, conventional and nuclear. While the terrorist threat is in the forefront today, it is not the only one. A nuclear device that wipes out an American city could be delivered by a terrorist suicide bomber or a missile launched by a sovereign nation. Either way, the explosion and destruction would make the casualties of 9/11, as terrible as they were, pale in number. The United States must be prepared to counter and defeat all these types of attacks.

2. **Solid and timely intelligence (especially "humint") is crucial:**
   9/11 represented, as the Intelligence Community prophetically forecast, a "catastrophic systemic intelligence failure". The key agencies the United States depends on to discern enemy actions, the FBI, CIA and NSA, did not come through. Lack of good human sources of intelligence was instrumental in the failure.

   This was not the first intelligence failure in U.S. history. Pearl Harbor stands out in many minds, but the Tet Offensive, the Chinese intervention in Korea, and the Battle of the Bulge are other examples. Intelligence surprises are to a certain point to be expected given the efforts of an opponent to mask his intentions and the vagaries inherent in intelligence gathering, analysis, and dissemination.

Past history and problems of intelligence gathering, however, do not alleviate the need to significantly improve U.S. intelligence capabilities. Some of this is a matter of resources, some an issue of coordination between agencies, and some a matter of policy (e.g. allowing the CIA to use potentially "dirty" sources of human intelligence). Without good intelligence it is impossible to prevent enemy attacks (terrorist or conventional) or make the U.S. assaults effective.

3. **Military action must be supported by diplomatic means**
In all types of wars it is necessary to gain allies and influence other nations to support ones' actions. The war on terrorism is no different. We have discussed above the many ways other nations can provide help to the United States in defeating terrorism and other threats. Rarely can military power or diplomatic finesse carry the day by themselves; when they are used in combination to support one another a nation can most effectively achieve its strategic objectives.

4. **Serious homeland defense is a necessity**
While the U.S. government has proven itself to be serious in attacking its enemies far from U.S. shores, it has moved much more slowly to make the United States less vulnerable to attack. As terrorists find themselves threatened with destruction many "fair day" terrorists will drop out of the movement. A hard core terrorist, however, will remain, and will seek to inflict the maximum damage on the United States. Terrorists are not the only threat; other nations militarily weaker than the United States may seek to damage it through unconventional means, using unexpected warfare tactics to achieve their objectives.

5. **Nationbuilding is not impossible**
Famous Civil War general, William T. Sherman, said, "The legitimate object of war is a more perfect peace." This is the essence of the American philosophy of warfare; the United States fights not only for survival but also for a higher moral purpose, freedom from tyranny. Defeating the enemy is just the first step; the United States has a history

of successful nationbuilding and should expend resources to do so. Thus the "more perfect peace" can be established and last longer, while bringing freedom to those whom were once oppressed. One can see this already in the war on terrorism by looking at the changes in Afghanistan after its people were liberated from the Taliban.

6. **Sun Tzu's principles provide a guide to winning all types of warfare**
Finally, as I believe I have shown, Sun Tzu's principles are applicable to all types of warfare. Terrorists, because they are weak militarily, will be likely to employ Sun Tzu's principles to gain advantage. Sun Tzu's principles can also be used to defeat terrorism, as well as win conventional conflicts.

Summary

9/11 has proven that Sun Tzu's principles are as important today for the United States in understanding the enemy and winning the war on terrorism as they were centuries ago for ancient Chinese rulers. The ideas contained in *The Art of War* shine as brilliantly today as ever.

I close with a final word from Sun Tzu:

- **Therefore, when I have won a victory I do not repeat my tactics but respond to different circumstances in an infinite variety of ways. (VI.26)**

NOTES

Introduction

1. Rick Atkinson, *Crusade: The Untold Story of the Persian Gulf War* (Boston and New York: Houghton Mifflin Company, 1993), 108.

2. Samuel B. Griffith, *Sun Tzu: The Art of War* (New York and Oxford: Oxford University Press, 1963), 1–12; Dennis and Ching Ping Bloodworth, *The Chinese Machiavelli* (NY: Farrar, Straus and Giroux, 1976), 90; Ralph D. Sawyer, *Sun Tzu: The Art of War* (Boulder and Oxford: Westview, 1994), 27, 151–62.

3. Bloodworth, *The Chinese Machiavelli*, 90.

4. Michael Pillsbury, *China Debates the Future Security Environment* (Washington, D.C.: National Defense University Press, 2000), xxxv–xxxvi.

5. Chin-Ning Chu, *The Asian Mindgame* (NY: Rawson Associates, 1991), 8.

6. Chu, *The Asian Mindgame*, 15.

Chapter 1: Win All Without Fighting

1. Robert D. Schulzinger, *A Time for War: The United States and Vietnam, 1941–1975* (New York and Oxford, Oxford University Press, 1997), 258–263.

2. James Clavell, *The Art of War by Sun Tzu* (Giles translation) (NY: Delacorte Press, 1983), 16.

3. Herbert Langer, *The Thirty Years' War* (Dorset Press, 1978), 7–9; J. M. Roberts, *A History of Europe* (NY: Penguin Press, 1996), 251–52.

4. Roberts, *A History of Europe*, 448–58; Keith Robins, *The First World War: The Outbreak, Events and Aftermath* (Oxford and New York: Oxford

University Press, 1984), 103–26; John Keegan, *The First World War* (London: Random House U.K. Limited, 1998), 48–49.

5. Geoffrey Blainey, *The Causes of War* (NY: The Free Press, 1973), 35–47.

6. Gordon A. Craig and Alexander L. George, *Force and Statecraft: Diplomatic Problems of Our Time* (New York and Oxford: Oxford University Press, 1983), 25–35; David Gates, *The Napoleonic Wars, 1803–1815* (New York and Oxford: Oxford University Press, 1997), 265–75.

7. Craig and George, *Force and Statecraft*, 102–15.

8. Gates, *The Napoleonic Wars*, 258–75.

9. Anthony Livesey, *Great Battles of World War I* (NY: Macmillan, 1989), 66–77.

10. Craig and George, *Force and Statecraft*, 80–86.

11. Nathan Miller, *The U.S. Navy: A History, Third Edition* (Annapolis: Naval Institute Press, 1997), 260–61.

12. Peter Connolly, *Greece and Rome at War* (London: Greenhill Books, 1981), 166–88; B. H. Liddell Hart, *Strategy* (Strategy, 1967), 24–33; Harold Lamb, *Hannibal* (NY: Doubleday, 1958), 87–128.

13. Robert Leckie, *George Washington's War: The Saga of the American Revolution* (NY: HarperCollins, 1992), 122–88 and 632–60.

Chapter 2: Avoid Strength, Attack Weakness

1. Rick Atkinson, *Crusade: The Untold Story of the Persian Gulf War* (Boston and New York: Houghton Mifflin, 1993), 333–35; General H. Norman Schwartzkopf, *It Doesn't Take a Hero* (NY: Bantam Books, 1992), 348.

2. Doyne Dawson, *The Origins of Western Warfare: Militarism and Morality in the Ancient World* (Boulder and Oxford: Westview, 1996), 47.

3. Victor Davis Hanson, *The Western Way of War: Infantry Battle in Classical Greece* (New York and Oxford: Oxford University Press, 1990), 27–28.

4. Stanley Lombardo, *Iliad: Homer* (Indianapolis and Cambridge: Hackett Publishing Company, 1997), 79 and 249.

5. Hanson, *The Western Way of War*, 27–39, 136–228.

6. Carl Von Clausewitz, *On War* (Edited and Translated by Michael Howard and Peter Paret) (Princeton: Princeton University Press, 1984), 3–58; excerpts on following pages, 258–262, 485; Larry H. Addington, *The Patterns of War Since the Eighteenth Century: Second Edition* (Bloomington and Indianapolis: Indiana University Press, 1994), 1–48.

7. Addington, *The Patterns of War Since the Eighteenth Century*, 68–94; Robert Leckie, *None Died in Vain: The Saga of the American Civil War* (New York: HarperPerennial, 1991), 154–74; William C. Davis, *Rebels and Yankees: The Battlefields of the Civil War* (London: Salamander Books, 1990), 88.

8. Alan Clark, *Barbarossa: The Russian–German Conflict, 1941–45* (New York: William Morrow, 1965), 204–48; Field Marshal Erich von Manstein,

Lost Victories: The War Memoirs of Hitler's Most Brilliant General (Novato, CA: Presidio Press, 1982), 289–365; Walter Goerlitz, *History of the German General Staff: 1657–1945* (New York: Barnes & Noble Books, 1995), 414–31; Matthew Cooper, *The German Army: 1933–1945* (Chelsea: Scarborough House, 1990), 422–40.

9. Nathan Miller, *The U.S. Navy: A History, Third Edition* (Annapolis: Naval Institute Press, 1997), 237–38.

10. Bruce I. Gudmundsson, *Stormtroop Tactics: Innovation in the German Army, 1914–1918* (Westport, CT: Praeger, 1989), 43–53 and 149–79; Addington, *The Patterns of War Since the Eighteenth Century*, 113–18, 162–71 and 178–80; John Laffin, *Jackboot: A History of the German Soldier 1713–1945* (NY: Barnes & Noble Books, 1994), 174–76.

11. Clark G. Reynolds, *History and the Sea: Essays on Maritime Strategies* (Columbia: University of South Carolina Press, 1989), 1–19; David Gates, *The Napoleonic Wars, 1803–1815* (New York and Oxford: Oxford University Press, 1997), 171–93; Harold Lamb, *Hannibal* (New York: Doubleday, 1958), 170.

12. Chris Cook and John Stevenson, *The Atlas of Modern Warfare* (New York: G. P. Putnam's Sons, 1978), 28–34.

13. Addington, *The Patterns of War Since the Eighteenth Century*, 243–44.

14. Williamson Murray, MacGregor Knox, and Alvin Bernstein, *The Making of Strategy: Rulers, States and War* (Cambridge: Cambridge University Press, 1994), 534–78.

15. Archer Jones, *The Art of War in the Western World* (New York and Oxford: Oxford University Press 1987), 518–38; Cooper, *The German Army 1933–1945*, 214–42; Addington, *The Patterns of War Since the Eighteenth Century*, 202–09.

16. Miller, *The U.S. Navy: A History*, 214–15; Robert B. Edgerton, *Warriors of the Rising Sun: A History of the Japanese Military* (New York & London: W. W. Norton & Co., 1997), 273–75.

17. Bruce W. Watson, Bruce George, Peter Tsouras, and B. L. Cyr, *Military Lessons of the Gulf War* (CA: Presidio Press, 1991), 64.

18. Addington, *The Patterns of War Since the Eighteenth Century*, 113–18; Byron Farwell, *Mr. Kipling's Army: All the Queen's Men* (New York & London: W. W. Norton & Co., 1981), 22.

19. Lawrence E. Babits, *A Devil of a Whipping: The Battle of Cowpens* (Chapel Hill: University of North Carolina Press, 1998), 55–149; Robert Leckie, *George Washington's War: The Saga of the American Revolution* (NY: HarperCollins, 1992), 507–22 and 593–604.

20. Dr. John Pimlott, *Wehrmacht: The Illustrated History of the German Army in WWII* (Osceola: Motorbooks International Publishers and Wholesalers, 1997), 75–83.

21. John MacDonald, *Great Battles of the Civil War* (NY: Macmillan Publishing Company, 1988), 68–79; Editors of Time-Life Books, *Brother Against Brother* (NY: Prentice Hall Press, 1990), 190–207; Richard Moe, *The Last Full*

Measure: The Life and Death of the First Minnesota Volunteers (NY: Avon Books, 1993), 212–13; Davis, *Rebels and Yankees*, 87–103.

Chapter 3: Deception and Foreknowledge

1. Lynn Montross, *War Through the Ages* (NY: Harper & Row, 1960), 52–53.

2. Colonel John Hughes-Wilson, *Military Intelligence Blunders* (London: Robinson Publishing, 1999), 5.

3. John G. Hubbell, *P.O.W.: A Definitive History of the American Prisoner-of-War Experience in Vietnam, 1964–1973* (NY: Reader's Digest Press, 1976), 536–38.

4. Russell Spurr, *Enter the Dragon: China's Undeclared War Against the U.S. In Korea, 1950–51* (NY: Newmarket Press, 1988), 127–71.

5. Simon Singh, *The Code Book: The Evolution of Secrecy from Mary, Queen of Scots to Quantum Cryptography* (NY: Doubleday, 1999), 107–15.

6. Ralph D. Sawyer, *Sun Pin: Military Methods* (Boulder: Westview, 1995), 5–8.

7. Robert Leckie, *George Washington's War: The Saga of the American Revolution* (NY: HarperCollins, 1992), 314–21; CIA Public Affairs, *Intelligence in the War of Independence* (Langley: CIA Publications), 36.

8. Ohio Historical Society Website (www.ohiohistory.org).

9. Hughes-Wilson, *Military Intelligence Blunders*, 11.

10. Nathan Miller, *The U.S. Navy: A History, Third Edition* (Annapolis: Naval Institute Press, 1997), 219–23.

11. Tom Clancy, *Into the Storm: A Study in Command* (NY: G. P. Putnam's Sons, 1997), 236.

12. David Gates, *The Napoleonic Wars, 1803–1815* (New York and Oxford: Oxford University Press, 1997), 198–218; Matthew Cooper, *The German Army: 1933–1945* (Chelsea: Scarborough House, 1978), 259–358.

13. Forrest C. Pogue, *George C. Marshall: Organizer of Victory 1943–1945* (NY: Viking Press, 1973), 388–89; John Carey, *Eyewitness to History* (NY: Avon Books, 1987), 592–93.

14. Noel Barber, *Sinister Twilight: The Fall of Singapore* (London: Arrow Books, 1988), 95–108; Richard Gough, *The Escape from Singapore* (London: William Kimber & Co., 1987), 48.

15. Michael Pillsbury, *China Debates the Future Security Environment* (Washington, D.C.: National Defense University Press, 2000), 203–56.

16. Hughes-Wilson, *Military Intelligence Blunders*, 4–14.

17. Rick Atkinson, *Crusade: The Untold Story of the Persian Gulf War* (Boston and New York: Houghton Mifflin Company, 1993), 234.

18. Andrew J. Nathan and Robert S. Ross, *The Great Wall and the Empty Fortress: China's Search for Security* (NY: W. W. Norton, 1997), 24–26.

19. Richard Overy, *Why the Allies Won* (New York: W. W. Norton,

1995), 134–71; Robert Cowley, *Experience of War* (NY: W. W. Norton, 1992), 472–80; Hughes-Wilson, *Military Intelligence Blunders*, 16–37.

20. David Fraser, *Knight's Cross: A Life of Field Marshal Erwin Rommel* (NY: HarperCollins, 1993), 164.

21. Tom Clancy with General Chuck Horner, *Every Man a Tiger* (NY: G. P. Putnam's Sons, 1999), 540.

22. Robert E. Neilson, *Sun Tzu and Information Warfare* (Washington, D.C.: National Defense University Press, 1997), 35–36.

Chapter 4: Speed and Preparation

1. Editors of American Heritage, *The Civil War* (NY: Golden Press, 1960), 55. Editors of Time-Life Books, *Brother Against Brother* (NY: Prentice Hall, 1990), 109.

2. Andrew J. Nathan and Robert S. Ross, *The Great Wall and the Empty Fortress: China's Search for Security* (NY: W. W. Norton, 1997), 15.

3. B. H. Liddell Hart, *History of the Second World War* (NY: G. P. Putnam's Sons, 1970), 65–74.

4. Eric Morris, *Tanks* (London: Octopus Books, 1975), 20–32.

5. Anthony Livesey, *Great Battles of World War I* (NY: Macmillan, 1989), 144–53.

6. Lynn Montross, *War Through the Ages* (NY: Harper & Row, 1960), 561–64.

7. R. W. L. Guisso, Catherine Pagani, and David Miller, *The First Emperor of China* (NY: Birch Lane Press, 1989), 64–78.

8. Montross, *War Through the Ages*, 16–25.

9. John Laffin, *Jackboot: A History of the German Soldier 1713–1945* (NY: Barnes & Nobles Books, 1994), 174–75.

10. David T. Zabecki, *Steel Wind: Colonel Georg Bruchmuller and the Birth of Modern Artillery* (Westport, CT: Praeger, 1994), 1–57.

11. John Walcott, "The Man To Watch," *U.S. News & World Report*, 21 August 1995, 19–22.

12. Colonel Trevor N. Dupuy, *Understanding Defeat* (NY: Paragon House, 1990), 85.

13. H. R. McMaster, *Dereliction of Duty: Lyndon Johnson, Robert McNamara, The Joint Chiefs of Staff and the Lies that Led to Viet Nam* (NY: HarperCollins, 1997), 89–92, and 155–58.

14. Carl Von Clausewitz, *On War* (Edited and Translated by Michael Howard and Peter Paret) (Princeton: Princeton University Press, 1984), 119–21.

15. Laffin, *Jackboot: A History of the German Soldier*, 160–68.

16. Montross, *War Through the Ages*, 48–51.

17. Tom Clancy, *Armored Cav: A Guided Tour of an Armored Cavalry Regiment* (NY: Berkley Press, 1994), 202–09.

18. Bruce I. Gudmundsson, *Stormtroop Tactics: Innovation in the German Army, 1914–1918* (NY: Praeger, 1989), 171–78.

19. While one may rightly question how an army that was so professional participated in or allowed terrible atrocities to occur during World War II, that discussion is beyond the scope of this book. When I relate the results of the German Army's strategy and tactics, I am focusing solely on battlefield performance. I am in no way condoning the atrocities that were committed.

20. Colonel Trevor N. Dupuy, *Future Wars: The World's Most Dangerous Flashpoints* (NY: Warner Books, 1993), 325.

21. Byron Farwell, *Queen Victoria's Little Wars* (NY: W. W. Norton, 1972), 68–72.

22. Bruce W. Watson, Bruce George, Peter Tsouras, and B. L. Cyr, *Military Lessons of the Gulf War* (CA: Presidio Press, 1991), 61, 71, 75, 123, and 171.

23. William H. Rave, *Spec Ops, Case Studies in Special Operations Warfare: Theory and Practice* (Novato, CA: Presidio Press, 1995), 1–25 and 333–78.

Chapter 5: Shaping the Enemy

1. Victor Davis Hanson, *The Wars of the Ancient Greeks* (London: Cassell, 1999), 93–105.

2. John Toland, *In Mortal Combat: Korea, 1950–1953* (NY: William Morrow, 1991), 35–37.

3. Dr. John Pimlott, *Wehrmacht: The Illustrated History of the German Army in WWII* (Osceola: Motorbooks International Publishers and Wholesalers, 1997), 117–27.

4. Harry Cook, *Samurai: The Story of a Warrior Tradition* (NY: Sterling Publishing Company, 1993), 68; Stephen Turnbull, *Samurai Warriors* (Poole, New York, and Sydney: Blandford Press, 1987), 70.

5. Ramon L. Jimenez, *Caesar Against Rome: The Great Roman Civil War* (Westport, CT: Praeger, 2000), 18–19.

6. Edward N. Luttwak, *The Grand Strategy of the Roman Empire* (Baltimore: John Hopkins University Press, 1976), 1–5; William Weir, *Fatal Victories* (Hamden, CT: Shoe String Press, 1993), 3–14.

7. *Compton's Interactive Encyclopedia* (Carlsbad, CA: Compton's New Media, Inc., 1992). Two additional points about both empires:

First, the idea of the Roman Empire lived on long after the fall of Rome itself, through both the Byzantine Empire in Constantinople (originally called "New Rome") and the Holy Roman Empire in Europe. A further tribute to the longevity of the idea of a continuing Roman Empire is the fact that the last time two rulers with the title of Caesar did battle was in the twentieth century. In World War I it was the armies of German Kaiser and the Russian Czar, each titled "Caesar."

Secondly, Cortez did have both the power of technology and mythology on his side. The Spanish had firearms, ships and horses, none of which the Aztecs had ever seen. Also, the Aztecs originally thought that Cortez was the incarnation of an Aztec god who had been prophesized to return in the year 1519. However, even with these advantages Cortez could never have beaten the tens of thousands of Aztec warriors without his Native American allies. They were just too numerous.

8. Williamson Murray, MacGregor Knox, and Alvin Bernstein, *The Making of Strategy: Rulers, States and War* (Cambridge: Cambridge University Press, 1994), 242–77 and 352–92.

9. Editors of Time-Life Books, *Brother Against Brother* (NY: Prentice Hall, 1990), 150.

10. Erich Eyck, *Bismarck and the German Empire* (NY: W. W. Norton, 1950), 58–138.

11. Gordon A. Craig and Alexander L. George, *Force and Statecraft, Diplomatic Problems of Our Time* (New York and Oxford: Oxford University Press, 1983), 117–37.

12. B. H. Liddell Hart, *History of the Second World War* (NY: G. P. Putnam's Sons, 1970), 145–52.

13. Henry Kissenger, *Diplomacy* (NY: Simon & Schuster, 1994), 97–100.

14. American Heritage Editors, *Texas and the War with Mexico* (NY: American Heritage Publishing Company, 1961), 94–148; Lynn Montross, *War Through the Ages* (NY: Harper & Row, 1960), 574–80.

15. Larry H. Addington, *The Patterns of War Since the Eighteenth Century: Second Edition* (Bloomington and Indianapolis: Indiana University Press, 1994), 270–73; Montross, *War Through the Ages*, 973–78.

16. William C. Davis, *Rebels and Yankees: The Battlefields of the Civil War* (London: Salamander Books, 1990), 195–240.

17. Samuel B. Griffith, *Sun Tzu: The Art of War* (New York and Oxford: Oxford University Press, 1963), 84.

18. Colonel J. D. Morelock, *Great Land Battles: From the Civil War to the Gulf War* (NY: The Berkley Publishing Group, 1994), 256–69.

19. Dee Brown, *Bury My Heart At Wounded Knee* (NY: Holt, Rinehart & Winston, 1970), 128–33.

20. Kissenger, *Diplomacy*, 473–77.

21. B. H. Liddell Hart, *Strategy* (London: Faber & Faber, 1954, 1967), 588 and 712–13.

Chapter 6: Character-based Leadership: Leading by Example

1. Colonel Trevor N. Dupuy, *Understanding Defeat: How to Recover from Loss in Battle to Gain Victory in War* (NY: Paragon House, 1990), 52–53.

2. Stephen E. Ambrose, *The Victors: Eisenhower and His Boys: The Men of World War II* (NY: Simon & Schuster, 1998), 41.

3. David Fraser, *Knight's Cross: A Life of Field Marshal Erwin Rommel* (NY: HarperCollins, 1993), 36–37.

4. Robert Leckie, *None Died in Vain: The Saga of the American Civil War* (NY: HarperCollins, 1990), 186–393.

5. Fraser, *Knight's Cross: A Life of Field Marshal Erwin Rommel*, 43, 69–73, and 307.

6. Edwin P. Hoyt, *The Last Kamikaze: The Story of Admiral Matome Ugaki* (Westport, CT: Praeger, 1993), vii–xvi.

7. General H. Norman Schwartzkopf, *It Doesn't Take a Hero* (NY: Bantam Books, 1992), 173.

8. Robert Leckie, *George Washington's War: The Saga of the American Revolution* (NY: HarperCollins, 1992), 433–44.

9. Leckie, *None Died in Vain: The Saga of the American Civil War*, 578–88.

10. United States Marine Corps, *Warfighting* (NY: Doubleday, 1989), 68.

11. These World War I Sturmtruppen are not to be confused with the German *Einsatzgruppen* (task groups) that followed behind the German Army in World War II and performed mass killings. The Sturmtruppen were elite soldiers.

12. Bruce I. Gudmundsson, *Stormtroop Tactics: Innovation in the German Army, 1914–1918* (NY: Praeger, 1989), 150.

13. Victor Davis Hanson, *The Wars of the Ancient Greeks* (London: Cassell, 1999), 82–105.

14. Larry H. Addington, *The Patterns of War Through the Eighteenth Century* (Bloomington and Indianapolis: Indiana University Press, 1990), 99.

15. Harry Cook, *Samurai: The Story of a Warrior Tradition* (NY: Sterling Publishing, 1993), 82–89.

16. Matthew Cooper, *The German Army: 1933–1945* (Chelsea, MI: Scarborough House, 1978), 111; Fraser, *Knight's Cross: A Life of Field Marshal Erwin Rommel*, 417.

17. H. R. McMaster, *Dereliction of Duty: Lyndon Johnson, Robert McNamara, The Joint Chiefs of Staff and the Lies that Led to Viet Nam* (NY: HarperCollins, 1997), 2–4.

18. Dennis and Ching Ping Bloodworth, *The Chinese Machiavelli* (NY: Farrar, Straus and Giroux, 1976), 207–11.

19. Williamson Murray, MacGregor Knox, and Alvin Bernstein, *The Making of Strategy: Rulers, States and War* (Cambridge: Cambridge University Press, 1994), 24–55.

Chapter 7: The Changing Character of War

1. CIA Global Trends 2015, December 2000, and National Defense Council Founcation World Conflict List 2000.

2. Geoffrey Blainey, *The Causes of War* (NY: The Free Press, 1973), 291–95.

3. Carl Von Clausewitz, *On War* (Edited and Translated by Michael Howard and Peter Paret) (Princeton: Princeton University Press, 1984), 87–89, 99, 258.

4. Williamson Murray, MacGregor Knox, and Alvin Bernstein, *The Making of Strategy: Rulers, States and War* (Cambridge: Cambridge University Press, 1994), 242–77 and 352–92.

Chapter 8: The War on Terrorism

1. Due to the relatively recent nature of the post-9/11 conflict as well as its unconventional form, history is still in the process of being made, much less written. Facts are still in short supply, while suppositions and postulations abound. Therefore, although I have tried to use reliable sources where available some of the information discussed here on strategies and tactics employed may prove later to be incorrect. If that proves to be the case I apologize in advance.

2. Geoffrey Blainey, *The Causes of War* (New York: The Free Press, 1973), 291–295.

3. Tom Clancy, Carl Stiner and Tony Koltz, *Shadow Warriors: Inside the Special Forces* (City: G.P. Putnam's Sons, 2002), 503–504.

4. Mark Bowden, *Black Hawk Down: A Story of Modern War* (New York: Penguin Books, 1999), 332–356.

5. Saxby Chambliss, Chairman of Subcommittee of Terrorism and Homeland Security, House Permanent Select Committee on Intelligence and Counterterrorism, *Counterterrorism Intelligence Capabilities and Performance Prior to 9–11*, i–x.

6. Michael Hirsh and Michael Isikoff, *What Went Wrong: The inside story of the missed signals and intelligence failures that raise a chilling question—did September 11th have to happen?*, Newsweek, May 27, 2002, 28.

7. Max Boot, *The Savage Wars of Peace: Small Wars and the Rise of American Power*, (New York: Basic Books, 2002), xiii–xx, 3–30, 99–128.

Original Translation of The Art of War

by Samuel B. Griffith

LIST OF ABBREVIATIONS OF WORKS
MENTIONED SEVERAL TIMES IN NOTES

BLS	*Book of Lord Shang* (Duyvendak)
CA	*La Chine Antique* (Maspero)
CC	*Chinese Classics* (Legge)
CKS	*Chan Kuo Shih* (Yang K'uan)
Dubs	*Hsün Tzu*
Duy	*Tao Te Ching* (Duyvendak)
GS	*Grammata Serica Recensa* (Karlgren)
HIWC	*Han (Shu) I Wen Chih*
HCP	*History of Chinese Philosophy* (Fung Yü-lan) (Bodde)
HFHD	*History of the Former Han Dynasty* (Dubs)
HFT	*Han Fei Tzu* (Liao)
Mao	*Collected Works of Mao Tse-tung*
OPW	*On the Protracted War* (Mao Tse-tung)
PTSC	*Pei T'ang Shu Ch'ao*
San I	*Japan, A Short Cultural History* (Sansom)
San II	*A History of Japan to 1334* (Sansom)
SC	*Shih Chi*
TC	*Tso Chuan*
TPYL	*T'ai P'ing Yü Lan*
TT	*T'ung Tien*
WSTK	*Wei Shu T'ung K'ao*

I

ESTIMATES†

SUN TZU said:

1. War is a matter of vital importance to the State; the province of life or death; the road to survival or ruin.* It is mandatory that it be thoroughly studied.

> *Li Ch'üan:* "Weapons are tools of ill omen." War is a grave matter; one is apprehensive lest men embark upon it without due reflection.

2. Therefore, appraise it in terms of the five fundamental factors and make comparisons of the seven elements later named.†† So you may assess its essentials.

3. The first of these factors is moral influence; the second, weather; the third, terrain; the fourth, command; and the fifth, doctrine.**

---

†The title means "reckoning," "plans," or "calculations." In the Seven Military Classics edition the title is "Preliminary Calculations." The subject first discussed is the process we define as an Estimate (or Appreciation) of the Situation.

*Or "for [the field of battle] is the place of life and death [and war] the road to survival or ruin."

††Sun Hsing-yen follows the *T'ung T'ien* here and drops the character *shih* ( ): "matters," "factors," or "affairs." Without it the verse does not make much sense.

**Here *Tao* ( ) is translated "moral influence." It is usually rendered as "The Way," or "The Right Way." Here it refers to the morality of government; specifically to that of the sovereign. If the sovereign governs justly, benevolently, and righteously, he follows the Right Path or the Right Way, and thus exerts a superior degree of moral influence. The character *fa* ( ), here rendered "doctrine," has as a primary meaning

Chang Yü: The systematic order above is perfectly clear. When troops are raised to chastise transgressors, the temple council first considers the adequacy of the rulers' benevolence and the confidence of their peoples; next, the appropriateness of nature's seasons, and finally the difficulties of the topography. After thorough deliberation of these three matters, a general is appointed to launch the attack.[†] After troops have crossed the borders, responsibility for laws and orders devolves upon the general.

4. By moral influence I mean that which causes the people to be in harmony with their leaders, so that they will accompany them in life and unto death without fear of mortal peril.[*]

Chang Yü: When one treats people with benevolence, justice, and righteousness, and reposes confidence in them, the army will be united in mind and all will be happy to serve their leaders. The Book of Changes says: "In happiness at overcoming difficulties, people forget the danger of death."

5. By weather I mean the interaction of natural forces; the effects of winter's cold and summer's heat and the conduct of military operations in accordance with the seasons.[††]

6. By terrain I mean distances, whether the ground is traversed with ease or difficulty, whether it is open or constricted, and the chances of life or death.

Mei Yao-ch'en: . . . When employing troops, it is essential to know beforehand the conditions of the terrain. Knowing the distances, one can make use of an indirect or a direct plan. If he knows the degree of ease or difficulty of traversing the ground, he can estimate the advantages of using infantry or cavalry. If he knows where the

---

"law" or "method." In the title of the work it is translated "Art." But in v. 8 Sun Tzu makes it clear that here he is talking about what we call doctrine.

[†]There are precise terms in Chinese that cannot be uniformly rendered by our word "attack." Chang Yü here uses a phrase that literally means "to chastise criminals," an expression applied to attack of rebels. Other characters have such precise meanings as "to attack by stealth," "to attack suddenly," "to suppress the rebellious," "to reduce to submission," &c.

[*]Or "Moral influence is that which causes the people to be in accord with their superiors. . . ." Ts'ao Ts'ao says the people are guided in the right way (of conduct) by "instructing" them.

[††]It is clear that the character *t'ien* ( ) (Heaven) is used in this verse in the sense of "weather," as it is today.

ground is constricted and where open he can calculate the size of force appropriate. If he knows where he will give battle he knows when to concentrate or divide his forces.[†]

7. By command I mean the general's qualities of wisdom, sincerity, humanity, courage, and strictness.

> *Li Ch'üan*: These five are the virtues of the general. Hence the army refers to him as "The Respected One."
>
> *Tu Mu*: . . . If wise, a commander is able to recognize changing circumstances and to act expediently. If sincere, his men will have no doubt of the certainty of rewards and punishments. If humane, he loves mankind, sympathizes with others, and appreciates their industry and toil. If courageous, he gains victory by seizing opportunity without hesitation. If strict, his troops are disciplined because they are in awe of him and are afraid of punishment.
>
> Shen Pao-hsu . . . said: "If a general is not courageous he will be unable to conquer doubts or to create great plans."

8. By doctrine I mean organization, control, assignment of appropriate ranks to officers, regulation of supply routes, and the provision of principal items used by the army.

9. There is no general who has not heard of these five matters. Those who master them win; those who do not are defeated.

10. Therefore in laying plans compare the following elements, appraising them with the utmost care.

11. If you say which ruler possesses moral influence, which commander is the more able, which army obtains the advantages of nature and the terrain, in which regulations and instructions are better carried out, which troops are the stronger;[*]

> *Chang Yü*: Chariots strong, horses fast, troops valiant, weapons sharp—so that when they hear the drums beat the attack they are happy, and when they hear the gongs sound the retirement they are enraged. He who is like this is strong.

12. Which has the better trained officers and men;

[†]"Knowing the ground of life and death . . ." is here rendered "If he knows where he will give battle."

[*]In this and the following two verses the seven elements referred to in v. 2 are named.

Tu Yu: . . . Therefore Master Wang said: "If officers are unaccustomed to rigorous drilling they will be worried and hesitant in battle; if generals are not thoroughly trained they will inwardly quail when they face the enemy."

13. And which administers rewards and punishments in a more enlightened manner;

Tu Mu: Neither should be excessive.

14. I will be able to forecast which side will be victorious and which defeated.

15. If a general who heeds my strategy is employed he is certain to win. Retain him! When one who refuses to listen to my strategy is employed, he is certain to be defeated. Dismiss him!

16. Having paid heed to the advantages of my plans, the general must create situations which will contribute to their accomplishment.† By "situations" I mean that he should act expediently in accordance with what is advantageous and so control the balance.

17. All warfare is based on deception.

18. Therefore, when capable, feign incapacity; when active, inactivity.

19. When near, make it appear that you are far away; when far away, that you are near.

20. Offer the enemy a bait to lure him; feign disorder and strike him.

Tu Mu: The Chao general Li Mu released herds of cattle with their shepherds; when the Hsiung Nu had advanced a short distance he feigned a retirement, leaving behind several thousand men as if abandoning them. When the Khan heard this news he was delighted, and at the head of a strong force marched to the place. Li Mu put most of his troops into formations on the right and left wings, made a horning attack, crushed the Huns and slaughtered over one hundred thousand of their horsemen.*

21. When he concentrates, prepare against him; where he is strong, avoid him.

---

†Emending *i* (   ) to *i* (   ). The commentators do not agree on an interpretation of this verse.

*The Hsiung Nu were nomads who caused the Chinese trouble for centuries. The Great Wall was constructed to protect China from their incursions.

22. Anger his general and confuse him.

> *Li Ch'üan*: If the general is choleric his authority can easily be upset. His character is not firm.
>
> *Chang Yü*: If the enemy general is obstinate and prone to anger, insult and enrage him, so that he will be irritated and confused, and without a plan will recklessly advance against you.

23. Pretend inferiority and encourage his arrogance.

> *Tu Mu*: Toward the end of the Ch'in dynasty, Mo Tun of the Hsiung Nu first established his power. The Eastern Hu were strong and sent ambassadors to parley. They said: "We wish to obtain T'ou Ma's thousand-*li* horse." Mo Tun consulted his advisers, who all exclaimed: "The thousand-*li* horse! The most precious thing in this country! Do not give them that!" Mo Tun replied: "Why begrudge a horse to a neighbor?" So he sent the horse.[†]
>
> Shortly after, the Eastern Hu sent envoys who said: "We wish one of the Khan's princesses." Mo Tun asked advice of his ministers who all angrily said: "The Eastern Hu are unrighteous! Now they even ask for a princess! We implore you to attack them!" Mo Tun said: "How can one begrudge his neighbor a young woman?" So he gave the woman.
>
> A short time later, the Eastern Hu returned and said: "You have a thousand *li* of unused land which we want." Mo Tun consulted his advisers. Some said it would be reasonable to cede the land, others that it would not. Mo Tun was enraged and said: "Land is the foundation of the State. How could one give it away?" All those who had advised doing so were beheaded.
>
> Mo Tun then sprang on his horse, ordered that all who remained behind were to be beheaded, and made a surprise attack on the Eastern Hu. The Eastern Hu were contemptuous of him and had made no preparations. When he attacked he annihilated them. Mo Tun then turned westward and attacked the Yueh Ti. To the south he annexed Lou Fan . . . and invaded Yen. He completely recovered the ancestral lands of the Hsiung Nu previously conquered by the Ch'in general Meng T'ien.[*]

[†]Mo Tun, or T'ou Ma or T'ouman, was the first leader to unite the Hsiung Nu. The thousand-*li* horse was a stallion reputedly able to travel a thousand *li* (about three hundred miles) without grass or water. The term indicates a horse of exceptional quality, undoubtedly reserved for breeding.

[*]Meng T'ien subdued the border nomads during the Ch'in, and began the con-

Ch'ên Hao: Give the enemy young boys and women to infatuate him, and jades and silks to excite his ambitions.

24. Keep him under a strain and wear him down.

Li Ch'üan: When the enemy is at ease, tire him.

Tu Mu: ... Toward the end of the Later Han, after Ts'ao Ts'ao had defeated Liu Pei, Pei fled to Yuan Shao, who then led out his troops intending to engage Ts'ao Ts'ao. T'ien Fang, one of Yuan Shao's staff officers, said: "Ts'ao Ts'ao is expert at employing troops; one cannot go against him heedlessly. Nothing is better than to protract things and keep him at a distance. You, General, should fortify along the mountains and rivers and hold the four prefectures. Externally, make alliances with powerful leaders; internally, pursue an agro-military policy.†† Later, select crack troops and form them into extraordinary units. Taking advantage of spots where he is unprepared, make repeated sorties and disturb the country south of the river. When he comes to aid the right, attack his left; when he goes to succor the left, attack the right; exhaust him by causing him continually to run about. ... Now if you reject this victorious strategy and decide instead to risk all on one battle, it will be too late for regrets." Yuan Shao did not follow this advice and therefore was defeated.**

25. When he is united, divide him.

Chang Yü: Sometimes drive a wedge between a sovereign and his ministers; on other occasions separate his allies from him. Make them mutually suspicious so that they drift apart. Then you can plot against them.

26. Attack where he is unprepared; sally out when he does not expect you.

Ho Yen-hsi: ... Li Ching of the T'ang proposed ten plans to be used against Hsiao Hsieh, and the entire responsibility of com-

---

struction of the Great Wall. It is said that he invented the writing-brush. This is probably not correct, but he may have improved the existing brush in some way.

††This refers to agricultural military colonies in remote areas in which soldiers and their families were settled. A portion of the time was spent cultivating the land, the remainder in drilling, training, and fighting when necessary. The Russians used this policy in colonizing Siberia. And it is in effect now in Chinese borderlands.

**During the period known as "The Three Kingdoms," Wei in the north and west, Shu in the south-west, and Wu in the Yangtze valley contested for empire.

manding the armies was entrusted to him. In the eighth month he collected his forces at K'uei Chou.[†]

As it was the season of the autumn floods the waters of the Yangtze were overflowing and the roads by the three gorges were perilous, Hsiao Hsieh thought it certain that Li Ching would not advance against him. Consequently he made no preparations.

In the ninth month Li Ching took command of the troops and addressed them as follows: "What is of the greatest importance in war is extraordinary speed; one cannot afford to neglect opportunity. Now we are concentrated and Hsiao Hsieh does not yet know of it. Taking advantage of the fact that the river is in flood, we will appear unexpectedly under the walls of his capital. As is said: 'When the thunder-clap comes, there is no time to cover the ears.' Even if he should discover us, he cannot on the spur of the moment devise a plan to counter us, and surely we can capture him."

He advanced to I Ling, and Hsiao Hsieh began to be afraid and summoned reinforcements from south of the river, but these were unable to arrive in time. Li Ching laid siege to the city and Hsieh surrendered.

"To sally forth where he does not expect you" means as when, toward its close, the Wei dynasty sent Generals Chung Hui and Teng Ai to attack Shu.[*] . . . In winter, in the tenth month, Ai left Yin P'ing and marched through uninhabited country for over seven hundred *li*, chiselling roads through the mountains and building suspension bridges. The mountains were high, the valleys deep, and this task was extremely difficult and dangerous. Also, the army, about to run out of provisions, was on the verge of perishing. Teng Ai wrapped himself in felt carpets and rolled down the steep mountain slopes; generals and officers clambered up by grasping limbs of trees. Scaling the precipices like strings of fish, the army advanced.

Teng Ai appeared first at Chiang Yu in Shu, and Ma Mou, the general charged with its defence, surrendered. Teng Ai beheaded Chu-ko Chan, who resisted at Mien-chu, and marched on Ch'eng Tu. The King of Shu, Liu Shan, surrendered.

27. These are the strategist's keys to victory. It is not possible to discuss them beforehand.

[†]K'uei Chou is in Ssu Ch'uan.
[*]This campaign was conducted about A.D. 255.

Mei Yao-ch'en: When confronted by the enemy, respond to changing circumstances and devise expedients. How can these be discussed beforehand?

28. Now if the estimates made in the temple before hostilities indicate victory it is because calculations show one's strength to be superior to that of his enemy; if they indicate defeat, it is because calculations show that one is inferior. With many calculations, one can win; with few one cannot. How much less chance of victory has one who makes none at all! By this means I examine the situation and the outcome will be clearly apparent.[†]

[†]A confusing verse difficult to render into English. In the preliminary calculations, some sort of counting devices were used. The operative character represents such a device, possibly a primitive abacus. We do not know how the various "factors" and "elements" named were weighted, but obviously the process of comparison of relative strengths was a rational one. It appears also that two separate calculations were made, the first on a national level, the second on a strategic level. In the former, the five basic elements named in v. 3 were compared; we may suppose that if the results of this were favorable, the military experts compared strengths, training, equity in administering rewards and punishments, and so on (the seven factors).

II

WAGING WAR

SUN TZU said:

1. Generally, operations of war require one thousand fast four-horse chariots, one thousand four-horse wagons covered in leather, and one hundred thousand mailed troops.

> *Tu Mu:* . . . In ancient chariot fighting, "leather-covered chariots" were both light and heavy. The latter were used for carrying halberds, weapons, military equipment, valuables, and uniforms. The *Ssu-ma Fa* said: "One chariot carries three mailed officers; seventy-two foot troops accompany it. Additionally, there are ten cooks and servants, five men to take care of uniforms, five grooms in charge of fodder, and five men to collect firewood and draw water. Seventy-five men to one light chariot, twenty-five to one baggage wagon, so that taking the two together one hundred men compose a company."[†]

2. When provisions are transported for a thousand *li* expenditures at home and in the field, stipends for the entertainment of advisers and visitors, the cost of materials such as glue and lacquer, and of chariots and armor, will amount to one thousand pieces of gold a day. After this money is in hand, one hundred thousand troops may be raised.[*]

[†]The ratio of combat to administrative troops was thus 3:1.

[*]Gold money was coined in Ch'u as early as 400 B.C., but actually Sun Tzu does not use the term "gold." He uses a term that meant "metallic currency."

Li Ch'üan: Now when the army marches abroad, the treasury will be emptied at home.

Tu Mu: In the army there is a ritual of friendly visits from vassal lords. That is why Sun Tzu mentions "advisers and visitors."

3. Victory is the main object in war.[†] If this is long delayed, weapons are blunted and morale depressed. When troops attack cities, their strength will be exhausted.

4. When the army engages in protracted campaigns the resources of the state will not suffice.

Chang Yü: . . . The campaigns of the Emperor Wu of the Han dragged on with no result and after the treasury was emptied he issued a mournful edict.

5. When your weapons are dulled and ardor damped, your strength exhausted and treasure spent, neighboring rulers will take advantage of your distress to act. And even though you have wise counsellors, none will be able to lay good plans for the future.

6. Thus, while we have heard of blundering swiftness in war, we have not yet seen a clever operation that was prolonged.

Tu Yu: An attack may lack ingenuity, but it must be delivered with supernatural speed.

7. For there has never been a protracted war from which a country has benefited.

Li Ch'üan: The Spring and Autumn Annals says: "War is like unto fire; those who will not put aside weapons are themselves consumed by them."

8. Thus those unable to understand the dangers inherent in employing troops are equally unable to understand the advantageous ways of doing so.

9. Those adept in waging war do not require a second levy of conscripts nor more than one provisioning.[*]

[†]I insert the character *kuei* (   ) following the "Seven Martial Classics." In the context the character has the sense of "what is valued" or "what is prized."

[*]The commentators indulge in lengthy discussions as to the number of provisionings. This version reads "they do not require three." That is, they require only two, that is, one when they depart and the second when they return. In the meanwhile they

10. They carry equipment from the homeland; they rely for provisions on the enemy. Thus the army is plentifully provided with food.

11. When a country is impoverished by military operations it is due to distant transportation; carriage of supplies for great distances renders the people destitute.

> *Chang Yü*: . . . If the army had to be supplied with grain over a distance of one thousand *li,* the troops would have a hungry look.[†]

12. Where the army is, prices are high; when prices rise the wealth of the people is exhausted. When wealth is exhausted the peasantry will be afflicted with urgent exactions.[*]

> *Chia Lin*: . . . Where troops are gathered the price of every commodity goes up because everyone covets the extraordinary profits to be made.[††]

13. With strength thus depleted and wealth consumed the households in the central plains will be utterly impoverished and seven-tenths of their wealth dissipated.

> *Li Ch'üan*: If war drags on without cessation, men and women will resent not being able to marry, and will be distressed by the burdens of transportation.

14. As to government expenditures, those due to broken-down chariots, worn-out horses, armor and helmets, arrows and crossbows, lances, hand and body shields, draft animals and supply wagons will amount to sixty percent of the total.[**]

15. Hence the wise general sees to it that his troops feed on the enemy, for one bushel of the enemy's provisions is equivalent to twenty of his; one hundredweight of enemy fodder to twenty hundredweight of his.

> *Chang Yü*: . . . In transporting provisions for a distance of one thousand *li,* twenty bushels will be consumed in delivering one to

---

live on the enemy. The TPYL version (following Ts'ao Ts'ao) reads: 'They do not require to be *again* provisioned," that is, during a campaign. I adopt this.

[†]This comment appears under V. 10 but seems more appropriate here.

[*]Or, "close to [where] the army [is]," (i.e., in the zone of operations) "buying is expensive; when buying is expensive . . ." The "urgent [or 'heavy'] exactions" refers to special taxes, forced contributions of animals and grain, and porterage.

[††]This comment, which appears under the previous verse, has been transposed.

[**]Here Sun Tzu uses the specific character for "crossbow."

the army. . . . If difficult terrain must be crossed even more is required.

16. The reason troops slay the enemy is because they are enraged.[†]

Ho Yen-hsi: When the Yen army surrounded Chi Mo in Ch'i, they cut off the noses of all the Ch'i prisoners.[*] The men of Ch'i were enraged and conducted a desperate defense. T'ien Tan sent a secret agent to say: "We are terrified that you people of Yen will exhume the bodies of our ancestors from their graves. How this will freeze our hearts!"

The Yen army immediately began despoiling the tombs and burning the corpses. The defenders of Chi Mo witnessed this from the city walls and with tears flowing wished to go forth to give battle, for rage had multiplied their strength by ten. T'ien Tan knew then that his troops were ready, and inflicted a ruinous defeat on Yen.

17. They take booty from the enemy because they desire wealth.

Tu Mu: . . . In the Later Han, Tu Hsiang, Prefect of Chin Chou, attacked the Kuei Chou rebels Pu Yang, P'an Hung, and others. He entered Nan Hai, destroyed three of their camps, and captured much treasure. However, P'an Hung and his followers were still strong and numerous, while Tu Hsiang's troops, now rich and arrogant, no longer had the slightest desire to fight.

Hsiang said: "Pu Yang and P'an Hung have been rebels for ten years. Both are well-versed in attack and defense. What we should really do is unite the strength of all the prefectures and then attack them. For the present the troops shall be encouraged to go hunting." Whereupon the troops both high and low went together to snare game.

As soon as they had left, Tu Hsiang secretly sent people to burn down their barracks. The treasures they had accumulated were completely destroyed. When the hunters returned there was not one who did not weep.

Tu Hsiang said: "The wealth and goods of Pu Yang and those with him are sufficient to enrich several generations. You gentlemen did not do your best. What you have lost is but a small bit of what is there. Why worry about it?"

[†]This seems out of place.
[*]This siege took place in 279 B.C.

When the troops heard this, they were all enraged and wished to fight. Tu Hsiang ordered the horses fed and everyone to eat in his bed, and early in the morning they marched on the rebels' camp.[†] Yang and Hung had not made preparations, and Tu Hsiang's troops made a spirited attack and destroyed them.

Chang Yü: ... In this Imperial Dynasty, when the Eminent Founder ordered his generals to attack Shu, he decreed: "In all the cities and prefectures taken, you should, in my name, empty the treasuries and public storehouses to entertain the officers and troops. What the State wants is only the land."

18. Therefore, when in chariot fighting more than ten chariots are captured, reward those who take the first. Replace the enemy's flags and banners with your own, mix the captured chariots with yours, and mount them.

19. Treat the captives well, and care for them.

Chang Yü: All the soldiers taken must be cared for with magnanimity and sincerity so that they may be used by us.

20. This is called "winning a battle and becoming stronger."

21. Hence what is essential in war is victory, not prolonged operations. And therefore the general who understands war is the Minister of the people's fate and arbiter of the nation's destiny.

Ho Yen-hsi: The difficulties in the appointment of a commander are the same today as they were in ancient times.[*]

[†]They ate a pre-cooked meal in order to avoid building fires to prepare breakfast.
[*]Ho Yen-hsi probably wrote this about A.D. 1050.

III

OFFENSIVE STRATEGY

SUN TZU said:

1. Generally in war the best policy is to take a state intact; to ruin it is inferior to this.

> *Li Ch'üan:* Do not put a premium on killing.

2. To capture the enemy's army is better than to destroy it; to take intact a battalion, a company or a five-man squad is better than to destroy them.

3. For to win one hundred victories in one hundred battles is not the acme of skill. To subdue the enemy without fighting is the acme of skill.

4. Thus, what is of supreme importance in war is to attack the enemy's strategy;[†]

> *Tu Mu:* . . . The Grand Duke said: "He who excels at resolving difficulties does so before they arise. He who excels in conquering his enemies triumphs before threats materialize."
> *Li Ch'üan:* Attack plans at their inception. In the Later Han, K'ou Hsün surrounded Kao Chun.* Chun sent his Planning Officer, Huang-fu Wen, to parley. Huang-fu Wen was stubborn and rude and K'ou Hsün beheaded him, and informed Kao Chun: "Your staff

---

[†]Not, as Giles translates, "to balk the enemy's plans."
*This took place during the first century A.D.

officer was without propriety. I have beheaded him. If you wish to submit, do so immediately. Otherwise defend yourself." On the same day, Chun threw open his fortifications and surrendered.

All K'ou Hsün's generals said: "May we ask, you killed his envoy, but yet forced him to surrender his city. How is this?"

K'ou Hsün said: "Huang-fu Wen was Kao Chun's heart and guts, his intimate counsellor. If I had spared Huang-fu Wen's life, he would have accomplished his schemes, but when I killed him, Kao Chun lost his guts. It is said: 'The supreme excellence in war is to attack the enemy's plans.' "

All the generals said: "This is beyond our comprehension."

5. Next best is to disrupt his alliances:[†]

> *Tu Yu*: Do not allow your enemies to get together.
> *Wang Hsi*: . . . Look into the matter of his alliances and cause them to be severed and dissolved. If an enemy has alliances, the problem is grave and the enemy's position strong; if he has no alliances the problem is minor and the enemy's position weak.

6. The next best is to attack his army.

> *Chia Lin*: . . . The Grand Duke said: "He who struggles for victory with naked blades is not a good general."
> *Wang Hsi*: Battles are dangerous affairs.
> *Chang Yü*: If you cannot nip his plans in the bud, or disrupt his alliances when they are about to be consummated, sharpen your weapons to gain the victory.

7. The worst policy is to attack cities. Attack cities only when there is no alternative.[*]

8. To prepare the shielded wagons and make ready the necessary arms and equipment requires at least three months; to pile up earthen ramps against the walls an additional three months will be needed.

9. If the general is unable to control his impatience and orders his troops to swarm up the wall like ants, one-third of them will be killed without taking the city. Such is the calamity of these attacks.

[†]Not, as Giles translates, "to prevent the junction of the enemy's forces."

[*]In this series of verses Sun Tzu is not discussing the art of generalship as Giles apparently thought. These are objectives or policies—*cheng* (   )—in order of relative merit.

Tu Mu: . . . In the later Wei, the Emperor T'ai Wu led one hundred thousand troops to attack the Sung general Tsang Chih at Yu T'ai. The Emperor first asked Tsang Chih for some wine.[†] Tsang Chih sealed up a pot full of urine and sent it to him. T'ai Wu was transported with rage and immediately attacked the city, ordering his troops to scale the walls and engage in close combat. Corpses piled up to the top of the walls and after thirty days of this the dead exceeded half his force.

10. Thus, those skilled in war subdue the enemy's army without battle. They capture his cities without assaulting them and overthrow his state without protracted operations.

Li Ch'üan: They conquer by strategy. In the Later Han the Marquis of Tsan, Tsang Kung, surrounded the "Yao" rebels at Yüan Wu, but during a succession of months was unable to take the city.[*] His officers and men were ill and covered with ulcers. The King of Tung Hai spoke to Tsang Kung, saying: "Now you have massed troops and encircled the enemy, who is determined to fight to the death. This is no strategy! You should lift the siege. Let them know that an escape route is open and they will flee and disperse. Then any village constable will be able to capture them!" Tsang Kung followed this advice and took Yüan Wu.

11. Your aim must be to take All-under-Heaven intact. Thus your troops are not worn out and your gains will be complete. This is the art of offensive strategy.

12. Consequently, the art of using troops is this: When ten to the enemy's one, surround him;

13. When five times his strength, attack him;

Chang Yü: If my force is five times that of the enemy I alarm him to the front, surprise him to the rear, create an uproar in the east and strike in the west.

[†]Exchange of gifts and compliments was a normal preliminary to battle.

[*]*Yao* ( ) connotes the supernatural. The Boxers, who believed themselves impervious to foreign lead, could be so described.

14. If double his strength, divide him.[†]

> *Tu Yu*: . . . If a two-to-one superiority is insufficient to manipulate the situation, we use a distracting force to divide his army. Therefore the Grand Duke said: "If one is unable to influence the enemy to divide his forces, he cannot discuss unusual tactics."

15. If equally matched you may engage him.

> *Ho Yen-hsi*: . . . In these circumstances only the able general can win.

16. If weaker numerically, be capable of withdrawing;

> *Tu Mu*: If your troops do not equal his, temporarily avoid his initial onrush. Probably later you can take advantage of a soft spot. Then rouse yourself and seek victory with determined spirit.
> *Chang Yü*: If the enemy is strong and I am weak, I temporarily withdraw and do not engage.[*] This is the case when the abilities and courage of the generals and the efficiency of troops are equal.
>
> If I am in good order and the enemy in disarray, if I am energetic and he careless, then, even if he be numerically stronger, I can give battle.

17. And if in all respects unequal, be capable of eluding him, for a small force is but booty for one more powerful.[††]

> *Chang Yü*: . . . Mencius said: "The small certainly cannot equal the large, nor can the weak match the strong, nor the few the many."[**]

18. Now the general is the protector of the state. If this protection is all-embracing, the state will surely be strong; if defective, the state will certainly be weak.

[†]Some commentators think this verse "means to divide one's own force," but that seems a less satisfactory interpretation, as the character *chih* ( ) used in the two previous verses refers to the enemy.

[*]Tu Mu and Chang Yü both counsel "temporary" withdrawal, thus emphasizing the point that offensive action is to be resumed when circumstances are propitious.

[††]Lit. "the strength of a small force is. . . ." This apparently refers to its weapons and equipment.

[**]CC II (Mencius), i, ch. 7.

Chang Yü: . . . The Grand Duke said: "A sovereign who obtains the right person prospers. One who fails to do so will be ruined."

19. Now there are three ways in which a ruler can bring misfortune upon his army:[†]

20. When ignorant that the army should not advance, to order an advance or ignorant that it should not retire, to order a retirement. This is described as "hobbling the army."

> *Chia Lin:* The advance and retirement of the army can be controlled by the general in accordance with prevailing circumstances. No evil is greater than commands of the sovereign from the court.

21. When ignorant of military affairs, to participate in their administration. This causes the officers to be perplexed.

> *Ts'ao Ts'ao:* . . . An army cannot be run according to rules of etiquette.
> *Tu Mu:* As far as propriety, laws, and decrees are concerned, the army has its own code, which it ordinarily follows. If these are made identical with those used in governing a state the officers will be bewildered.
> *Chang Yü:* Benevolence and righteousness may be used to govern a state but cannot be used to administer an army. Expediency and flexibility are used in administering an army, but cannot be used in governing a state.

22. When ignorant of command problems to share in the exercise of responsibilities. This engenders doubts in the minds of the officers.*

> *Wang Hsi:* . . . If one ignorant of military matters is sent to participate in the administration of the army, then in every movement there will be disagreement and mutual frustration and the entire army will be hamstrung. That is why Pei Tu memorialized the

---

[†]Here I have transposed the characters meaning "ruler" and "army," otherwise the verse would read that there are three ways in which an army can bring misfortune upon the sovereign.

*Lit. "Not knowing [or "not understanding" or "ignorant of"] [where] authority [lies] in the army"; or "ignorant of [matters relating to exercise of] military authority. . . ." The operative character is "authority" or "power."

throne to withdraw the Army Supervisor; only then was he able to pacify Ts'ao Chou.[†]

Chang Yü: In recent times court officials have been used as Supervisors of the Army and this is precisely what is wrong.

23. If the army is confused and suspicious, neighboring rulers will cause trouble. This is what is meant by the saying: "A confused army leads to another's victory."[*]

Meng: . . . The Grand Duke said: "One who is confused in purpose cannot respond to his enemy."
Li Ch'üan: . . . The wrong person cannot be appointed to command. . . . Lin Hsiang-ju, the Prime Minister of Chao, said: "Chao Kua is merely able to read his father's books, and is as yet ignorant of correlating changing circumstances. Now Your Majesty, on account of his name, makes him the commander-in-chief. This is like glueing the pegs of a lute and then trying to tune it."

24. Now there are five circumstances in which victory may be predicted.

25. He who knows when he can fight and when he cannot will be victorious.

26. He who understands how to use both large and small forces will be victorious.

Tu Yu: There are circumstances in war when many cannot attack few, and others when the weak can master the strong. One able to manipulate such circumstances will be victorious.

27. He whose ranks are united in purpose will be victorious.

Tu Yu: Therefore Mencius said: "The appropriate season is not as important as the advantages of the ground; these are not as important as harmonious human relations."[††]

[†]The "Army Supervisors" of the T'ang were in fact political commissars. Pei Tu became Prime Minister in A.D. 815 and in 817 requested the throne to recall the supervisor assigned him, who must have been interfering in army operations.

[*]"Feudal Lords" is rendered "neighboring rulers." The commentators agree that a confused army robs itself of victory.

[††]CC II (Mencius), ii, ch. I, p. 85.

28. He who is prudent and lies in wait for an enemy who is not, will be victorious.

> *Ch'ên Hao*: Create an invincible army and await the enemy's moment of vulnerability.
> *Ho Yen-hsi*: . . . A gentleman said: "To rely on rustics and not prepare is the greatest of crimes; to be prepared beforehand for any contingency is the greatest of virtues."

29. He whose generals are able and not interfered with by the sovereign will be victorious.

> *Tu Yu*: . . . Therefore Master Wang said: "To make appointments is the province of the sovereign; to decide on battle, that of the general."
> *Wang Hsi*: . . . A sovereign of high character and intelligence must be able to know the right man, should place the responsibility on him, and expect results.
> *Ho Yen-hsi*: . . . Now in war there may be one hundred changes in each step. When one sees he can, he advances; when he sees that things are difficult, he retires. To say that a general must await commands of the sovereign in such circumstances is like informing a superior that you wish to put out a fire. Before the order to do so arrives the ashes are cold. And it is said one must consult the Army Supervisor in these matters! This is as if in building a house beside the road one took advice from those who pass by. Of course the work would never be completed![†]
>
> To put a rein on an able general while at the same time asking him to suppress a cunning enemy is like tying up the Black Hound of Han and then ordering him to catch elusive hares. What is the difference?

30. It is in these five matters that the way to victory is known.

31. Therefore I say: "Know the enemy and know yourself; in a hundred battles you will never be in peril.

[†]A paraphrase of an ode that Legge renders:
> They are like one taking counsel with wayfarers about building a house
> Which consequently will never come to completion.
>
> (CC IV, ii, p. 332, Ode I.)

32. When you are ignorant of the enemy but know yourself, your chances of winning or losing are equal.

33. If ignorant both of your enemy and of yourself, you are certain in every battle to be in peril."

> *Li Ch'üan*: Such people are called "mad bandits." What can they expect if not defeat?

IV

DISPOSITIONS†

SUN TZU said:

1. Anciently the skillful warriors first made themselves invincible and awaited the enemy's moment of vulnerability.

2. Invincibility depends on one's self; the enemy's vulnerability on him.

3. It follows that those skilled in war can make themselves invincible but cannot cause an enemy to be certainly vulnerable.

> *Mei Yao-ch'en*: That which depends on me, I can do; that which depends on the enemy cannot be certain.

4. Therefore it is said that one may know how to win, but cannot necessarily do so.

5. Invincibility lies in the defense; the possibility of victory in the attack.*

6. One defends when his strength is inadequate; he attacks when it is abundant.

7. The experts in defense conceal themselves as under the ninefold

---

†The character *hsing* (　) means "shape," "form," or "appearance" or in a more restricted sense, "disposition" or "formation." The Martial Classics edition apparently followed Ts'ao Ts'ao and titled the chapter *Chun Hsing* (　　), "Shape [or "Dispositions"] of the Army." As will appear, the character connotes more than mere physical dispositions.

*"Invincibility is [means] defense; the ability to conquer is [means] attack."

earth; those skilled in attack move as from above the ninefold heavens. Thus they are capable both of protecting themselves and of gaining a complete victory.[†]

> *Tu Yu*: Those expert at preparing defenses consider it fundamental to rely on the strength of such obstacles as mountains, rivers and foothills. They make it impossible for the enemy to know where to attack. They secretly conceal themselves as under the nine-layered ground.
>
> Those expert in attack consider it fundamental to rely on the seasons and the advantages of the ground; they use inundations and fire according to the situation. They make it impossible for an enemy to know where to prepare. They release the attack like a lightning bolt from above the nine-layered heavens.

8. To foresee a victory which the ordinary man can foresee is not the acme of skill;

> *Li Ch'üan*: . . . When Han Hsin destroyed Chao State he marched out of the Well Gorge before breakfast. He said: "We will destroy the Chao army and then meet for a meal." The generals were despondent and pretended to agree. Han Hsin drew up his army with the river to its rear. The Chao troops climbed upon their breastworks and, observing this, roared with laughter and taunted him: "The General of Han does not know how to use troops!" Han Hsin then proceeded to defeat the Chao army and after break-fasting beheaded Lord Ch'eng An.
>
> This is an example of what the multitude does not comprehend.[*]

9. To triumph in battle and be universally acclaimed "Expert" is not the acme of skill, for to lift an autumn down requires no great strength; to distinguish between the sun and moon is no test of vision; to hear the thunderclap is no indication of acute hearing.[††]

> *Chang Yü*: By "autumn down" Sun Tzu means rabbits' down, which on the coming of autumn is extremely light.

[†]The concept that Heaven and Earth each consist of "layers" or "stages" is an ancient one.

[*]Han Hsin placed his army in "death ground." He burned his boats and smashed his cooking pots. The river was at the rear, the Chao army to the front. Han Hsin had to conquer or drown.

[††]To win a hard-fought battle or to win one by luck is no mark of skill.

10. Anciently those called skilled in war conquered an enemy easily conquered.[†]

11. And therefore the victories won by a master of war gain him neither reputation for wisdom nor merit for valor.

Tu Mu: A victory gained before the situation has crystallized is one the common man does not comprehend. Thus its author gains no reputation for sagacity. Before he has bloodied his blade the enemy state has already submitted.

Ho Yen-hsi: . . . When you subdue your enemy without fighting who will pronounce you valorous?

12. For he wins his victories without erring. "Without erring" means that whatever he does ensures his victory; he conquers an enemy already defeated.

Ch'ên Hao: In planning, never a useless move; in strategy, no step taken in vain.

13. Therefore the skillful commander takes up a position in which he cannot be defeated and misses no opportunity to master his enemy.

14. Thus a victorious army wins its victories before seeking battle; an army destined to defeat fights in the hope of winning.

Tu Mu: . . . Duke Li Ching of Wei said: "Now, the supreme requirements of generalship are a clear perception, the harmony of his host, a profound strategy coupled with far-reaching plans, an understanding of the seasons and an ability to examine the human factors. For a general unable to estimate his capabilities or comprehend the arts of expediency and flexibility when faced with the opportunity to engage the enemy will advance in a stumbling and hesitant manner, looking anxiously first to his right and then to his left, and be unable to produce a plan. Credulous, he will place confidence in unreliable reports, believing at one moment this and at another that. As timorous as a fox in advancing or retiring, his groups will be scattered about. What is the difference between this and driving innocent people into boiling water or fire? Is this not exactly like driving cows and sheep to feed wolves or tigers?"

[†]The enemy was conquered easily because the experts previously had created appropriate conditions.

15. Those skilled in war cultivate the *Tao* and preserve the laws and are therefore able to formulate victorious policies.

> *Tu Mu*: The *Tao* is the way of humanity and justice; "laws" are regulations and institutions. Those who excel in war first cultivate their own humanity and justice and maintain their laws and institutions. By these means they make their governments invincible.

16. Now the elements of the art of war are first, measurement of space; second, estimation of quantities; third, calculations; fourth, comparisons; and fifth, chances of victory.

17. Measurements of space are derived from the ground.

18. Quantities derive from measurement, figures from quantities, comparisons from figures, and victory from comparisons.

> *Ho Yen-hsi*:[†] "Ground" includes both distances and type of terrain; "measurement" is calculation. Before the army is dispatched, calculations are made respecting the degree of difficulty of the enemy's land; the directness and deviousness of its roads; the number of his troops; the quantity of his war equipment and the state of his morale. Calculations are made to see if the enemy can be attacked and only after this is the population mobilized and troops raised.

19. Thus a victorious army is as a hundredweight balanced against a grain; a defeated army as a grain balanced against a hundredweight.

20. It is because of disposition that a victorious general is able to make his people fight with the effect of pent-up waters which, suddenly released, plunge into a bottomless abyss.

> *Chang Yü*: The nature of water is that it avoids heights and hastens to the lowlands. When a dam is broken, the water cascades with irresistible force. Now the shape of an army resembles water. Take advantage of the enemy's unpreparedness; attack him when he does not expect it; avoid his strength and strike his emptiness, and like water, none can oppose you.

[†]This comment appears in the text after V. 18. The factors enumerated are qualities of "shape."

V

ENERGY†

SUN TZU said:

1. Generally, management of many is the same as management of few. It is a matter of organization.*

> Chang Yü: To manage a host one must first assign responsibilities to the generals and their assistants, and establish the strengths of ranks and files. . . .
>
> One man is a single; two, a pair; three, a trio. A pair and a trio make a five,†† which is a squad; two squads make a section; five sections, a platoon; two platoons, a company; two companies, a battalion; two battalions, a regiment; two regiments, a group; two groups, a brigade; two brigades, an army.** Each is subordinate to the superior and controls the inferior. Each is properly trained. Thus one may manage a host of a million men just as he would a few.

---

†*Shih* (   ), the title of this chapter, means "force," "influence," "authority," "energy." The commentators take it to mean "energy" or "potential" in some contexts and "situation" in others.

*Fen Shu (   ) is literally "division of [or by] numbers" (or "division and numbering"). Here translated "organization."

††Suggestive that the "pair" and the "trio" carried different weapons.

**A ten-man section; one hundred to the company; two hundred to the battalion; four hundred to the regiment; eight hundred to the group; sixteen hundred to the brigade; thirty-two hundred to the army. This apparently reflects organization at the time Chang Yü was writing. The English terms for the units are arbitrary.

2. And to control many is the same as to control few. This is a matter of formations and signals.

> *Chang Yü:* ... Now when masses of troops are employed, certainly they are widely separated, and ears are not able to hear acutely nor eyes to see clearly. Therefore officers and men are ordered to advance or retreat by observing the flags and banners and to move or stop by signals of bells and drums. Thus the valiant shall not advance alone, nor shall the coward flee.

3. That the army is certain to sustain the enemy's attack without suffering defeat is due to operations of the extraordinary and the normal forces.[†]

> *Li Ch'üan:* The force which confronts the enemy is the normal; that which goes to his flanks the extraordinary. No commander of an army can wrest the advantage from the enemy without extraordinary forces.
> *Ho Yen-hsi:* I make the enemy conceive my normal force to be the extraordinary and my extraordinary to be the normal. Moreover, the normal may become the extraordinary and vice versa.

4. Troops thrown against the enemy as a grindstone against eggs is an example of a solid acting upon a void.

> *Ts'ao Ts'ao:* Use the most solid to attack the most empty.

5. Generally, in battle, use the normal force to engage; use the extraordinary to win.

6. Now the resources of those skilled in the use of extraordinary forces are as infinite as the heavens and earth; as inexhaustible as the flow of the great rivers.[*]

7. For they end and recommence; cyclical, as are the movements of the sun and moon. They die away and are reborn; recurrent, as are the passing seasons.

[†]The concept expressed by *cheng* ( ), "normal" (or "direct") and *ch'i* ( ), "extraordinary" (or "indirect") is of basic importance. The normal (*cheng*) force fixes or distracts the enemy; the extraordinary (*ch'i*) forces act when and where their blows are not anticipated. Should the enemy perceive and respond to a *ch'i* maneuver in such a manner as to neutralize it, the maneuver would automatically become *cheng*.

[*]Sun Tzu uses the characters *chiang* ( ) and *ho* ( ), which I have rendered "the great rivers."

8. The musical notes are only five in number but their melodies are so numerous that one cannot hear them all.

9. The primary colors are only five in number but their combinations are so infinite that one cannot visualize them all.

10. The flavors are only five in number but their blends are so various that one cannot taste them all.

11. In battle there are only the normal and extraordinary forces, but their combinations are limitless; none can comprehend them all.

12. For these two forces are mutually reproductive; their interaction as endless as that of interlocked rings. Who can determine where one ends and the other begins?

13. When torrential water tosses boulders, it is because of its momentum;

14. When the strike of a hawk breaks the body of its prey, it is because of timing.[†]

> *Tu Yu*: Strike the enemy as swiftly as a falcon strikes its target. It surely breaks the back of its prey for the reason that it awaits the right moment to strike. Its movement is regulated.

15. Thus the momentum of one skilled in war is overwhelming, and his attack precisely regulated.[*]

16. His potential is that of a fully drawn crossbow; his timing, the release of the trigger.[††]

17. In the tumult and uproar the battle seems chaotic, but there is no disorder; the troops appear to be milling about in circles but cannot be defeated.[**]

> *Li Ch'üan*: In battle all appears to be turmoil and confusion. But the flags and banners have prescribed arrangements; the sounds of the cymbals, fixed rules.

[†]Or regulation of its distance from the prey.
[*]Following Tu Mu.
[††]Here again the specific character meaning "crossbow" is used.
[**]Sun Tzu's onomatopoetic terms suggest the noise and confusion of battle.

18. Apparent confusion is a product of good order; apparent cowardice, of courage; apparent weakness, of strength.[†]

> *Tu Mu*: The verse means that if one wishes to feign disorder to entice an enemy he must himself be well-disciplined. Only then can he feign confusion. One who wishes to simulate cowardice and lie in wait for his enemy must be courageous, for only then is he able to simulate fear. One who wishes to appear to be weak in order to make his enemy arrogant must be extremely strong. Only then can he feign weakness.

19. Order or disorder depends on organization; courage or cowardice on circumstances; strength or weakness on dispositions.

> *Li Ch'üan*: Now when troops gain a favorable situation the coward is brave; if it be lost, the brave become cowards. In the art of war there are no fixed rules. These can only be worked out according to circumstances.

20. Thus, those skilled at making the enemy move do so by creating a situation to which he must conform; they entice him with something he is certain to take, and with lures of ostensible profit they await him in strength.

21. Therefore a skilled commander seeks victory from the situation and does not demand it of his subordinates.

> *Ch'ên Hao*: Experts in war depend especially on opportunity and expediency. They do not place the burden of accomplishment on their men alone.

22. He selects his men and they exploit the situation*

> *Li Ch'üan*: . . . Now, the valiant can fight; the cautious defend, and the wise counsel. Thus there is none whose talent is wasted.
> *Tu Mu*: . . . Do not demand accomplishment of those who have no talent.
>   When Ts'ao Ts'ao attacked Chang Lu in Han Chung, he left Generals Chang Liao, Li Tien, and Lo Chin in command of over one thousand men to defend Ho Fei. Ts'ao Ts'ao sent instructions

---

[†]Following Tu Mu.

*The text reads: "Thus he is able to select men. . . ." That is, men capable of exploiting any situation. A system of selection not based on nepotism or favoritism is the inference.

to the Army Commissioner, Hsieh Ti, and wrote on the edge of the envelope: "Open this only when the rebels arrive." Soon after, Sun Ch'üan of Wu with one hundred thousand men besieged Ho Fei. The generals opened the instructions and read: "If Sun Ch'üan arrives, Generals Chang and Li will go out to fight. General Lo will defend the city. The Army Commissioner shall not participate in the battle.[†] All the other generals should engage the enemy."

Chang Liao said: "Our Lord is campaigning far away, and if we wait for the arrival of reinforcements the rebels will certainly destroy us. Therefore the instructions say that before the enemy is assembled we should immediately attack him in order to blunt his keen edge and to stabilize the morale of our own troops. Then we can defend the city. The opportunity for victory or defeat lies in this one action."

Li Tien and Chang Liao went out to attack and actually defeated Sun Ch'üan, and the morale of the Wu army was rubbed out. They returned and put their defenses in order and the troops felt secure. Sun Ch'üan assaulted the city for ten days but could not take it and withdrew.

The historian Sun Sheng in discussing this observed: "Now war is a matter of deception. As to the defense of Ho Fei, it was hanging in the air, weak and without reinforcements. If one trusts solely to brave generals who love fighting, this will cause trouble. If one relies solely on those who are cautious, their frightened hearts will find it difficult to control the situation."

Chang Yü: Now the method of employing men is to use the avaricious and the stupid, the wise and the brave, and to give responsibility to each in situations that suit him. Do not charge people to do what they cannot do. Select them and give them responsibilities commensurate with their abilities.

24. He who relies on the situation uses his men in fighting as one rolls logs or stones. Now the nature of logs and stones is that on stable ground they are static; on unstable ground, they move. If square, they stop; if round, they roll.

25. Thus, the potential of troops skillfully commanded in battle may be compared to that of round boulders which roll down from mountain heights.

[†]Ts'ao Ts'ao took care to keep the political officer out of the picture!

Tu Mu: . . . Thus one need use but little strength to achieve much.

Chang Yü: . . . Li Ching said: "In war there are three kinds of situation:

When the general is contemptuous of his enemy and his officers love to fight, their ambitions soaring as high as the azure clouds and their spirits as fierce as hurricanes, this is situation in respect to morale.

When one man defends a narrow mountain defile which is like sheep's intestines or the door of a dog-house, he can withstand one thousand. This is situation in respect to terrain.

When one takes advantage of the enemy's laxity, his weariness, his hunger and thirst, or strikes when his advanced camps are not settled, or his army is only half-way across a river, this is situation in respect to the enemy."

Therefore when using troops, one must take advantage of the situation exactly as if he were setting a ball in motion on a steep slope. The force applied is minute but the results are enormous."

VI

WEAKNESSES AND STRENGTHS

SUN TZU said:

1. Generally, he who occupies the field of battle first and awaits his enemy is at ease; he who comes later to the scene and rushes into the fight is weary.

2. And therefore those skilled in war bring the enemy to the field of battle and are not brought there by him.

3. One able to make the enemy come of his own accord does so by offering him some advantage. And one able to prevent him from coming does so by hurting him.

> *Tu Yu*: . . . If you are able to hold critical points on his strategic roads the enemy cannot come. Therefore Master Wang said: "When a cat is at the rat hole, ten thousand rats dare not come out; when a tiger guards the ford, ten thousand deer cannot cross."

4. When the enemy is at ease, be able to weary him; when well fed, to starve him; when at rest, to make him move.

5. Appear at places to which he must hasten; move swiftly where he does not expect you.

6. That you may march a thousand *li* without wearying yourself is because you travel where there is no enemy.

> *Ts'ao Ts'ao*: Go into emptiness, strike voids, bypass what he defends, hit him where he does not expect you.

7. To be certain to take what you attack is to attack a place the enemy does not protect. To be certain to hold what you defend is to defend a place the enemy does not attack.

8. Therefore, against those skilled in attack, an enemy does not know where to defend; against the experts in defense, the enemy does not know where to attack.

9. Subtle and insubstantial, the expert leaves no trace; divinely mysterious, he is inaudible. Thus he is master of his enemy's fate.

> *Ho Yen-hsi*: . . . I make the enemy see my strengths as weaknesses and my weaknesses as strengths while I cause his strengths to become weaknesses and discover where he is not strong. . . . I conceal my tracks so that none can discern them; I keep silence so that none can hear me.

10. He whose advance is irresistible plunges into his enemy's weak positions; he who in withdrawal cannot be pursued moves so swiftly that he cannot be overtaken.

> *Chang Yü*: . . . Come like the wind, go like the lightning.

11. When I wish to give battle, my enemy, even though protected by high walls and deep moats, cannot help but engage me, for I attack a position he must succor.

12. When I wish to avoid battle I may defend myself simply by drawing a line on the ground; the enemy will be unable to attack me because I divert him from going where he wishes.

> *Tu Mu*: Chu-ko Liang camped at Yang P'ing and ordered Wei Yen and various generals to combine forces and go down to the east. Chu-ko Liang left only ten thousand men to defend the city while he waited for reports. Ssŭ-ma I said: "Chu-ko Liang is in the city; his troops are few; he is not strong. His generals and officers have lost heart." At this time Chu-ko Liang's spirits were high as usual. He ordered his troops to lay down their banners and silence their drums, and did not allow his men to go out. He opened the four gates and swept and sprinkled the streets.
>
> Ssŭ-ma I suspected an ambush, and led his army in haste to the Northern Mountains.
>
> Chu-ko Liang remarked to his Chief of Staff: "Ssŭ-ma I thought I had prepared an ambush and fled along the mountain

ranges." Ssŭ-ma I later learned of this and was overcome with regrets.[†]

13. If I am able to determine the enemy's dispositions while at the same time I conceal my own then I can concentrate and he must divide. And if I concentrate while he divides, I can use my entire strength to attack a fraction of his.[*] There, I will be numerically superior. Then, if I am able to use many to strike few at the selected point, those I deal with will be in dire straits.[††]

> *Tu Mu*: . . . Sometimes I use light troops and vigorous horsemen to attack where he is unprepared, sometimes strong crossbowmen and bow-stretching archers to snatch key positions, to stir up his left, overrun his right, alarm him to the front, and strike suddenly into his rear.
>
> In broad daylight I deceive him by the use of flags and banners and at night confuse him by beating drums. Then in fear and trembling he will divide his forces to take precautionary measures.

14. The enemy must not know where I intend to give battle. For if he does not know where I intend to give battle he must prepare in a great many places. And when he prepares in a great many places, those I have to fight in any one place will be few.

15. For if he prepares to the front his rear will be weak, and if to the rear, his front will be fragile. If he prepares to the left, his right will be vulnerable and if to the right, there will be few on his left. And when he prepares everywhere he will be weak everywhere.[**]

> *Chang Yü*: He will be unable to fathom where my chariots will actually go out, or where my cavalry will actually come from, or where my infantry will actually follow up, and therefore he will disperse and divide and will have to guard against me everywhere. Consequently his force will be scattered and weakened and his

---

[†]This story provides the plot for a popular Chinese opera. Chu-ko Liang sat in a gate tower and played his lute while the porters swept and sprinkled the streets and Ssŭ-ma I's host hovered on the outskirts. Ssŭ-ma I had been fooled before by Chu-ko Liang and would be fooled again.

[*]Lit. "one part of his."

[††]Karlgren GS 1120m for "dire straits."

[**]Lit. "if there is no place he does not make preparations there is no place he is not vulnerable." The double negative makes the meaning emphatically positive.

strength divided and dissipated, and at the place I engage him I can use a large host against his isolated units.

16. One who has few must prepare against the enemy; one who has many makes the enemy prepare against him.

17. If one knows where and when a battle will be fought his troops can march a thousand *li* and meet on the field. But if one knows neither the battleground nor the day of battle, the left will be unable to aid the right, or the right, the left; the van to support the rear, or the rear, the van. How much more is this so when separated by several tens of *li*, or, indeed, by even a few!

> *Tu Yü*: Now those skilled in war must know where and when a battle will be fought. They measure the roads and fix the date. They divide the army and march in separate columns. Those who are distant start first, those who are near by, later. Thus the meeting of troops from distances of a thousand *li* takes place at the same time. It is like people coming to a city market.[†]

18. Although I estimate the troops of Yüeh as many, of what benefit is this superiority in respect to the outcome?[*]

[†]Tu Mu tells the following interesting story to illustrate the point:
Emperor Wu of the Sung sent Chu Ling-shih to attack Ch'iao Tsung in Shu. The Emperor Wu said: "Last year Liu Ching-hsuan went out of the territory inside the river heading for Huang Wu. He achieved nothing and returned. The rebels now think that I should come from outside the river but surmise that I will take them unaware by coming from inside the river. If this is the case they are certain to defend Fu Ch'eng with heavy troops and guard the interior roads. If I go to Huang Wu, I will fall directly into their trap. Now, I will move the main body outside the river and take Ch'eng Tu, and use distracting troops towards the inside of the river. This is a wonderful plan for controlling the enemy."

Yet he was worried that his plan would be known and that the rebels would learn where he was weak and where strong. So he handed a completely sealed letter to Ling Shih. On the envelope he wrote "Open when you reach Pai Ti." At this time the army did not know how it was to be divided or from where it would march.

When Ling Shih reached Pai Ti, he opened the letter which read: "The main body of the army will march together from outside the river to take Ch'eng Tu. Tsang Hsi and Chu Lin from the central river road will take Kuang Han. Send the weak troops embarked in more than ten high boats from within the river toward Huang Wu."

Chiao Tsung actually used heavy troops to defend within the river and Ling Shh exterminated him.

[*]These references to Wu and Yüeh are held by some critics to indicate the date of composition of the text.

19. Thus I say that victory can be created. For even if the enemy is numerous, I can prevent him from engaging.

> *Chia Lin*: Although the enemy be numerous, if he does not know my military situation, I can always make him urgently attend to his own preparations so that he has no leisure to plan to fight me.

20. Therefore, determine the enemy's plans and you will know which strategy will be successful and which will not;

21. Agitate him and ascertain the pattern of his movement.

22. Determine his dispositions and so ascertain the field of battle.[†]

23. Probe him and learn where his strength is abundant and where deficient.

24. The ultimate in disposing one's troops is to be without ascertainable shape. Then the most penetrating spies cannot pry in nor can the wise lay plans against you.

25. It is according to the shapes that I lay the plans for victory, but the multitude does not comprehend this. Although everyone can see the outward aspects, none understands the way in which I have created victory.

26. Therefore, when I have won a victory I do not repeat my tactics but respond to circumstances in an infinite variety of ways.

27. Now an army may be likened to water, for just as flowing water avoids the heights and hastens to the lowlands, so an army avoids strength and strikes weakness.

28. And as water shapes its flow in accordance with the ground, so an army manages its victory in accordance with the situation of the enemy.

29. And as water has no constant form, there are in war no constant conditions.

30. Thus, one able to gain the victory by modifying his tactics in accordance with the enemy situation may be said to be divine.

31. Of the five elements, none is always predominant; of the four seasons, none lasts forever; of the days, some are long and some short, and the moon waxes and wanes.

[†]Lit. "the field of life and death."

VII

MANEUVER†

SUN TZU said:

1. Normally, when the army is employed, the general first receives his commands from the sovereign. He assembles the troops and mobilizes the people. He blends the army into a harmonious entity and encamps it.*

> Li Ch'üan: He receives the sovereign's mandate and in compliance with the victorious deliberations of the temple councils reverently executes the punishments ordained by Heaven.

2. Nothing is more difficult than the art of maneuver. What is difficult about maneuver is to make the devious route the most direct and to turn misfortune to advantage.

3. Thus, march by an indirect route and divert the enemy by enticing him with a bait. So doing, you may set out after he does and arrive before him. One able to do this understands the strategy of the direct and the indirect.

---

†Lit. "struggle" or "contest of the armies" as each strives to gain an advantageous position.

*This verse can be translated as I have, following Li Ch'uan and Chia Lin, or "He encamps the army so that the Gates of Harmony confront one another" following Ts'ao Ts'ao and Tu Mu. After assembling the army, the first task of a commander would be to organize it, or to "harmonize" its diverse elements.

Ts'ao Ts'ao: ... Make it appear that you are far off. You may start after the enemy and arrive before him because you know how to estimate and calculate distances.

Tu Mu: He who wishes to snatch an advantage takes a devious and distant route and makes of it the short way. He turns misfortune to his advantage. He deceives and fools the enemy to make him dilatory and lax, and then marches on speedily.[†]

4. Now both advantage and danger are inherent in manuever.[*]

Ts'ao Ts'ao: One skilled will profit by it; if he is not, it is dangerous.

5. One who sets the entire army in motion to chase an advantage will not attain it.

6. If he abandons the camp to contend for advantage the stores will be lost.

Tu Mu: If one moves with everything the stores will travel slowly and he will not gain the advantage. If he leaves the heavy baggage behind and presses on with the light troops, it is to be feared the baggage would be lost.

7. It follows that when one rolls up the armor and sets out speedily, stopping neither day nor night and marching at double time for a hundred *li,* the three commanders will be captured. For the vigorous troops will arrive first and the feeble straggle along behind, so that if this method is used only one-tenth of the army will arrive.[††]

Tu Mu: ... Normally, an army marches thirty *li* in a day, which is one stage. In a forced march of double distance it covers two stages. You can cover one hundred *li* only if you rest neither day nor night. If the march is conducted in this manner the troops will be taken prisoner. ... When Sun Tzu says that if this method is

---

[†]This comment appears under v. 2 in the text.

[*]Giles based his reading on the TT and translated: "Maneuvering with an army is advantageous; with an undisciplined multitude most dangerous." Sun Hsing-yen also thought this was the meaning of the verse. This too literal translation completely misses the point. Ts'ao Ts'ao's interpretation is surely more satisfactory. The verse is a generalization that introduces what follows. A course of action that may appear advantageous usually contains within itself the seeds of disadvantage. The converse is also true.

[††]By "rolling up armor" Sun Tzu undoubtedly meant that heavy individual equipment would be bundled together and left at base.

used only one out of ten will arrive he means that when there is no alternative and you must contend for an advantageous position, you select the most robust man of ten to go first while you order the remainder to follow in the rear. So of ten thousand men you select one thousand who will arrive at dawn. The remainder will arrive continuously, some in late morning and some in mid-afternoon, so that none is exhausted and all arrive in succession to join those who preceded them. The sound of their marching is uninterrupted. In contending for advantage, it must be for a strategically critical point. Then, even one thousand will be sufficient to defend it until those who follow arrive.

8. In a forced march of fifty *li* the commander of the van will fall, and using this method but half the army will arrive. In a forced march of thirty *li,* but two-thirds will arrive.[†]

9. It follows that an army which lacks heavy equipment, fodder, food and stores will be lost.[*]

> *Li Ch'üan:* . . . The protection of metal walls is not as important as grain and food.

10. Those who do not know the conditions of mountains and forests, hazardous defiles, marshes and swamps, cannot conduct the march of an army;

11. Those who do not use local guides are unable to obtain the advantages of the ground.

> *Tu Mu:* The *Kuan Tzu* says: "Generally, the commander must thoroughly acquaint himself beforehand with the maps so that he knows dangerous places for chariots and carts, where the water is too deep for wagons; passes in famous mountains,[††] the principal rivers, the locations of highlands and hills; where rushes, forests, and reeds are luxuriant; the road distances; the size of cities and

---

[†]This may also be rendered as "The general of the Upper Army [as distinguished from the generals commanding the Central and Lower Armies] will be defeated" or "will be checked." Here the Upper Army would refer to the advance guard when the three divisions of the army marched in column. In other words, the advantages and disadvantages of forced marches must be carefully weighed, and the problem of what should be carried and what left in a secure base considered.

[*]The verse that follows this one repeats a previous verse and is a *non sequitur* here. It has been dropped.

[††]"Famous" because of their strategic significance.

towns; well-known cities and abandoned ones, and where there are flourishing orchards. All this must be known, as well as the way boundaries run in and out. All these facts the general must store in his mind; only then will he not lose the advantage of the ground."

Li Ching said: ". . . We should select the bravest officers and those who are most intelligent and keen, and using local guides, secretly traverse mountain and forest noiselessly and concealing our traces. Sometimes we make artificial animals' feet to put on our feet; at others we put artificial birds on our hats and quietly conceal ourselves in luxuriant undergrowth. After this, we listen carefully for distant sounds and screw up our eyes to see clearly. We concentrate our wits so that we may snatch an opportunity. We observe the indications of the atmosphere; look for traces in the water to know if the enemy has waded a stream, and watch for movement of the trees which indicates his approach."

Ho Yen-hsi: . . . Now, if having received instructions to launch a campaign, we hasten to unfamiliar land where cultural influence has not penetrated and communications are cut, and rush into its defiles, is it not difficult? If I go with a solitary army the enemy awaits me vigilantly. For the situations of an attacker and a defender are vastly different. How much more so when the enemy concentrates on deception and uses many misleading devices! If we have made no plans we plunge in headlong. By braving the dangers and entering perilous places we face the calamity of being trapped or inundated. Marching as if drunk, we may run into an unexpected fight. When we stop at night we are worried by false alarms; if we hasten along unprepared we fall into ambushes. This is to plunge an army of bears and tigers into the land of death. How can we cope with the rebels' fortifications, or sweep him out of his deceptive dens?

Therefore in the enemy's country, the mountains, rivers, highlands, lowlands, and hills which he can defend as strategic points; the forests, reeds, rushes, and luxuriant grasses in which he can conceal himself; the distances over the roads and paths, the size of cities and towns, the extent of the villages, the fertility or barrenness of the fields, the depth of irrigation works, the amounts of stores, the size of the opposing army, the keenness of weapons—all must be fully known. Then we have the enemy in our sights and he can be easily taken.

12. Now war is based on deception. Move when it is advantageous

and create changes in the situation by dispersal and concentration of forces.[†]

13. When campaigning, be swift as the wind; in leisurely march, majestic as the forest; in raiding and plundering, like fire; in standing, firm as the mountains.* As unfathomable as the clouds, move like a thunderbolt.

14. When you plunder the countryside, divide your forces.[††] When you conquer territory, divide the profits.**

15. Weigh the situation, then move.

16. He who knows the art of the direct and the indirect approach will be victorious. Such is the art of maneuvering.

17. The Book of Military Administration says: "As the voice cannot be heard in battle, drums and bells are used. As troops cannot see each other clearly in battle, flags and banners are used."[‡]

18. Now gongs and drums, banners and flags are used to focus the attention of the troops. When the troops can be thus united, the brave cannot advance alone, nor can the cowardly withdraw. This is the art of employing a host.

> *Tu Mu*: . . . The Military Law states: "Those who when they should advance do not do so and those who when they should retire do not do so are beheaded."
>
> When Wu Ch'i fought against Ch'in, there was an officer who before battle was joined was unable to control his ardor. He advanced and took a pair of heads and returned. Wu Ch'i ordered him beheaded.
>
> The Army Commissioner admonished him, saying: "This is a talented officer; you should not behead him." Wu Ch'i replied: "I am confident he is an officer of talent, but he is disobedient."
>
> Thereupon he beheaded him.

[†]Mao Tse-tung paraphrases this verse several times.

*Adopted as his slogan by the Japanese warrior Takeda Shingen.

[††]Yang P'ing-an emends and reads: "Thus wherever your banners point, the enemy is divided." There does not seem to be any justification for this change.

**Rather than "divide the profits" Yang P'ing-an reads: "defend it to the best advantage." The text does not substantiate this rendering.

[‡]This verse is interesting because in it Sun Tzu names a work that antedates his own.

19. In night fighting use many torches and drums, in day fighting many banners and flags in order to influence the sight and hearing of our troops.[†]

> *Tu Mu*: . . . Just as large formations include smaller ones, so large camps include smaller ones. The army of the van, rear, right and left has each its own camp. These form a circle round the headquarters of the commander-in-chief in the center. All the camps encompass the headquarters. The several corners are hooked together so that the camp appears like the *Pi Lei* constellation.[*]
>
> The distance between camps is not greater than one hundred paces or less than fifty. The roads and paths join to enable troops to parade. The fortifications face each other so that each can assist the others with bows and crossbows.
>
> At every crossroad a small fort is built; on top firewood is piled; inside there are concealed tunnels. One climbs up to these by ladders; sentries are stationed there. After darkness, if a sentry hears drumbeats on the four sides of the camp he sets off the beacon fire. Therefore if the enemy attacks at night he may get in at the gates, but everywhere there are small camps, each firmly defended, and to the east, west, north or south he does not know which to attack.
>
> In the camp of the commander-in-chief or in the smaller camps, those who first know the enemy has come allow them all to enter; they then beat the drums and all the camps respond. At all the small forts beacon fires are lit, making it as light as day. Whereupon the officers and troops close the gates of the camps and man the fortifications and look down upon the enemy. Strong crossbows and powerful bows shoot in all directions. . . .
>
> Our only worry is that the enemy will not attack at night, for if he does he is certain to be defeated.

20. Now an army may be robbed of its spirit and its commander deprived of his courage.[††]

> *Ho Yen-hsi*: . . . Wu Ch'i said: "The responsibility for a martial host of a million lies in one man. He is the trigger of its spirit."

[†]Or "the enemy," it is not clear which. Possibly both. Tu Mu's comment is not particularly relevant to the verse but is included because it indicates a remarkably high degree of skill in the science of castramentation.

[*]Markal? *Pi* is Alpharatz.

[††]Or "of his wits," I am not sure which.

Mei Yao-ch'en: . . . If an army has been deprived of its morale, its general will also lose his heart.

Chang Yü: Heart is that by which the general masters. Now order and confusion, bravery and cowardice, are qualities dominated by the heart. Therefore the expert at controlling his enemy frustrates him and then moves against him. He aggravates him to confuse him and harasses him to make him fearful. Thus he robs his enemy of his heart and of his ability to plan.

21. During the early morning spirits are keen, during the day they flag, and in the evening thoughts turn toward home.[†]

22. And therefore those skilled in war avoid the enemy when his spirit is keen and attack him when it is sluggish and his soldiers homesick. This is control of the moral factor.

23. In good order they await a disorderly enemy; in serenity, a clamorous one. This is control of the mental factor.

Tu Mu: In serenity and firmness they are not destroyed by events.
Ho Yen-hsi: For the lone general who with subtlety must control a host of a million against an enemy as fierce as tigers, advantages and disadvantages are intermixed. In the face of countless changes he must be wise and flexible; he must bear in mind all possibilities. Unless he is stout of heart and his judgment not confused, how would he be able to respond to circumstances without coming to his wits' end? And how settle affairs without being bewildered? When unexpectedly confronted with grave difficulties, how could he not be alarmed? How could he control the myriad matters without being confused?

24. Close to the field of battle, they await an enemy coming from afar; at rest, an exhausted enemy; with well-fed troops, hungry ones. This is control of the physical factor.

25. They do not engage an enemy advancing with well-ordered banners nor one whose formations are in impressive array. This is control of the factor of changing circumstances.[*]

26. Therefore, the art of employing troops is that when the enemy

---

[†]Mei Yao-ch'en says that "morning," "day," and "evening" represent the phases of a long campaign.

[*]Or the "circumstantial factor." "They" in these verses refers to those skilled in war.

occupies high ground, do not confront him; with his back resting on hills, do no oppose him.

27. When he pretends to flee, do not pursue.

28. Do not attack his *élite* troops.

29. Do not gobble proffered baits.

> *Mei Yao-ch'en*: The fish which covets bait is caught; troops who covet bait are defeated.
> *Chang Yü*: The "Three Strategies" says: "Under fragrant bait there is certain to be a hooked fish."

30. Do not thwart an enemy returning homewards.

31. To a surrounded enemy you must leave a way of escape.

> *Tu Mu*: Show him there is a road to safety, and so create in his mind the idea that there is an alternative to death. Then strike.
> *Ho Yen-hsi*: When Ts'ao Ts'ao surrounded Hu Kuan he issued an order: "When the city is taken, the defenders will be buried." For month after month it did not fall. Ts'ao Jen said: "When a city is surrounded it is essential to show the besieged that there is a way to survival. Now, Sir, as you have told them they must fight to the death everyone will fight to save his own skin. The city is strong and has a plentiful supply of food. If we attack them many officers and men will be wounded. If we persevere in this it will take many days. To encamp under the walls of a strong city and attack rebels determined to fight to the death is not a good plan!" Ts'ao Ts'ao followed this advice, and the city submitted.

32. Do not press an enemy at bay.

> *Tu Yu*: Prince Fu Ch'ai said: "Wild beasts, when at bay, fight desperately. How much more is this true of men! If they know there is no alternative they will fight to the death."
> During the reign of Emperor Hsüan of the Han, Chao Ch'ung-kuo was suppressing a revolt of the Ch'iang tribe. The Ch'iang tribesmen saw his large army, discarded their heavy baggage, and set out to ford the Yellow River. The road was through narrow defiles, and Ch'ung Kuo drove them along in a leisurely manner.
> Someone said: "We are in pursuit of great advantage but proceed slowly."

Ch'ung-kuo replied: "They are desperate. I cannot press them. If I do this easily they will go without even looking around. If I press them they will turn on us and fight to the death."

All the generals said: "Wonderful!"

33. This is the method of employing troops.

VIII

THE NINE VARIABLES

SUN TZU said:

1. In general, the system of employing troops is that the commander receives his mandate from the sovereign to mobilize the people and assemble the army.[†]

2. You should not encamp in low-lying ground.

3. In communicating ground, unite with your allies.

4. You should not linger in desolate ground.

5. In enclosed ground, resourcefulness is required.

6. In death ground, fight.

7. There are some roads not to follow; some troops not to strike; some cities not to assault; and some ground which should not be contested.

> *Wang Hsi*: In my opinion, troops put out as bait, *élite* troops, and an enemy in well-regulated and imposing formation should not be attacked.

[†]As Sun Tzu uses almost identical words to introduce Chapter vii, Yang P'ing-an would drop this. He would also drop v. 2–6 inclusive, as they occur later in discussion of the "Nine Grounds," and replace them with v. 26–32 inclusive from Chapter vii. Where Sun Tzu uses a negative in v. 2–6, it is not the peremptory form he used previously. Hence I do not feel justified in accepting the emendations proposed. The "Nine Variables" are then expressed in v. 2–7 inclusive.

Tu Mu: Probably this refers to an enemy in a strategic position behind lofty walls and deep moats with a plentiful store of grain and food, whose purpose is to detain my army. Should I attack the city and take it, there would be no advantage worth mentioning; if I do not take it the assault will certainly grind down the power of my army. Therefore I should not attack it.

8. There are occasions when the commands of the sovereign need not be obeyed.[†]

Ts'ao Ts'ao: When it is expedient in operations, the general need not be restricted by the commands of the sovereign.
Tu Mu: The *Wei Liao Tzu* says: "Weapons are inauspicious instruments; strife contrary to virtue; the general, the Minister of Death, who is not responsible to the heavens above, to the earth beneath, to the enemy in his front, or to the sovereign in his rear."
Chang Yü: Now King Fu Ch'ai said: "When you see the correct course, act; do not wait for orders."

9. A general thoroughly versed in the advantages of the nine variable factors knows how to employ troops.

Chia Lin: The general must rely on his ability to control the situation to his advantage as opportunity dictates. He is not bound by established procedures.

10. The general who does not understand the advantages of the nine variable factors will not be able to use the ground to his advantage even though familiar with it.

Chia Lin: . . . A general prizes opportune changes in circumstances.

11. In the direction of military operations one who does not understand the tactics suitable to the nine variable situations will be unable to use his troops effectively, even if he understands the "five advantages."[*]

Chia Lin: . . . The "five variations" are the following: A road, although it may be the shortest, is not to be followed if one knows it is dangerous and there is the contingency of ambush.
An army, although it may be attacked, is not to be attacked if

---

[†]A catch-all that covers the variable circumstances previously enumerated.

[*]A confusing verse that baffles all the commentators. If Chia Lin is correct, the "five advantages" must be the situations named in v. 2–6 inclusive.

it is in desperate circumstances and there is the possibility that the enemy will fight to the death.

A city, although isolated and susceptible to attack, is not to be attacked if there is the probability that it is well stocked with provisions, defended by crack troops under command of a wise general, that its ministers are loyal and their plans unfathomable.

Ground, although it may be contested, is not to be fought for if one knows that, after getting it, it will be difficult to defend, or that he gains no advantage by obtaining it, but will probably be counter-attacked and suffer casualties.

The orders of a sovereign, although they should be followed, are not to be followed if the general knows they contain the danger of harmful superintendence of affairs from the capital.

These five contingencies must be managed as they arise and as circumstances dictate at the time, for they cannot be settled beforehand.

12. And for this reason, the wise general in his deliberations must consider both favorable and unfavorable factors.[†]

Ts'ao Ts'ao: He ponders the dangers inherent in the advantages, and the advantages inherent in the dangers.

13. By taking into account the favorable factors, he makes his plan feasible; by taking into account the unfavorable, he may resolve the difficulties.[*]

Tu Mu: . . . If I wish to take advantage of the enemy I must perceive not just the advantage in doing so but must first consider the ways he can harm me if I do.

Ho Yen-hsi: Advantage and disadvantage are mutually reproductive. The enlightened deliberate.

14. He who intimidates his neighbours does so by inflicting injury upon them.

Chia Lin: Plans and projects for harming the enemy are not confined to any one method. Sometimes entice his wise and virtuous men away so that he has no counselors. Or send treacherous people

---

[†]Sun Tzu says these are "mixed."

[*]Sun Tzu says that by taking account of the favorable factors the plan is made "trustworthy" or "reliable." "Feasible" (or "workable") is as close as I can get it.

to his country to wreck his administration. Sometimes use cunning deceptions to alienate his ministers from the sovereign. Or send skilled craftsmen to encourage his people to exhaust their wealth. Or present him with licentious musicians and dancers to change his customs. Or give him beautiful women to bewilder him.

15. He wearies them by keeping them constantly occupied, and makes them rush about by offering them ostensible advantages.

16. It is a doctrine of war not to assume the enemy will not come, but rather to rely on one's readiness to meet him; not to presume that he will not attack, but rather to make one's self invincible.

> *Ho Yen-hsi*: ... The "Strategies of Wu" says: "When the world is at peace, a gentleman keeps his sword by his side."

17. There are five qualities which are dangerous in the character of a general.

18. If reckless, he can be killed;

> *Tu Mu*: A general who is stupid and courageous is a calamity. Wu Ch'i said: "When people discuss a general they always pay attention to his courage. As far as a general is concerned, courage is but one quality. Now a valiant general will be certain to enter an engagement recklessly and if he does so he will not appreciate what is advantageous."

19. If cowardly, captured;

> *Ho Yen-hsi*: The *Ssu-ma Fa* says: "One who esteems life above all will be overcome with hesitancy. Hesitancy in a general is a great calamity."

20. If quick-tempered you can make a fool of him;

> *Tu Yu*: An impulsive man can be provoked to rage and brought to his death. One easily angered is irascible, obstinate, and hasty. He does not consider difficulties.
> *Wang Hsi*: What is essential in the temperament of a general is steadiness.

21. If he has too delicate a sense of honor you can calumniate him;

> *Mei Yao-ch'en*: One anxious to defend his reputation pays no regard to anything else.

22. If he is of a compassionate nature you can harass him.

Tu Mu: He who is humanitarian and compassionate and fears only casualties cannot give up temporary advantage for a long-term gain and is unable to let go this in order to seize that.

23. Now these five traits of character are serious faults in a general and in military operations are calamitous.

24. The ruin of the army and the death of the general are inevitable results of these shortcomings. They must be deeply pondered.

IX

MARCHES

Sun Tzu said:

1. Generally when taking up a position and confronting the enemy, having crossed the mountains, stay close to valleys. Encamp on high ground facing the sunny side.†

2. Fight downhill; do not ascend to attack.*

3. So much for taking position in mountains.

4. After crossing a river you must move some distance away from it.

5. When an advancing enemy crosses water do not meet him at the water's edge. It is advantageous to allow half his force to cross and then strike.

> *Ho Yen-hsi:* During the Spring and Autumn period the Duke of Sung came to Hung to engage the Ch'u army. The Sung army had deployed before the Ch'u troops had completed crossing the river. The Minister of War said: "The enemy is many, we are but few. I request permission to attack before he has completed his crossing." The Duke of Sung replied: "You cannot."
>
> When the Ch'u army had completed the river crossing but had not yet drawn up its formations, the Minister again asked permis-

---

†Lit. "Looking in the direction of growth, camp in a high place." The commentators explain that *sheng* (   ), "growth," means *yang* (   ), "sunny"—that is, the south.

*The TT reading is adopted. Otherwise: "In mountain warfare, do not ascend to attack."

sion to attack and the Duke replied: "Not yet. When they have drawn up their army we will attack."

The Sung army was defeated, the Duke wounded in the thigh, and the officers of the Van annihilated.[†]

6. If you wish to give battle, do not confront your enemy close to the water.[*] Take position on high ground facing the sunlight. Do not take position downstream.

7. This relates to taking up positions near a river.

8. Cross salt marshes speedily. Do not linger in them. If you encounter the enemy in the middle of a salt marsh you must take position close to grass and water with trees to your rear.[††]

9. This has to do with taking up position in salt marshes.

10. In level ground occupy a position which facilitates your action. With heights to your rear and right, the field of battle is to the front and the rear is safe.[**]

11. This is how to take up position in level ground.

12. Generally, these are advantageous for encamping in the four situations named.[‡] By using them the Yellow Emperor conquered four sovereigns.[‡‡]

13. An army prefers high ground to low; esteems sunlight and dislikes shade. Thus, while nourishing its health, the army occupies a firm position. An army that does not suffer from countless diseases is said to be certain of victory.[§]

[†]The source of Mao Tse-tung's remark: "We are not like the Duke of Sung."

[*]The commentators say that the purpose of retiring from the banks or shores is to lure the enemy to attempt a crossing.

[††]Possibly salt flats from time to time inundated, as one sees in north and east China, rather than the salt marshes negotiable only by boat, with which we are more familiar.

[**]Sun Tzu says: "To the front, death; to the rear, life." The right flank was the more vulnerable; shields were carried on the left arm.

[‡]That is, the methods described are to be used in encamping the army. Chang Yü takes the verses to relate to encamping but then proceeds to quote Chu-ko Liang on fighting in such places.

[‡‡]Supposed to have reigned 2697–2597 B.C.

[§]Lit. "the one hundred diseases."

14. When near mounds, foothills, dikes or embankments, you must take position on the sunny side and rest your right and rear on them.

15. These methods are all advantageous for the army, and gain the help the ground affords.[†]

16. Where there are precipitous torrents, "Heavenly Wells," "Heavenly Prisons," "Heavenly Nets," "Heavenly Traps," and "Heavenly Cracks," you must march speedily away from them. Do not approach them.

> *Ts'ao Ts'ao*: Raging waters in deep mountains are "precipitous torrents." A place surrounded by heights with low-lying ground in the center is called a "Heavenly Well." When you pass through mountains and the terrain resembles a covered cage it is a "Heavenly Prison." Places where troops can be entrapped and cut off are called "Heavenly Nets." Where the land is sunken, it is a "Heavenly Trap." Where mountain gorges are narrow and where the road is sunken for several tens of feet, this is a "Heavenly Crack."

17. I keep a distance from these and draw the enemy toward them. I face them and cause him to put his back to them.

18. When on the flanks of the army there are dangerous defiles or ponds covered with aquatic grasses where reeds and rushes grow, or forested mountains with dense tangled undergrowth you must carefully search them out, for these are places where ambushes are laid and spies are hidden.

19. When the enemy is near by but lying low he is depending on a favorable position. When he challenges to battle from afar he wishes to lure you to advance, for when he is in easy ground he is in an advantageous position.[*]

20. When the trees are seen to move the enemy is advancing.

21. When many obstacles have been placed in the undergrowth, it is for the purpose of deception.

22. Birds rising in flight is a sign that the enemy is lying in ambush;

[†]The verse that immediately follows this in the text reads: "When rain falls in the upper reaches of a river and foaming water descends those who wish to ford must wait until the waters subside." This is obviously out of place here. I suspect it is part of the commentary that has worked its way into the text.

[*]Another version seems to have read: ". . . is offering an ostensible advantage."

when the wild animals are startled and flee he is trying to take you unaware.

23. Dust spurting upward in high straight columns indicates the approach of chariots. When it hangs low and is widespread infantry is approaching.

> *Tu Mu*: When chariots and cavalry travel rapidly they come one after another like fish on a string and therefore the dust rises high in slender columns.
>
> *Chang Yü*: . . . Now when the army marches there should be patrols out to the front to observe. If they see dust raised by the enemy, they must speedily report this to the commanding general.

24. When dust rises in scattered areas the enemy is bringing in firewood; when there are numerous small patches which seem to come and go he is encamping the army.[†]

25. When the enemy's envoys speak in humble terms, but he continues his preparations, he will advance.

> *Chang Yü*: When T'ien Tan was defending Chi Mo the Yen general Ch'i Che surrounded it. T'ien Tan personally handled the spade and shared in the labor of the troops. He sent his wives and concubines to enroll in the ranks and divided his own food to entertain his officers. He also sent women to the city walls to ask for terms of surrender. The Yen general was very pleased. T'ien Tan also collected twenty-four thousand ounces of gold, and made the rich citizens send a letter to the Yen general which said: "The city is to be surrendered immediately. Our only wish is that you will not make our wives and concubines prisoners." The Yen army became increasingly relaxed and negligent and T'ien Tan sallied out of the city and inflicted a crushing defeat on them.

26. When their language is deceptive but the enemy pretentiously advances, he will retreat.

27. When the envoys speak in apologetic terms, he wishes a respite.[*]

[†]Li Ch'üan's reading, "bringing in firewood," is adopted. They are dragging bundles of firewood. The comments that interrupt this verse are devoted to discussions of how people collect firewood!

[*]This verse, out of place in the text, has been moved to the present context.

28. When without a previous understanding the enemy asks for a truce, he is plotting.

> *Ch'ên Hao:* . . . If without reason one begs for a truce it is assuredly because affairs in his country are in a dangerous state and he is worried and wishes to make a plan to gain a respite. Or otherwise he knows that our situation is susceptible to his plots and he wants to forestall our suspicions by asking for a truce. Then he will take advantage of our unpreparedness.

29. When light chariots first go out and take position on the flanks the enemy is forming for battle.

> *Chang Yü:* In the "Fish Scale Formation" chariots are in front, infantry behind them.

30. When his troops march speedily and he parades his battle chariots he is expecting to rendezvous with reinforcements.[†]

31. When half his force advances and half withdraws he is attempting to decoy you.

32. When his troops lean on their weapons, they are famished.

33. When drawers of water drink before carrying it to camp, his troops are suffering from thirst.

34. When the enemy sees an advantage but does not advance to seize it, he is fatigued.[*]

35. When birds gather above his camp sites, they are empty.

> *Ch'ên Hao:* Sun Tzu is describing how to distinguish between the true and the false in the enemy's aspect.

36. When at night the enemy's camp is clamorous, he is fearful.[††]

> *Tu Mu:* His troops are terrified and insecure. They are boisterous to reassure themselves.

37. When his troops are disorderly, the general has no prestige.

[†]This is not exactly clear. He expects to rendezvous with reinforcing troops? Or are his dispersed detachments concentrating?

[*]The fact that this series of verses is expressed in elementary terms does not restrain the commentators, who insist on explaining each one at considerable length.

[††]See Plutarch's description in "Alexander" of the Persian camp the night before the battle of Gaugemala.

Ch'ên Hao: When the general's orders are not strict and his deportment undignified, the officers will be disorderly.

38. When his flags and banners move about constantly he is in disarray.

Tu Mu: Duke Chuang of Lu defeated Ch'i at Ch'ang Sho. Tsao Kuei requested permission to pursue. The Duke asked him why. He replied: "I see that the ruts of their chariots are confused and their flags and banners drooping. Therefore I wish to pursue them."

39. If the officers are short-tempered they are exhausted.

Ch'ên Hao: When the general lays on unnecessary projects, everyone is fatigued.
Chang Yü: When administration and orders are inconsistent, the men's spirits are low, and the officers exceedingly angry.

40. When the enemy feeds grain to the horses and his men meat and when his troops neither hang up their cooking pots nor return to their shelters, the enemy is desperate.[†]

Wang Hsi: The enemy feeds grain to the horses and the men eat meat in order to increase their strength and powers of endurance. If the army has no cooking pots it will not again eat. If the troops do not go back to their shelters they have no thoughts of home and intend to engage in decisive battle.

41. When the troops continually gather in small groups and whisper together the general has lost the confidence of the army.[*]

42. Too frequent rewards indicate that the general is at the end of his resources; too frequent punishments that he is in acute distress.[††]

43. If the officers at first treat the men violently and later are fearful of them, the limit of indiscipline has been reached.[**]

[†]Chang Yü says that when an army "burns its boats" and "smashes its cooking pots" it is at bay and will fight to the death.
[*]Comments under this verse are principally devoted to explaining the terms used. Most of the commentators agree that when the men gather together and carry on whispered conversations they are criticizing their officers. Mei Yao-ch'en observes that they are probably planning to desert. The verse that immediately follows is a paraphrase of this one, and is dropped.
[††]Ho Yen-hsi remarks that in the management of his affairs the general should seek a balance of tolerance and severity.
[**]Or "at first to bluster but later to be in fear of the enemy's host"? Ts'ao Ts'ao, Tu Mu, Wang Hsi and Chang Yü all take the *ch'i* (   ) here to refer to the enemy,

44. When the enemy troops are in high spirits, and, although facing you, do not join battle for a long time, nor leave, you must thoroughly investigate the situation.

45. In war, numbers alone confer no advantage. Do not advance relying on sheer military power.[†]

46. It is sufficient to estimate the enemy situation correctly and to concentrate your strength to capture him.[*] There is no more to it than this. He who lacks foresight and underestimates his enemy will surely be captured by him.

47. If troops are punished before their loyalty is secured they will be disobedient. If not obedient, it is difficult to employ them. If troops are loyal, but punishments are not enforced, you cannot employ them.

48. Thus, command them with civility and imbue them uniformly with martial ardor and it may be said that victory is certain.

49. If orders which are consistently effective are used in instructing the troops, they will be obedient. If orders which are not consistently effective are used in instructing them, they will be disobedient.

50. When orders are consistently trustworthy and observed, the relationship of a commander with his troops is satisfactory.

but this thought does not follow the preceding verse too well. Tu Yu's interpretation, which I adopt, seems better.

[†]"For it is not by the numbers of the combatants but by their orderly array and their bravery that prowess in war is wont to be measured." Procopius, *History of the Wars,* p. 347.

[*]Ts'ao Ts'ao misinterprets *tsu* (　) here in the phrase *tsu i* (　　) meaning "it is sufficient." His mistake obviously confused the commentators and none cared to take issue with him. Wang Hsi starts off bravely enough by saying: "I think those who are skilled in creating changes in the situation by concentration and dispersion need only gather their forces together and take advantage of a chink in the enemy's defenses to gain the victory," but in the end allows Ts'ao Ts'ao's prestige to overcome his own better judgment.

X

TERRAIN[†]

SUN TZU said:

1. Ground may be classified according to its nature as accessible, entrapping, indecisive, constricted, precipitous, and distant.*

2. Ground which both we and the enemy can traverse with equal ease is called accessible. In such ground, he who first takes high sunny positions convenient to his supply routes can fight advantageously.

3. Ground easy to get out of but difficult to return to is entrapping. The nature of this ground is such that if the enemy is unprepared and you sally out you may defeat him. If the enemy is prepared and you go out and engage, but do not win, it is difficult to return. This is unprofitable.

4. Ground equally disadvantageous for both the enemy and ourselves to enter is indecisive. The nature of this ground is such that although the enemy holds out a bait I do not go forth but entice him by marching off. When I have drawn out half his force, I can strike him advantageously.

[†]"Topography" or "conformation of the ground."
*Mei Yao-ch'en defines "accessible" ground as that in which roads meet and cross; "entrapping" ground as net-like; "indecisive" ground as that in which one gets locked with the enemy; "constricted" ground as that in which a valley runs between two mountains; "precipitous" ground as that in which there are mountains, rivers, foothills, and ridges, and "distant" ground as level. Sun Tzu uses "distant" to indicate that there is a considerable distance between the camps of the two armies.

> *Chang Yü*: . . . Li Ching's "Art of War" says: "In ground which offers no advantage to either side we should lure the enemy by feigned departure, wait until half his force has come out, and make an intercepting attack."

5. If I first occupy constricted ground I must block the passes and await the enemy. If the enemy first occupies such ground and blocks the defiles I should not follow him; if he does not block them completely I may do so.

6. In precipitous ground I must take position on the sunny heights and await the enemy.[†] If he first occupies such ground I lure him by marching off; I do not follow him.

> *Chang Yü*: If one should be the first to occupy a position in level ground, how much more does this apply to difficult and dangerous places![*] How can such terrain be given to the enemy?

7. When at a distance from an enemy of equal strength it is difficult to provoke battle and unprofitable to engage him in his chosen position.[††]

8. These are the principles relating to six different types of ground. It is the highest responsibility of the general to inquire into them with the utmost care.

> *Mei Yao-ch'en*: Now the nature of the ground is the fundamental factor in aiding the army to set up its victory.

9. Now when troops flee, are insubordinate,[**] distressed, collapse in disorder or are routed, it is the fault of the general. None of these disasters can be attributed to natural causes.

10. Other conditions being equal, if a force attacks one ten times its size, the result is flight.

[†]Generally I have translated the *Yang* of *Yin-Yang* as "south" or "sunny," and *Yin* as "north" or "shady." In the context of Sun Tzu these terms have no cosmic connotations.

[*]*Hsien* (   ) means a "narrow pass," hence "dangerous" and by implication "strategic."

[††]The phrase following "engage" is added to clarify Sun Tzu's meaning.

[**]The character rendered "insubordinate" is *shih* (   ), "to unstring a bow"; hence, "lax," "remiss," "loose." The commentators make it clear that in this context the character means "insubordinate."

Tu Mu: When one is to be used to attack ten we should first compare the wisdom and the strategy of the opposing generals, the bravery and cowardice of the troops, the question of weather, of the advantages offered by the ground, whether the troops are well fed or hungry, weary or rested.

11. When troops are strong and officers weak the army is insubordinate.

Tu Mu: The verse is speaking of troops and non-commissioned officers[†] who are unruly and overbearing, and generals and commanders who are timid and weak.

In the present dynasty at the beginning of the Ch'ang Ch'ing reign period* T'ien Pu was ordered to take command in Wei for the purpose of attacking Wang T'ing-ch'ou. Pu had grown up in Wei and the people there held him in contempt, and several tens of thousands of men all rode donkeys about the camp. Pu was unable to restrain them. He remained in his position for several months and when he wished to give battle, the officers and troops dispersed and scattered in all directions. Pu cut his own throat.

12. When the officers are valiant and the troops ineffective the army is in distress.[††]

13. When senior officers are angry and insubordinate, and on encountering the enemy rush into battle with no understanding of the feasibility of engaging and without awaiting orders from the commander, the army is in a state of collapse.

Ts'ao Ts'ao: "Senior officers" means subordinate generals. If . . . in a rage they attack the enemy without measuring the strength of both sides, then the army is assuredly in a state of collapse.

14. When the general is morally weak and his discipline not strict, when his instructions and guidance are not enlightened, when there are no consistent rules to guide the officers and men and when the formations are slovenly the army is in disorder.**

[†]*Wu* (   ) denotes a file of five men or the leader of such a file; a corporal; a non-commissioned officer.

*A.D. 820–825.

[††]Bogged down or sinking, as in a morass. The idea is that if the troops are weak the efforts of the officers are as vain as if the troops were in a bog.

**The term rendered "slovenly" is literally "vertically and horizontally."

Chang Yü: . . . Chaos self-induced.

15. When a commander unable to estimate his enemy uses a small force to engage a large one, or weak troops to strike the strong, or when he fails to select shock troops for the van, the result is rout.

> *Ts'ao Ts'ao*: Under these conditions he commands "certain-to-flee" troops.
> *Ho Yen-hsi*: . . . In the Han the "Gallants from the Three Rivers" were "Sword Friends" of unusual talent. In Wu the shock troops were called "Dissolvers of Difficulty"; in Ch'i "Fate Deciders"; in the T'ang "Leapers and Agitators." These were various names applied to shock troops; nothing is more important in the tactics of winning battles than to employ them.[†]
>
> Generally when all the troops are encamped together the general selects from every camp its high-spirited and valiant officers who are distinguished by agility and strength and whose martial accomplishments are above the ordinary. These are grouped to form a special corps. Of ten men, but one is selected; of ten thousand, one thousand.
> *Chang Yü*: . . . Generally in battle it is essential to use *élite* troops as the vanguard sharp point. First, because this strengthens our own determination; second, because they blunt the enemy's edge.

16. When any of these six conditions prevails the army is on the road to defeat. It is the highest responsibility of the general that he examine them carefully.

17. Conformation of the ground is of the greatest assistance in battle. Therefore, to estimate the enemy situation and to calculate distances and the degree of difficulty of the terrain so as to control victory are virtues of the superior general. He who fights with full knowledge of these factors is certain to win; he who does not will surely be defeated.

18. If the situation is one of victory but the sovereign has issued orders not to engage, the general may decide to fight. If the situation is such that he cannot win, but the sovereign has issued orders to engage, he need not do so.

[†]Unfortunately the functions of the "Leapers and Agitators" are not explained. Undoubtedly one may have been to arouse the ardor of the troops by wild gyrating and acrobatic sword play for which the Chinese are justly renowned, and possibly at the same time to impress the enemy with their ferocity and skill.

19. And therefore the general who in advancing does not seek personal fame, and in withdrawing is not concerned with avoiding punishment, but whose only purpose is to protect the people and promote the best interests of his sovereign, is the precious jewel of the state.

> *Li Ch'üan*: . . . Such a general has no personal interest.
> *Tu Mu*: . . . Few such are to be had.

20. Because such a general regards his men as infants they will march with him into the deepest valleys. He treats them as his own beloved sons and they will die with him.

> *Li Ch'üan*: If he cherishes his men in this way he will gain their utmost strength. Thus, the Viscount of Ch'u needed but to speak a word and the soldiers felt as if clad in warm silken garments.[†]
> *Tu Mu*: During the Warring States when Wu Ch'i was a general he took the same food and wore the same clothes as the lowliest of his troops. On his bed there was no mat; on the march he did not mount his horse; he himself carried his reserve rations. He shared exhaustion and bitter toil with his troops.
> *Chang Yü*: . . . Therefore the Military Code says: "The general must be the first in the toils and fatigues of the army. In the heat of summer he does not spread his parasol nor in the cold of winter don thick clothing. In dangerous places he must dismount and walk. He waits until the army's wells have been dug and only then drinks; until the army's food is cooked before he eats; until the army's fortifications have been completed, to shelter himself."[*]

21. If a general indulges his troops but is unable to employ them; if he loves them but cannot enforce his commands; if the troops are disorderly and he is unable to control them, they may be compared to spoiled children, and are useless.

> *Chang Yü*: . . . If one uses kindness exclusively the troops become like arrogant children and cannot be employed. This is the reason Ts'ao Ts'ao cut off his own hair and so punished himself.[††] . . . Good commanders are both loved and feared.

[†]The Viscount commiserated with those suffering from the cold. His words were enough to comfort the men and raise their flagging spirits.

[*]Military essays and codes were generally entitled *Ping Fa*. Chang Yü does not identify the one from which he quotes.

[††]After having issued orders that his troops were not to damage standing grain,

22. If I know that my troops are capable of striking the enemy, but do not know that he is invulnerable to attack, my chance of victory is but half.

23. If I know that the enemy is vulnerable to attack, but do not know that my troops are incapable of striking him, my chance of victory is but half.

24. If I know that the enemy can be attacked and that my troops are capable of attacking him, but do not realize that because of the conformation of the ground I should not attack, my chance of victory is but half.

25. Therefore when those experienced in war move they make no mistakes; when they act, their resources are limitless.

26. And therefore I say: "Know the enemy, know yourself; your victory will never be endangered. Know the ground, know the weather; your victory will then be total."

Ts'ao Ts'ao carelessly permitted his own grazing horse to trample it. He thereupon ordered himself to be beheaded. His officers tearfully remonstrated, and Ts'ao Ts'ao then inflicted upon himself this symbolic punishment to illustrate that even a commander-in-chief is amenable to military law and discipline.

XI

THE NINE VARIETIES OF GROUND†

SUN TZU said:

1. In respect to the employment of troops, ground may be classified as dispersive, frontier, key, communicating, focal, serious, difficult, encircled, and death.*

2. When a feudal lord fights in his own territory, he is in dispersive ground.

> *Ts'ao Ts'ao:* Here officers and men long to return to their nearby homes.

3. When he makes but a shallow penetration into enemy territory he is in frontier ground.††

4. Ground equally advantageous for the enemy or me to occupy is key ground.**

---

†The original arrangement of this chapter leaves much to be desired. Many verses are not in proper context; others are repetitious and may possibly be ancient commentary that has worked its way into the text. I have transposed some verses and eliminated those that appear to be accretions.

*There is some confusion here. The "accessible" ground of the preceding chapter is defined in the same terms as "communicating" ground.

††Lit. "light" ground, possibly because it is easy to retire or because the officers and men think lightly of deserting just as the expedition is getting under way.

**This is contestable ground, or, as Tu Mu says, "strategically important."

5. Ground equally accessible to both the enemy and me is communicating.

> *Tu Mu*: This is level and extensive ground in which one may come and go, sufficient in extent for battle and to erect opposing fortifications.

6. When a state is enclosed by three other states its territory is focal. He who first gets control of it will gain the support of All-under-Heaven.[†]

7. When the army has penetrated deep into hostile territory, leaving far behind many enemy cities and towns, it is in serious ground.

> *Ts'ao Ts'ao*: This is ground difficult to return from.

8. When the army traverses mountains, forests, precipitous country, or marches through defiles, marshlands, or swamps, or any place where the going is hard, it is in difficult ground.[*]

9. Ground to which access is constricted, where the way out is tortuous, and where a small enemy force can strike my larger one is called "encircled."[††]

> *Tu Mu*: . . . Here it is easy to lay ambushes and one can be utterly defeated.

10. Ground in which the army survives only if it fights with the courage of desperation is called "death."

> *Li Ch'üan*: Blocked by mountains to the front and rivers to the rear, with provisions exhausted. In this situation it is advantageous to act speedily and dangerous to procrastinate.

11. And therefore, do not fight in dispersive ground; do not stop in the frontier borderlands.

12. Do not attack an enemy who occupies key ground; in communicating ground do not allow your formations to become separated.[**]

[†]The Empire is always described as "All-under-Heaven."

[*]The commentators indulge in some discussion respecting the interpretation of the character rendered "difficult." Several want to restrict the meaning to ground susceptible to flooding.

[††]The verb may be translated as "tie down" rather than "strike."

[**]Ts'ao Ts'ao says they must be "closed up."

13. In focal ground, ally with neighbouring states; in deep ground, plunder.†

14. In difficult ground, press on; in encircled ground, devise stratagems; in death ground, fight.

15. In dispersive ground I would unify the determination of the army.*

16. In frontier ground I would keep my forces closely linked.

> *Mei Yao-ch'en*: On the march the several units are connected; at halts the camps and fortified posts are linked together.

17. In key ground I would hasten up my rear elements.

> *Ch'ên Hao*: What the verse means is that if . . . the enemy, relying on superior numbers, comes to contest such ground, I use a large force to hasten into his rear.††
>
> *Chang Yü*: . . . Someone has said that the phrase means "to set out after the enemy and arrive before him."**

18. In communicating ground I would pay strict attention to my defenses.

19. In focal ground I would strengthen my alliances.

> *Chang Yü*: I reward my prospective allies with valuables and silks and bind them with solemn covenants. I abide firmly by the treaties and then my allies will certainly aid me.

20. In serious ground I would ensure a continuous flow of provisions.

21. In difficult ground I would press on over the roads.

22. In encircled ground I would block the points of access and egress.

> *Tu Mu*: It is military doctrine that an encircling force must leave a gap to show the surrounded troops there is a way out, so that they will not be determined to fight to the death. Then, taking

---

†Li Ch'üan thinks the latter half should read "do not plunder," as the principal object when in enemy territory is to win the affection and support of the people.

*This and the nine verses that immediately follow have been transposed to this context. In the text they come later in the chapter.

††The question is, whose "rear" is Sun Tzu talking about? Ch'ên Hao is reading something into the verse as it stands in present context.

**The "someone" is Mei Yao-ch'en, who takes *hou* ( ) to mean "after" in the temporal sense.

advantage of this, strike. Now, if I am in encircled ground, and the enemy opens a road in order to tempt my troops to take it, I close this means of escape so that my officers and men will have a mind to fight to the death.[†]

23. In death ground I could make it evident that there is no chance of survival. For it is the nature of soldiers to resist when surrounded; to fight to the death when there is no alternative, and when desperate to follow commands implicitly.

24. The tactical variations appropriate to the nine types of ground, the advantages of close or extended deployment, and the principles of human nature are matters the general must examine with the greatest care.[*]

25. Anciently, those described as skilled in war made it impossible for the enemy to unite his van and his rear; for his elements both large and small to mutually cooperate; for the good troops to succor the poor and for superiors and subordinates to support each other.[††]

26. When the enemy's forces were dispersed they prevented him from assembling them; when concentrated, they threw him into confusion.

> *Meng*: Lay on many deceptive operations. Be seen in the west and march out of the east; lure him in the north and strike in the south. Drive him crazy and bewilder him so that he disperses his forces in confusion.
>
> *Chang Yü*: Take him unaware by surprise attacks where he is unprepared. Hit him suddenly with shock troops.

27. They concentrated and moved when it was advantageous to do so;[**] when not advantageous, they halted.

28. Should one ask: "How do I cope with a well-ordered enemy host

---

[†]A long story relates that Shen Wu of the Later Wei, when in such a position, blocked the only escape road for his troops with the army's livestock. His forces then fought desperately and defeated an army of two hundred thousand.

[*]This verse is followed by seven short verses that again define terms previously defined in v. 2 to 10 inclusive. This appears to be commentary that has worked its way into the text.

[††]The implication is that even were the enemy able to concentrate, internal dissensions provoked by the skilled general would render him ineffective.

[**]Lit. "They concentrated where it was advantageous to do so and then acted. When it was not advantageous they stood fast." In another commentary Shih Tzu-mei says not to move unless there is advantage in it.

about to attack me?" I reply: "Seize something he cherishes and he will conform to your desires."†

29. Speed is the essence of war. Take advantage of the enemy's unpreparedness; travel by unexpected routes and strike him where he has taken no precautions.

> *Tu Mu*: This summarizes the essential nature of war . . . and the ultimate in generalship.

> *Chang Yü*: Here Sun Tzu again explains . . . that the one thing esteemed is divine swiftness.

30. The general principles applicable to an invading force are that when you have penetrated deeply into hostile territory your army is united, and the defender cannot overcome you.

31. Plunder fertile country to supply the army with plentiful provisions.

32. Pay heed to nourishing the troops; do not unnecessarily fatigue them. Unite them in spirit; conserve their strength. Make unfathomable plans for the movements of the army.

33. Throw the troops into a position from which there is no escape and even when faced with death they will not flee. For if prepared to die, what can they not achieve? Then officers and men together put forth their utmost efforts. In a desperate situation they fear nothing; when there is no way out they stand firm. Deep in a hostile land they are bound together, and there, where there is no alternative, they will engage the enemy in hand-to-hand combat.*

34. Thus, such troops need no encouragement to be vigilant. Without extorting their support the general obtains it; without inviting their affection he gains it; without demanding their trust he wins it.††

35. My officers have no surplus of wealth but not because they disdain worldly goods; they have no expectation of long life but not because they dislike longevity.

---

†Comments between question and answer omitted.

*There are several characters in Chinese that basically mean "to fight." That used here implies "close combat."

††This refers to the troops of a general who nourishes them, who unites them in spirit, who husbands their strength, and who makes unfathomable plans.

Wang Hsi: . . . When officers and men care only for worldly riches they will cherish life at all costs.

36. On the day the army is ordered to march the tears of those seated soak their lapels; the tears of those reclining course down their cheeks.

Tu Mu: All have made a covenant with death. Before the day of battle the order is issued: "Today's affair depends upon this one stroke. The bodies of those who do not put their lives at stake will fertilize the fields and become carrion for the birds and beasts."

37. But throw them into a situation where there is no escape and they will display the immortal courage of Chuan Chu and Ts'ao Kuei.[†]

38. Now the troops of those adept in war are used like the "Simultaneously Responding" snake of Mount Ch'ang. When struck on the head its tail attacks; when struck on the tail, its head attacks, when struck in the center both head and tail attack.[*]

39. Should one ask: "Can troops be made capable of such instantaneous co-ordination?" I reply: "They can." For, although the men of Wu and Yüeh mutually hate one another, if together in a boat tossed by the wind they would cooperate as the right hand does with the left.

40. It is thus not sufficient to place one's reliance on hobbled horses or buried chariot wheels.[††]

41. To cultivate a uniform level of valor is the object of military administration.[**] And it is by proper use of the ground that both shock and flexible forces are used to the best advantage.[‡]

Chang Yü: If one gains the advantage of the ground then even weak and soft troops can conquer the enemy. How much more so

---

[†]The exploits of these heroes are recounted in SC, ch. 68.

[*]This mountain was anciently known as Mt. Hêng. During the reign of the Emperor Wên (Liu Hêng) of the Han (179–159 B.C.) the name was changed to "Ch'ang" to avoid the taboo. In all existing works "Hêng" was changed to "Ch'ang."

[††]Such "Maginot Line" expedients are not in themselves sufficient to prevent defending troops from fleeing.

[**]Lit. "To equalize courage [so that it is that of] one [man] is the right way of administration."

[‡]Chang Yü makes it clear why terrain should be taken into account when troops are disposed. The difference in quality of troops can be balanced by careful sector assignment. Weak troops can hold strong ground, but might break if posted in a position less strong.

if they are tough and strong! That both may be used effectively is because they are disposed in accordance with the conditions of the ground.

42. It is the business of a general to be serene and inscrutable, impartial and self-controlled.[†]

> *Wang Hsi*: If serene he is not vexed; if inscrutable, unfathomable; if upright, not improper; if self-controlled, not confused.

43. He should be capable of keeping his officers and men in ignorance of his plans.

> *Ts'ao Ts'ao*: . . . His troops may join him in rejoicing at the accomplishment, but they cannot join him in laying the plans.

44. He prohibits superstitious practices and so rids the army of doubts. Then until the moment of death there can be no troubles.[*]

> *Ts'ao Ts'ao*: Prohibit talk of omens and of supernatural portents. Rid plans of doubts and uncertainties.
> *Chang Yü*: The *Ssu-ma Fa* says: "Exterminate superstitions."

45. He changes his methods and alters his plans so that people have no knowledge of what he is doing.

> *Chang Yü*: Courses of action previously followed and old plans previously executed must be altered.

46. He alters his camp-sites and marches by devious routes, and thus makes it impossible for others to anticipate his purpose.[††]

47. To assemble the army and throw it into a desperate position is the business of the general.

[†]Giles translated: "It is the business of a general to be quiet and thus ensure secrecy; upright and just and thus maintain order." The commentators do not agree, but none takes it in this sense, nor does the text support this rendering. I follow Ts'ao Ts'ao and Wang Hsi.

[*]The　　 at the end of this sentence is emended to read　　, which means a natural or "heaven sent" calamity. Part of Ts'ao Ts'ao's comment that is omitted indicates that various texts were circulating in his time.

[††]Or perhaps, "makes it impossible for the enemy to learn *his* plans." But Mei Yao-ch'en thinks the meaning is that the enemy will thus be rendered incapable of laying plans. Giles infers that the general, by altering his camps and marching by devious routes, can prevent the enemy "from anticipating his purpose," which seems the best. The comments do not illuminate the point at issue.

48. He leads the army deep into hostile territory and there releases the trigger.[†]

49. He burns his boats and smashes his cooking pots; he urges the army on as if driving a flock of sheep, now in one direction, now in another, and none knows where he is going.[*]

50. He fixes a date for rendezvous and after the troops have met, cuts off their return route just as if he were removing a ladder from beneath them.

51. One ignorant of the plans of neighboring states cannot prepare alliances in good time; if ignorant of the conditions of mountains, forests, dangerous defiles, swamps, and marshes he cannot conduct the march of an army; if he fails to make use of native guides he cannot gain the advantages of the ground. A general ignorant of even one of these three matters is unfit to command the armies of a Hegemonic King.[††]

> Ts'ao Ts'ao: These three matters have previously been elaborated. The reason Sun Tzu returns to the subject is that he strongly disapproved of those unable to employ troops properly.

52. Now when a Hegemonic King attacks a powerful state he makes it impossible for the enemy to concentrate. He overawes the enemy and prevents his allies from joining him.[**]

> Mei Yao-ch'en: In attacking a great state, if you can divide your enemy's forces your strength will be more than sufficient.

53. It follows that he does not contend against powerful combinations nor does he foster the power of other states. He relies for the attainment

---

[†]"Release" of a trigger, or mechanism, is the usual meaning of the expression *fa chi* (   ). The idiom has been translated: "puts into effect his expedient plans." Wang Hsi says that when the trigger is released "there is no return" (of the arrow or bolt). Lit. this verse reads: "He leads the army deep into the territory of the Feudal Lords and there releases the trigger" (or "puts into effect his expedient plans"). Giles translates the phrase in question as "shows his hand," that is, takes irrevocable action.

[*]Neither his own troops nor the enemy can fathom his ultimate design.

[††]Emending   —"[these] four or five [matters]"—to read   — "these three [matters]."

[**]This verse and next present problems. Chang Yü thinks the verse means that if the troops of a Hegemonic King (or a ruler who aspires to such status) attack hastily (or recklessly, or without forethought) *his* allies will not come to *his* aid. The other commentators interpret the verse as I have.

of his aims on his ability to overawe his opponents. And so he can take the enemy's cities and overthrow the enemy's state.[†]

> *Ts'ao Ts'ao*: By "Hegemonic King" is meant one who does not ally with the feudal lords. He breaks up the alliances of All–under–Heaven and snatches the position of authority. He uses prestige and virtue to attain his ends.[*]
>
> *Tu Mu*: The verse says if one neither covenants for the help of neighbors nor develops plans based on expediency but in further-ance of his personal aims relies only on his own military strength to overawe the enemy country then his own cities can be captured and his own state overthrown.[††]

54. Bestow rewards without respect to customary practice; publish or-ders without respect to precedent.[**] Thus you may employ the entire army as you would one man.

> *Chang Yü*: . . . If the code respecting rewards and punishments is clear and speedily applied then you may use the many as you do the few.

55. Set the troops to their tasks without imparting your designs; use them to gain advantage without revealing the dangers involved. Throw them into a perilous situation and they survive; put them in death ground and they will live. For when the army is placed in such a situation it can snatch victory from defeat.

56. Now the crux of military operations lies in the pretense of accom-modating one's self to the designs of the enemy.[‡]

[†]The commentators differ in their interpretations of this verse. Giles translates: "Hence he does not strive to ally himself with all and sundry nor does he foster the power of other states. He carries out his own secret designs, keeping his antagonists in awe. Thus he is able to capture their cities and overthrow their kingdoms." But I feel that Sun Tzu meant that the "Hegemonic King" need not contend against "powerful combinations" because he isolates his enemies. He does not permit them to form "pow-erful combinations."

[*]Possibly Giles derived his interpretation from this comment.

[††]Also a justifiable interpretation, which illustrates how radically the commentators frequently differ.

[**]This verse, obviously out of place, emphasizes that the general in the field need not follow prescribed procedures in recognition of meritorious service but should be-stow timely rewards. The general need not follow customary law in respect to admin-istration of his army.

[‡]Possibly too free a translation, but the commentators agree that this is the idea Sun Tzu tries to convey. I follow Tu Mu.

57. Concentrate your forces against the enemy and from a distance of a thousand *li* you can kill his general.[†] This is described as the ability to attain one's aim in an artful and ingenious manner.

58. On the day the policy to attack is put into effect, close the passes, rescind the passports,[*] have no further intercourse with the enemy's envoys and exhort the temple council to execute the plans.[††]

59. When the enemy presents an opportunity, speedily take advantage of it.[**] Anticipate him in seizing something he values and move in accordance with a date secretly fixed.

60. The doctrine of war is to follow the enemy situation in order to decide on battle.[‡]

61. Therefore at first be shy as a maiden. When the enemy gives you an opening be swift as a hare and he will be unable to withstand you.

[†]I follow Ts'ao Ts'ao here. A strategist worthy of the name defeats his enemy from a distance of one thousand *li* by anticipating his enemy's plans.

[*]Lit. "break the tallies." These were carried by travelers and were examined by the Wardens of the Passes. Without a proper tally no one could legally enter or leave a country.

[††]The text is confusing. It seems literally to read: "From [the rostrum of] the temple, exhort [the army?] [the people?] to execute the plans." The commentators are no help.

[**]Another difficult verse. Some commentators think it should read: "When the enemy sends spies, immediately let them enter." The difficulty is in the idiom *k'ai ho* (   ), literally, "to open the leaf of a door," thus, "to present an opportunity [to enter]." Ts'ao Ts'ao says the idiom means "a cleavage," "a gap," or "a space." Then, he goes on, "you must speedily enter." Other commentators say the idiom means "spies" or "secret agents." I follow Ts'ao Ts'ao.

[‡]The commentators again disagree: v. 58–61 are susceptible to varying translations or interpretations.

XII

ATTACK BY FIRE

SUN TZU said:

1. There are five methods of attacking with fire. The first is to burn personnel; the second, to burn stores; the third, to burn equipment; the fourth, to burn arsenals; and the fifth, to use incendiary missiles.[†]

2. To use fire, some medium must be relied upon.

   Ts'ao Ts'ao: Rely upon traitors among the enemy.[*]
   Chang Yü: All fire attacks depend on weather conditions.

3. Equipment for setting fires must always be at hand.

   Chang Yü: Implements and combustible materials should be prepared beforehand.

4. There are suitable times and appropriate days on which to raise fires.

5. "Times" means when the weather is scorching hot; "days" means when the moon is in Sagittarius, Alpharatz, *I,* or *Chen* constellations, for these are days of rising winds.[††]

[†]There is a mistake in the text here. Tu Yu emends and explains that flame-tipped arrows are fired into the enemy's barracks or camp by strong crossbowmen. Other commentators vary in their interpretations, but Tu Yu's emendation is logical.

[*]"among the enemy" added. Ch'ên Hao remarks that one does not only rely on traitors.

[††]Sun Hsing-yen has emended the original text in accordance with the TT and YL, but the original seems better and I follow it. I cannot place the *I* and *Chen* constellations.

6. Now in fire attacks one must respond to the changing situation.

7. When fire breaks out in the enemy's camp immediately coordinate your action from without. But if his troops remain calm bide your time and do not attack.

8. When the fire reaches its height, follow up if you can. If you cannot do so, wait.

9. If you can raise fires outside the enemy camp, it is not necessary to wait until they are started inside. Set fires at suitable times.[†]

10. When fires are raised up-wind do not attack from down-wind.

11. When the wind blows during the day it will die down at night.[*]

12. Now the army must know the five different fire-attack situations and be constantly vigilant.[††]

13. Those who use fire to assist their attacks are intelligent; those who use inundations are powerful.

14. Water can isolate an enemy but cannot destroy his supplies or equipment.[**]

15. Now to win battles and take your objectives, but to fail to exploit these achievements is ominous and may be described as "wasteful delay."[‡]

16. And therefore it is said that enlightened rulers deliberate upon the plans, and good generals execute them.

17. If not in the interests of the state, do not act. If you cannot succeed, do not use troops. If you are not in danger, do not fight.[‡‡]

18. A sovereign cannot raise an army because he is enraged, nor can a general fight because he is resentful. For while an angered man may

---

[†]A warning not to be cooked in your own fire is to be inferred from the last sentence.

[*]Following Chang Yü.

[††]Following Tu Mu.

[**]Following Ts'ao Ts'ao.

[‡]Mei Yao-ch'en is the only commentator who caught Sun Tzu's meaning: situations must be exploited.

[‡‡]The commentators make it clear that war is to be used only as a last resort.

again be happy, and a resentful man again be pleased, a state that has perished cannot be restored, nor can the dead be brought back to life.

19. Therefore, the enlightened ruler is prudent and the good general is warned against rash action.† Thus the state is kept secure and the army preserved.

†Last three words added. Rage and resentment lead to rash action.

XIII

EMPLOYMENT OF SECRET AGENTS†

SUN TZU said:

1. Now when an army of one hundred thousand is raised and dispatched on a distant campaign the expenses borne by the people together with the disbursements of the treasury will amount to a thousand pieces of gold daily. There will be continuous commotion both at home and abroad, people will be exhausted by the requirements of transport, and the affairs of seven hundred thousand households will be disrupted.*

> *Ts'ao Ts'ao*: Anciently, eight families comprised a community. When one family sent a man to the army, the remaining seven contributed to its support. Thus, when an army of one hundred thousand was raised those unable to attend fully to their own ploughing and sowing amounted to seven hundred thousand households.

2. One who confronts his enemy for many years in order to struggle for victory in a decisive battle yet who, because he begrudges rank, honors and a few hundred pieces of gold, remains ignorant of his ene-

---

†The character used in the title means "the space between" two objects (such as a crack between two doors) and thus "cleavage," "division," or "to divide." It also means "spies," "spying," or "espionage."

*I have translated "to a distance of one thousand *li*" as "on a distant campaign." The figure need not be taken as specific.

my's situation, is completely devoid of humanity. Such a man is no general; no support to his sovereign; no master of victory.

3. Now the reason the enlightened prince and the wise general conquer the enemy whenever they move and their achievements surpass those of ordinary men is foreknowledge.

> *Ho Yen-hsi*: The section in the Rites of Chou entitled "Military Officers" names "The Director of National Espionage." This officer probably directed secret operations in other countries.[†]

4. What is called "foreknowledge" cannot be elicited from spirits, nor from gods, nor by analogy with past events, nor from calculations. It must be obtained from men who know the enemy situation.

5. Now there are five sorts of secret agents to be employed. These are native, inside, doubled, expendable, and living.[*]

6. When these five types of agents are all working simultaneously and none knows their method of operation, they are called "The Divine Skein" and are the treasure of a sovereign.[††]

7. Native agents are those of the enemy's country people whom we employ.

8. Inside agents are enemy officials whom we employ.

> *Tu Mu*: Among the official class there are worthy men who have been deprived of office; others who have committed errors and have been punished. There are sycophants and minions who are covetous of wealth. There are those who wrongly remain long in lowly office; those who have not obtained responsible positions, and those whose sole desire is to take advantage of times of trouble to extend the scope of their own abilities. There are those who are two-faced, changeable, and deceitful, and who are always sitting on the fence. As far as all such are concerned you can secretly inquire after their welfare, reward them liberally with gold and silk, and so tie them to you. Then you may rely on them to seek out the real facts of the situation in their country, and to ascertain its plans

---

[†]Probably an appeal to the authority of tradition to support the legitimacy of espionage and subversion which are contrary to the spirit of Confucian teaching.

[*]I use "expendable" in lieu of "death."

[††]The idea is that information may be gathered in as fish are by pulling on a single cord and so drawing together the various threads of a net.

directed against you. They can as well create cleavages between the sovereign and his ministers so that these are not in harmonious accord.

9. Doubled agents are enemy spies whom we employ.

Li Ch'üan: When the enemy sends spies to pry into my accomplishments or lack of them, I bribe them lavishly, turn them around, and make them my agents.

10. Expendable agents are those of our own spies who are deliberately given fabricated information.

Tu Yu: We leak information which is actually false and allow our own agents to learn it. When these agents operating in enemy territory are taken by him they are certain to report this false information. The enemy will believe it and make preparations accordingly. But our actions will of course not accord with this, and the enemy will put the spies to death.

Chang Yü: . . . In our dynasty Chief of Staff Ts'ao once pardoned a condemned man whom he then disguised as a monk, and caused to swallow a ball of wax and enter Tangut. When the false monk arrived he was imprisoned. The monk told his captors about the ball of wax and soon discharged it in a stool. When the ball was opened, the Tanguts read a letter transmitted by Chief of Staff Ts'ao to their Director of Strategic Planning. The chieftain of the barbarians was enraged, put his minister to death, and executed the spy monk. This is the idea. But expendable agents are not confined to only one use. Sometimes I send agents to the enemy to make a covenant of peace and then I attack.

11. Living agents are those who return with information.

Tu Yu: We select men who are clever, talented, wise, and able to gain access to those of the enemy who are intimate with the sovereign and members of the nobility. Thus they are able to observe the enemy's movements and to learn of his doings and his plans. Having learned the true state of affairs they return and tell us. Therefore they are called "living" agents.

Tu Mu: These are people who can come and go and communicate reports. As living spies we must recruit men who are intelligent but appear to be stupid; who seem to be dull but are strong in heart; men who are agile, vigorous, hardy, and brave; well-versed in lowly matters and able to endure hunger, cold, filth, and humiliation.

12. Of all those in the army close to the commander none is more intimate than the secret agent; of all rewards none more liberal than those given to secret agents; of all matters none is more confidential than those relating to secret operations.

> *Mei Yao-ch'en*: Secret agents receive their instructions within the tent of the general, and are intimate and close to him.
> *Tu Mu*: These are "mouth to ear" matters.

13. He who is not sage and wise, humane and just, cannot use secret agents. And he who is not delicate and subtle cannot get the truth out of them.

> *Tu Mu*: The first essential is to estimate the character of the spy to determine if he is sincere, truthful, and really intelligent. Afterwards, he can be employed. . . . Among agents there are some whose only interest is in acquiring wealth without obtaining the true situation of the enemy, and only meet my requirements with empty words.† In such a case I must be deep and subtle. Then I can assess the truth or falsity of the spy's statements and discriminate between what is substantial and what is not.
> *Mei Yao-ch'en*: Take precautions against the spy having been turned around.

14. Delicate indeed! Truly delicate! There is no place where espionage is not used.

15. If plans relating to secret operations are prematurely divulged the agent and all those to whom he spoke of them shall be put to death.*

> *Ch'ên Hao*: . . . They may be killed in order to stop their mouths and prevent the enemy hearing.

16. Generally in the case of armies you wish to strike, cities you wish to attack, and people you wish to assassinate, you must know the names of the garrison commander, the staff officers, the ushers, gate keepers, and the bodyguards. You must instruct your agents to inquire into these matters in minute detail.

---

†Such agents are now aptly described as "paper mills."

*Giles translated: "If a secret piece of news is divulged by a spy before the time is ripe. . . ." Sun Tzu is not talking about "news" here but about espionage affairs, or matters or plans relating to espionage.

Tu Mu: If you wish to conduct offensive war you must know the men employed by the enemy. Are they wise or stupid, clever or clumsy? Having assessed their qualities, you prepare appropriate measures. When the King of Han sent Han Hsin, Ts'ao Ts'an, and Kuan Ying to attack Wei Pao he asked: "Who is the commander-in-chief of Wei?" The reply was: "Po Chih." The King said: "His mouth still smells of his mother's milk. He cannot equal Han Hsin. Who is the Cavalry commander?" The reply was: "Feng Ching." The King said: "He is the son of General Feng Wu-che of Ch'in. Although worthy, he is not the equal of Kuan Ying. And who is the infantry commander?" The reply was: "Hsiang T'o." The King said: "He is no match for Ts'ao Ts'an. I have nothing to worry about."

17. It is essential to seek out enemy agents who have come to conduct espionage against you and to bribe them to serve you. Give them instructions and care for them.† Thus doubled agents are recruited and used.

18. It is by means of the doubled agent that native and inside agents can be recruited and employed.

Chang Yü: This is because the doubled agent knows those of his own countrymen who are covetous as well as those officials who have been remiss in office. These we can tempt into our service.

19. And it is by this means that the expendable agent, armed with false information, can be sent to convey it to the enemy.

Chang Yü: It is because doubled agents know in what respects the enemy can be deceived that expendable agents may be sent to convey false information.

20. It is by this means also that living agents can be used at appropriate times.

21. The sovereign must have full knowledge of the activities of the five sorts of agents. This knowledge must come from the doubled agents, and therefore it is mandatory that they be treated with the utmost liberality.

---

†These agents, according to Giles' translation, are to be "tempted with bribes, led away and comfortably housed."

22. Of old, the rise of Yin was due to I Chih, who formerly served the Hsia; the Chou came to power through Lu Yu, a servant of the Yin.[†]

Chang Yü: I Chih was a minister of Hsia who went over to the Yin. Lu Wang was a minister of Yin who went over to the Chou.

23. And therefore only the enlightened sovereign and the worthy general who are able to use the most intelligent people as agents are certain to achieve great things. Secret operations are essential in war; upon them the army relies to make its every move.

Chia Lin: An army without secret agents is exactly like a man without eyes or ears.

[†]Several of the commentators are outraged that these worthies are described by Sun Tzu as "spies" or "agents," but of course they were.

BIBLIOGRAPHY TO SUN TZU
TRANSLATION

I

Books in English

Aston, W. G. *The Nihongi*. Transactions and Proceedings of the Japan Society, Supplement I. London, 1896. Kegan Paul.

De Bary, William T., and others. *Sources of Chinese Tradition*. New York, 1960. Columbia University Press.

Baynes, Cary F. *The I Ching, or Book of Changes*. The Richard Wilhelm Translation. London, 1951. Routledge & Kegan Paul.

Calthrop, Captain E. F. *The Book of War*. London, 1908. John Murray.

Carlson, Evans F. *Twin Stars of China*. New York, 1940. Dodd, Mead & Co.

Cheng, Lin. *The Art of War*. Shanghai, China, 1946. The World Book Company Ltd.

Dubs, Professor Homer H. (trans.). *History of the Former Han Dynasty* (3 vols.). Baltimore, Md., 1946, 1955. The Waverly Press.

———— *Hsün Tze, The Moulder of Ancient Confucianism*. London, 1927. Arthur Probsthain.

———— *The Works of Hsün Tze*. London, 1928. Arthur Probsthain.

Duyvendak, J. J. L. *Tao Te Ching*. The Book of the Way and Its Virtue. London, 1954. John Murray.

———— *The Book of Lord Shang*. London, 1928. Arthur Probsthain.

Fitzgerald, C. P. *China, A Short Cultural History* (rev. ed.). London, 1950. The Cresset Press Ltd.

Fung, Yu-lan. *A History of Chinese Philosophy* (trans. Bodde). Princeton, 1952. Princeton University Press.

Gale, Esson M. (trans.). *Discourses on Salt and Iron*. Sinica Leidensia, vol. ii. Leiden, 1931. E. J. Brill Ltd.

Giles, Lionel (trans.). *Sun Tzu on the Art of War*. London, 1910. Luzac & Co.

Granet, Marcel. *Chinese Civilization.* London, 1957. Routledge & Kegan Paul Ltd.

Legge, James. *The Chinese Classics.* London, 1861. Trubner & Co.

Liang, Ch'i-ch'ao. *Chinese Political Thought.* London, 1930. Kegan Paul; Trench, Trubner & Co. Ltd.

Liao, W. K. (trans.). *The Complete Works of Han Fei-tzu* (2 vols.). London, 1939 (vol. i); 1959 (vol. ii). Arthur Probsthain.

McCullogh, Helen Craig (trans.). *The Taiheiki. A Chronicle of Medieval Japan.* New York, 1959. Columbia University Press.

Machell-Cox, E. *Principles of War by Sun Tzu.* Colombo, Ceylon. A Royal Air Force Welfare Publication.

Mao Tse-tung. *Selected Works.* London, 1955. Lawrence & Wishart.

———— *Strategic Problems in the Anti-Japanese Guerrilla War.* Peking, 1954. Foreign Language Press.

Mei, Y. P. *Motse, the Neglected Rival of Confucius.* London, 1934. Arthur Probsthain.

———— *The Ethical and Political Works of Motse.* London, 1929. Arthur Probsthain.

Müller, Max F. (ed.). *The Sacred Books of the East* (vol. xv): *The Yi King* (trans. Legge). Oxford, 1882. The Clarendon Press.

Murdoch, James. *A History of Japan* (3rd impression). London, 1949. Routledge & Kegan Paul Ltd.

Payne, Robert. *Mao Tse-tung, Ruler of Red China.* London, 1951. Secker & Warburg.

Ryusaka, Tsunuda, de Bery, and Keene. *Sources of the Japanese Tradition.* New York, 1958. Columbia University Press.

Sadler, Professor A. L. *The Makers of Modern Japan.* London, 1937. George Allen & Unwin Ltd.

———— *Three Military Classics of China.* Sydney, Australia, 1944. Australasian Medical Publishing Co. Ltd.

Sansom, George B. *A History of Japan to 1334* (San II). London, 1958. The Cresset Press.

———— *Japan, A Short Cultural History* (2nd impression, revised) (San I). London, 1952. The Cresset Press Ltd.

Schwartz, Benjamin I. *Chinese Communism and The Rise of Mao* (3rd printing). Cambridge, Mass., 1958. Harvard University Press.

Snow, Edgar. *Red Star over China* (Left Book Club Edition). London, 1937. Victor Gollancz Ltd.

Tjan Tjoe Som (Tseng, Chu-sen). *The Comprehensive Discussions in The White Tiger Hall.* Leiden, 1952. E. J. Brill.

Waley, Arthur. *The Analects of Confucius.* London, 1938. George Allen & Unwin Ltd.

Walker, Richard L. *The Multi-State System of Ancient China.* Hamden, Conn., 1953. The Shoe String Press.

Watson, Burton. *Ssu-ma Ch'ien, Grand Historian of China.* New York, 1958. Columbia University Press.

II

Monographs and Articles in English

Bodde, Dirk. *Statesman, Patriot and General in Ancient China.* New Haven, Conn., 1943. A Publication of the American Oriental Society.

Chang, Ch'i-yün. *China's Ancient Military Geography.* Chinese Culture, vii, no. 3. Taipeh, December 1959.

Extracts from China Mainland Magazines. "Fragmentary Notes on the Way Comrade Mao Tse-tung Pursued his Studies in his Early Days." American Consulate General. Hong Kong, 191, 7 December 1959.

Lanciotti, Lionello. *Sword Casting and Related Legends in China, I, II.* East and West, Year VI, N. 2, N. 4. Rome, 1955, 1956.

Needham, J. *The Development of Iron and Steel Technology in China.* London, 1958. The Newcomen Society.

North, Robert C. "The Rise of Mao Tse-tung." *The Far Eastern Quarterly,* vol. xi, no. 2, February 1952.

Rowley, Harold H. *The Chinese Philosopher Mo Ti* (reprint from *Bulletin of the John Rylands Library,* vol. xxxi, no. 2, November 1948). Manchester, 1948. The Manchester University Press.

Selections from China Mainland Magazines. "Comrade Lin Piao in the Period of Liberation War in the Northeast." American Consulate General. Hong Kong, 217, 11 July 1960.

Teng, Ssu-yü. *New Light on the History of the T'aip'ing Rebellion.* Cambridge, Mass., 1950. Harvard University Press.

Van Straelen, H. *Yoshida Shoin.* Monographies du T'oung Pao, vol. ii. Leiden, 1952. E. J. Brill.

III

Books, Monographs and Articles in Western Languages
(other than English)

Amiot, J. J. L. *Mémoires concernant l'histoire, les sciences, les arts les mœurs, les usages, etc. des Chinois.* Chez Nyon l'aîné. Paris, 1782.

Ashiya, Mizuyo. *Der Chinesische Kriegsphilosoph der Vorchristlichen Zeit.* Wissen und Wehr, 1939, 416–27.

Chavannes, Edouard. *Les Mémoires historiques de Se-ma Ts'ien.* Paris. Ernest Leroux.

Cholet, E. *L'Art militaire dans l'antiquité chinoise.* Paris, 1922. Charles-Lavauzelle.

Cotenson, G. de. "L'Art militaire des Chinois, d'après leurs classiques." *Le Nouvelle Revue*. Paris, August 1900.

Gaillois, Brig.-Gen. R. *Lois de la guerre en Chine*. Preuves, 1956.

Konrad, N. I. *Wu Tzu*. Traktat o Voennom Iskusstve. Moscow, 1958. Publishing House of Eastern Literature.

———— *Sun Tzu*. Traktat o Voennom Iskusstve. Moscow, 1950. Publishing House of the Academy of Science USSR.

Maspero, Henri. *La Chine Antique* (Nouvelle éd.). Paris, 1955. Imprimerie Nationale.

Nachin, L. (ed.). *Sun Tse et les anciens Chinois Ou Tse et Se Ma Fa*. Paris, 1948. Editions Berger-Levrault.

Sidorenko, J. I. *Ssun-ds' Traktat über Die Kriegskunst*. Berlin, 1957. Ministerium Für Nationale Verteidigung.

IV

Works in Chinese

Chan Kuo Shih.

Yang K'uan. "A History of the Warring States." People's Press. Shanghai, 1956.

Chao Chu Sun Tzu Shih San P'ien.

Chao Pen-hsüeh. "Chao (Pen-hsueh's) Commentary on the Thirteen Chapters of Sun Tzu." Peiyang Military Academy Press. Peking, 1905.

Chin I Hsin P'ien Sun Tzu Ping Fa.

Kuo Hua-jo. "A Modern Translation of Sun Tzu's Art of War with New Chapter Arrangement." People's Press. Peking, 1957.

Ch'in Ting Ku Chin T'u Shu Chi Ch'eng.

Chung Hua Shu Chü. Short Title: *T'u Shu*. "Photographic reproduction of the Palace Edition of 1731. Chapter 83 "Military Canon." Shanghai, 1934.

Chung Kuo Ping Ch'i Shih Kao.

Chou Wei and San Lien Shu Tien. "A Draft History of Chinese Weapons." Peking, 1957.

Ku Chin Wei Shu K'ao Pu Cheng.

Huang Yun-mei. "A Further Inquiry into Apocryphal Books both Ancient and Modern." Shantung People's Press, 1959.

Pei T'ang Shu Ch'ao.

Yü Shih-nan. "Selected Passages Transcribed in the Northern Hall." (558–638).

Shih Ch'i Hsuan.

Wang Po-hsiang. "Selections from the Historical Records." People's Literary Press. Peking, 1958.

Ssu-ma Fa.

Chung Hua Shu Chü. "The Art of War of Ssu-ma Jang-chiu." *Ssu Pu Pei Yao*, ed. Shanghai.

Sun Tzu Shih San P'ien Chiao Chien Chi Yao.

Yang P'ing-an. "Notes on the Collation of Sun Tzu's Thirteen Chapters." *Peking University Journal of the Humanities*, no. i, 1958.

Sun Tzu Chi Chiao.

Yang P'ing-an and Chung Hua Shu Chu. "A Collated Critical Study of Sun Tzu." Shanghai, 1959.

Sun Tzu.

Chung Hua Shu Chü and Sun Hsing-yen. The Sun Tzu with Commentaries. *Ssu Pu Pei Yao*, ed. Shanghai, 1931.

Sun-Wu Ping Fa.

Ta Chung Shu Chü. "The Arts of War of Sun (Tzu) and Wu (Ch'i)." Shanghai, 1931.

T'ai P'ing Yü Lan.

Li Fang, 3rd series. *Ssu Pu Tsung K'an*, chs. 270–359. Commercial Press. Shanghai, 1935.

T'ung Chih.

Cheng Ch'iao. Facsimile Reproduction of Palace ed. of 1859, ch. 68.

T'ung Tien.

Tu Yu. Facsimile Reproduction of Palace ed. of 1859, chs. 148–62.

Wei Shu T'ung K'ao.

Chang Hsin-cheng. "A Comprehensive Study of Apocryphal Books" (rev. ed.). Commercial Press. Shanghai, 1957.

Wu Ch'i Ping Fa.

Chung Hua Shu Chü. "The Art of War of Wu Ch'i." *Ssu Pu Pei Yao* ed. Shanghai, 1931.

Wu Ching Tsung Yao.

Tseng Kung-liang. "Essentials of the Martial Classics." *Ssu K'u Ch'uan Shu* ed.

INDEX

Sun Tzu and the Art of Modern Warfare